y then not ash.^d of Gos bec of its Ungness - Unique

The Gospel is Unique in its Simplicity & Sere

In ord to und. math^s. yrs of study are nec.,

A child cannot fathom mys^s of astron,

An uncivd. heathen c^d. nev mast the prob^s of m

chief gl & beauty of Gos is its Simpl^ty & in this Uni

such easy terms? The Simplicity of the Gos is

man had made the Gos. he w^d. made it so diff.

w diff^t. Gos as presented in the W^d. "Ho ev. 1 that thirsteth ...

II Because of the Power of the Gospel.

Its Power to overcome Obstacles in the first centuries.

Consid the diffs. faced: no means of rapid transport^n, no printed B^s, no guar^s fr Missy Soc, no

Chs at home beh^d. them, no prev^s. tri^s. to spur them on; but ev where faced with rel^s fanat^m. & pred.

Consid the succ^s & vict^s. won: In 1 gen^r. Gos carr^d. to all parts of the kn E; back of

heathendom broken, idol overthrown; thous^s converted Ch^s est^d. ev where.

Consid the means employed: This succ not achieved by sup^r. hum wis - preachers uneal

hermen: not won by force of arms but by Sword of Sp. Not by imperial edict but by Gos.

Its Power to survive the Assaults of its Enem^s & of Time. Tx - power

the early ages ev. poss. attempt was made to ster Gos, but unsucc^ly thro the 19 cent.

Xtn era Gos. has survived tho' most of its contemp^s. lory since dead. In 20th cent

is not out of date but new, fresh, appro' Why these thgs? How a/c Gos is the pow of God

Its Power to save men fr. Hell & Transform their lives. Tx.

The word "salvation" denotes & implies a danger to be del^d. from.

Hear very little of it in these days: "Flee fr the wrath to come" effete message.

Ill^ns. of its power to transform: Paul, Bunyan, Pastor Hsi Tx - power

Its Power to hold its Converts

This strikingly ill^s. Tx. Early converts in Rom arena refused to apostasise.

Protestant Xtians in middle ages at Smithfields refused to recant

Converted heathen today cast off by rel^s & bitterly persec^d, remain true to Xt.

What is the cause of this heroism? Tx - Gos. is the Power of God.

III Because of the Blessings which the Gospel bestows

Forgiveness of sins. 2 Peace of heart & conscience. 3 Eternal life.

Daily provis^n. for all our need in time. 5 Ultimately being made like Xt.

& living with Him for ever in Glory.

Application:

The Invitation - to "everyone that believeth"

Gos is suit for all Ages, Nationalities Indiv^s, because all need a Sav^r.

The Limitation - to "everyone that believeth": none else benefit.

y have been born of & reared by Xtn parents, taught in S.S^s & sit und preach^g of Gos,

t unless bel. profits noth^g - prove by analogy.

Appropriation "believing" means "receiv^g" John 1^12. 4 Exhortation Mark 8^35.

THE LIFE OF
ARTHUR W. PINK

By the Same Author:

D. Martyn Lloyd-Jones: The First Forty Years

D. Martyn Lloyd-Jones: The Fight of Faith
(the two-volume authorized biography)

Evangelicalism Divided: A Record of Crucial Change in the Years 1950 to 2000

The Forgotten Spurgeon

Jonathan Edwards: A New Biography

Pentecost–Today? The Biblical for Understanding Revival

The Puritan Hope: Revival and the Interpretation of Prophecy

Revival and Revivalism: The Making and Marring of American Evangelicalism 1750–1858

Spurgeon v. Hyper-Calvinism: The Battle for Gospel Preaching

Wesley and Men Who Followed

THE LIFE OF
ARTHUR W. PINK

Revised and Enlarged Edition

Iain H. Murray

THE BANNER OF TRUTH TRUST

THE BANNER OF TRUTH TRUST
3 Murrayfield Road, Edinburgh EH12 6EL, UK
P O Box 621, Carlisle, PA 17013, USA

*

© Iain H. Murray 2004
First edition 1981
Revised and enlarged edition 2004

ISBN 0 85151 883 4

*

Typeset in 12/14 pt Galliard at the
Banner of Truth Trust, Edinburgh
Printed in Great Britain at
The University Press,
Cambridge

TO THE FEW WHO, IN FAITH AND PRAYER,
SUPPORTED THE MINISTRY OF
STUDIES IN THE SCRIPTURES
(1922–53)

when its Editor stood practically alone; who with him saw 'hard things' and drank 'the wine of astonishment' (*Psa.* 60:3); and who, under God, served to prepare the way for a renewal of doctrinal Christianity.

'It was a most joyous ministry to be counted worthy to serve the Lord's dear people – verily the cream of the earth today.'

VERA E. PINK
23 April 1954

Contents

Illustrations

Preface to Enlarged Edition

In these pages I have returned to the *Life of Arthur W. Pink* which I wrote nearly a quarter of a century ago. My reasons for the present revision and enlargement are threefold.

First, there is some more information on Pink available to me than there was in 1981. A number of Pink's own notebooks and manuscripts were not in my hands at that date. Further many letters written by him between 1917 and 1920 have now come into the public domain. For the latter we are indebted to Richard P. Belcher of Columbia, South Carolina, who undertook their publication in *Letters from Spartanburg* and *Letters of an Itinerant Preacher*. Dr Belcher has also contributed valuable additions to the understanding of Pink in his biography, *Arthur W. Pink: Born to Write* (1982, and his current enlarged edition of the same title). It may be that still more sources of information will come to light and, if so, the writer and the present publishers would be glad to hear of them.

Second, opportunity to reflect on my first edition of the biography, as well as perhaps on Dr Belcher's *Born to Write*, has left me with the impression that there was too much attention given to the unusual in Pink. Anything extraordinary or unique in an individual always tends to gain over-much attention from biographers and can thus distort the picture presented. If we erred in this regard it happened in part because of our incomplete knowledge. Not only did Pink write very little about himself, there is almost no surviving correspondence of a personal nature – nothing, for instance, between him and those who knew him best such as his parents and his wife.

Presumably on the basis of the limited information in our biographies, opinions have sometimes been expressed about Arthur Pink which give no true impression of the man. In a recent article in an Australian magazine entitled 'Ten Years on and Still a Calvinist', the author wrote of his concerns when he first became a Calvinist: 'Would I', he asked himself, 'become a schismatic, breaking fellowship with an increasingly large number of people until there was just me and my copy of Arthur Pink's *Collected Works* left?'[1] I hope this revision may do something to remove such misconceptions. The real Pink was a man who could write: 'We should view God's children, separated as they now are by party partitions and denominational walls, as members of the same family, and sharing a common interest. Let our hearts embrace and our prayers include the entire household of faith.'[2]

I do not deny that there is the unusual in Pink's life, and that is one reason he gave why 'We shall not relate our own spiritual history . . . There are probably some things about our conversion and some things in our subsequent spiritual history which have been duplicated in very few others, if they should look for parallel in themselves.'[3] He had no wish that anyone should take the events of his life as an example for themselves.

[1] Rory Shiner in *The Briefing* (Matthias Media, October 2003), p. 5.
[2] *Studies in the Scriptures*, 1947, p. 229.
[3] A. W. Pink, *Spiritual Growth or Christian Progress* (Grand Rapids: Baker,

Third, there are good reasons why the fullest possible biographical information should be set down. For one thing, the widespread circulation of his writings after his death made him one of the most influential evangelical authors in the second half of the twentieth century. Yet his life has been little known. When Donald McKinnon, Lady Margaret Professor of Divinity at Cambridge, was addressing the Divinity Faculty and others in Edinburgh in 1974 there was only one who could respond to his question, 'Does anyone here know Pink?'[4] Still today his life is sometimes unreported where you would expect to find it. There is no entry for him in the *Twentieth Century Dictionary of Christian Biography*, edited by J. D. Douglas (Grand Rapids: Baker; Carlisle: Paternoster, 1995).[5] We are reminded of the words of a Puritan, 'There will be a resurrection of reputations as well as bodies.'

The life of Pink tells us much that is for the glory of God. No Christian can know him without appreciation and profit. He was led by God along a difficult path, and could say, 'Much failure attached to us at every point', but we can now see how he was guided to be a God-honouring witness in a day of much superficiality. We are humbled in the presence of his love of Scripture and his single-minded devotion to Christ. While the portrait we have attempted in these pages is still incomplete we believe it will be of help to fellow pilgrims who are all called to live by faith.

1971), p. 34. Another reason why he had no concern to leave records of himself was 'We are not so conceited as to imagine that our own particular conversion and the ups and downs of our Christian life are of sufficient importance to narrate.'

[4] Surprised at the question, Ian Hamilton queried if he meant A. W. Pink.

[5] There is an entry, however, in the *Biographical Dictionary of Evangelicals*, edited by Timothy A. Larsen (Downers Grove, IL: IVP, 2003).

Our thanks are due to numbers for their help on points of detail in this revision and particularly I must mention Tom White, Ralph Ireland and Mrs Margaret Siddans for her excellent editorial care.

IAIN H. MURRAY
Edinburgh, 31 May 2004

Preface to the First Edition

'The Editor', writes Arthur Pink in the December 1945 issue of his monthly magazine *Studies in the Scriptures*, 'was brought up by parents who taught him it was bad manners to talk about himself. It has ever been his supreme aim, either when preaching or writing, to occupy those he ministered unto with God, his Word, and his Christ rather than with himself.'

To this aim he adhered, and so, although *Studies in the Scriptures* ran to thirty-two volumes (1922–53), it contains little to be gleaned by any biographer. What little there is in that source I have tried to make use of in these pages, but without the additional help of a number of friends this short *Life* would have been impossible. Chiefly, I have to thank Mr Ray Levick of Sydney for his articles on Pink in *Reformation Today* and for the manuscript letters by A. W. Pink which he obtained for us on loan from friends in Australia. Ninety-five letters from Pink's pen supplied by Mr and Mrs Lowell Green have been invaluable. The *Banner of Truth* magazine commenced just two years after the closure of *Studies* and an eager reader of *Studies*, Mr Douglas Craig of Swansea, became one of its principal supporters. Mr Craig has loaned us his most treasured literary possession, a full set of *Studies* (the only such set known to us in Britain!), and also supplied much which has been of help in the preparation of these pages.

While on a visit to Sydney in September 1980 it was a pleasure to meet a few who remembered Pink's ministry with much appreciation. To Mr Alan L. McKerrell of Dural, Sydney, I am indebted for the opportunity to examine the Minute Book of the independent church (now defunct) which Pink helped to form in 1927. Although A. W. Pink died as comparatively recently as 1952 there are few alive who knew him personally. This has led us to prize all the more the aid of Mr and Mrs Charles Pressel of York, Pennsylvania, who first welcomed the Pinks to their home in 1922. The help of others, some of whom are not named in these pages, is also gratefully acknowledged.

My work was made a great deal easier by the preliminary labours of my colleague Dr Sinclair Ferguson who took the major responsibility in the editing of *Letters of A. W. Pink* published by the Trust in 1978. As ever, I must thank Mr S. M. Houghton for his checking of this publication both at manuscript and at proof stages. The Rev. Peter Lewis of Nottingham has assisted me with information on Pink's childhood homes in that city.

In a real sense the life-work of Arthur Pink is unfinished, for his writings are now being read by far larger numbers than those who saw the original magazine. It is almost exclusively from that magazine, and since 1953, that publishers across the world have drawn the material which is now so widely known in book form.

For the present writer the preparation of these pages has been a spiritual refreshment. Pink's words stirred many of us years ago, but we knew very little of his history. To know him is to love and respect him as a humble and faithful servant of Jesus Christ.

IAIN MURRAY
30 April 1981

1

A Spiritualist Medium Becomes a Christian

Arthur Walkington Pink was born on April 1, 1886 in Nottingham, beside the River Trent, and in the Midlands of what was then accounted 'the richest country of the world'. Queen Victoria had reigned over a rising prosperity for half a century, and the government of Robert Cecil, third marquess of Salisbury, ruled a quarter of the earth. The political agitations of fifty years earlier, when Nottingham Castle had been destroyed in the riots of the poor and starving, were things of the past, and the city was now sharing in the social progress that saw the introduction of such amenities as public baths, libraries, parks and tramways.

Nottingham, with a population at this date of about 200,000, had not been left out of the industrial revolution. There were several iron foundries, and local manufactures included lace, clothing and bicycles. Even so the surrounding county remained largely unspoiled. A large part of its fifty miles by twenty was taken up with arable farming — corn, wheat, barley and oats — while such ancient woodlands as Sherwood Forest still remained.

The Christian churches in general shared the national mood of optimism. Voices raised in warning were few, yet they would be remembered long after spokesmen for popular opinion were forgotten. Approaching the conclusion of his long ministry, J. C. Ryle, the Bishop of Liverpool, was ready to assert 'that in hardness, unbelief, superstition, and self-righteousness, the Christian Churches, as a whole, are little better than the Jewish Church of our Lord's time'.[1]

Among the few who agreed with Ryle was C. H. Spurgeon. In the month Pink was born, the fifty-one year old Baptist preacher wrote in his magazine *The Sword and the Trowel* an article entitled, 'A Word for the Hour'. It included the words:

> An abiding consolation in these evil days is to be found in the fact that the Holy Spirit is working in the same manner as ever. A conversion to-day bears all the marks which authenticated a conversion five hundred years ago . . . It matters not how much the wise men of this world deride the gospel of our Lord Jesus, it still arouses the careless, guides the despondent, renews the guilty and sanctifies the believing . . . While this is the case, what means this clamour for advanced thought? Can there be an advance upon a revelation which is complete? Is there anything better than Jesus Christ, the same yesterday, today, and for ever? In patience let us possess our souls, resting not in talent and learning and influence for the progress of the gospel, but in the Holy Spirit alone. He can raise up leaders of eminence if other Pauls are needed. He can find learned pens if other Augustines are required. He never fails, nor even pauses, for lack of instruments.

[1] J. C. Ryle, *Expository Thoughts on Luke*, vol. 2 (1877, reprinted Edinburgh: Banner of Truth, 1997), p. 325.

Arthur Pink's parents may have read these words for it was into such homes that the 20,000 copies of Spurgeon's monthly were circulated. His father, Thomas Clement Pink, was some thirty-eight years of age at the time of Arthur's birth, his own birth having taken place near Nottingham in 1849. Of Thomas Pink's life very little is known. It is clear that he had passed through sorrow, for the census of 1881 gave his dwelling as 15 Cobden Road, Chesterfield, at which time he was married to Sarah Augusta, aged twenty-eight, who came from County Sligo in Ireland. Sarah Pink must have died soon after that date, for by 1884 Thomas Pink had moved to Nottingham where he married Agnes Ann Hunt of Belper, in that year. When their eldest son, Arthur, was born two years later, they were living at 4 Claremont Terrace, Francis Street, Nottingham.

Arthur Pink's birth certificate gave the father's profession as a 'corn dealer' while a local trade directory for 1887 lists him as a 'corn miller'.

He was self-employed and at least part of his business was the provision of corn cake as cattle food. That he worked hard and prospered can be judged from the fact that when Arthur was five the family moved to a more commodious home at 9 Newstead Grove, and on this point we also have his son's own words:

> The father of the writer was an exceptionally busy business man: so busy that for over thirty years he never had more than three consecutive days' holidays. He was a corn merchant, and after returning from market attended to much of the clerical work in person, so that for years he did not cease till 11:50 Saturday night.[2]

[2] *Studies in the Scriptures*, 1944, p. 387, hereafter to be referred to as *Studies*.

The census of 1901 gives Thomas Pink as fifty-two years of age, his wife, fifty-one, and the family now contained three children: Arthur, aged fourteen; Frank, aged thirteen; and Agnes Louise, aged eleven. His profession remained the same.

Arthur Pink tells us more about the Christian commitment of his parents, including the fact that his mother devoted him to Christ before he was born. The Bible was taken very seriously. 'We had', he recalled in later years, 'a daily delivery of mail, including Sunday, which often contained important business letters, but none were opened on the Lord's Day. No Sunday newspapers ever entered our home – not even when the Boer war was on. When we were little all our toys were put away on Saturday night and pictorial editions of Bunyan's *Pilgrim's Progress* and Foxe's *Book of Martyrs*, etc. were brought out.'[3]

Of course such practices were followed in many Victorian homes, but in the house in Claremont Terrace the discipline was accompanied by his parents' warmth of devotion to Christ. 'As a boy', writes Pink again, 'I several times asked my father why he spent so much pains in shining his shoes, and each time he answered, "I am polishing them as though the Lord Jesus was going to wear them."'

After the quotation already given on the late hour to which his father often worked on Saturdays, Pink continued:

> Yet he did not lie in bed Sabbath mornings, but took his children to hear God's Word preached. He did not send them to 'Sunday school' while he took a nap in the afternoon, but gathered us around him

[3] *Studies*, 1931, p. 140.

> and spent a couple of hours in reading to us from the Scriptures, from Foxe's *Book of Martyrs*, Bunyan's *Pilgrim's Progress*, etc. Every day he conducted family worship, and when we were too little to sit up for the evening our godly mother took us around her knee and prayed with us.

Other memories of Sundays were of how 'the day began by our father reading to us God's Word', and also of how 'quite a little of the time was spent in the singing of hymns'. In later years Pink was often to quote a verse which he first learned in childhood,

> A Sabbath well spent
> brings a week of content,
> and strength for the toils of the morrow,
> but a Sabbath profaned,
> whate'er may be gained,
> is a certain forerunner of sorrow.[4]

When Arthur was sixteen he overheard and remembered a conversation between his parents which gives us another brief glimpse into his father's character. Coming down to breakfast on a spring morning in the year 1902, Arthur found his parents already at the table and his father reading a newspaper that carried news of preparations for the first coronation in Britain for sixty-four years. 'In the middle of breakfast he turned to my mother and said, "Oh, I am sorry to see this worded like that." And she said, "What is it?" "Why," he said, "here is a proclamation that on a certain date Prince Edward will be crowned king at Westminster and there is no *Deo*

[4] He was to write a long series of articles on 'The Holy Sabbath' in *Studies*, 1939 and 1940.

volente, God willing."' The words stuck in Arthur's mind for the very reason that on the appointed date the future Edward VII was ill with appendicitis and the coronation had to be postponed.[5]

Our knowledge of Pink's childhood and youth is practically a total blank. Whether he attended the nearest local school to Newstead Grove, whether he sat with many other youths in the summer sunshine at Trent Bridge to watch cricket, whether he had one of Nottingham's latest bicycles with which to ride in Sherwood – all these and other such things are unrecorded. Academically Pink's education appears to have been good and, unlike many children of that period, he stayed at school until he was sixteen. Certainly his later life shows that he had a trained and disciplined mind, and that such subjects as English literature and general history were ones with which he was familiar. He appears to have had a particular interest in music and could speak of himself as 'a trained musician, both vocally and instrumentally'.[6]

What is clear is that as Arthur and his younger brother, Frank, and sister who was known by her second name, Louise, grew up, their early training in the Scriptures showed no signs of bearing fruit. Slowly all three children appear to have drifted into lives of unbelief. In Arthur's case it seems he was influenced by young people who had no such background as his own. In later memories of this time he refers to 'the godless companions of our youth', and says that during energetic and thoughtless days among them there were 'a number of occasions when he was in imminent peril, brought face to face with death'. Whatever these escapades were, they were probably

[5] *Studies*, 1926, p. 16.
[6] *Letters of A. W. Pink* (Edinburgh: Banner of Truth, 1978), p. 62.

unknown to his parents. But to their grief there was another development in his life that they could not miss. Not only did their eldest son turn from their faith, he turned to Theosophy.

Theosophy is a cult which, although only formed into a Society in 1875, claims a special knowledge (*theosophia* – divine wisdom) which is supposedly preserved from generation to generation by a brotherhood of initiates. At the beginning of the twentieth century its best-known British publication, the monthly magazine *Lucifer*, indicated clearly enough its anti-Christian nature. Its leading journal *The Theosophist*, at that time published monthly at the Society's headquarters in Madras, India, promoted in esoteric form the 'wisdom' of eastern religions, including belief in reincarnation. While denying the personality of God (and the supernatural in Christianity), Theosophy claimed to be able to unify all religions and to establish a universal brotherhood. Its main 'messenger' in the nineteenth century was the Russian, Helena Blavatsky (1831–1891), and she was followed by Annie Besant (1847–1933), who left her clergyman husband in 1873 for a life in politics, mysticism and eastern religions. From 1907 to her death she was President of the Theosophical Society.

What drew Pink to Theosophy is unknown. Perhaps, as in the case of others, it was the Society's claim to experience occult phenomena, and certainly their practices were allied to Spiritualism. In a later address on the subject Pink spoke of Spiritualism, that is, belief in communication with the spirits of those dead, as the 'pioneer' to Theosophy. Many, he said, were attracted to the occult simply by curiosity, and then by a desire to investigate the proof it offered of the existence of the spirit world. 'Nearly every spiritist I have met', he wrote, 'began by being a blank unbeliever in its phenomena.' Then, when 'they see its phenomena are real, they accept the explanation given'.[7]

This could well be autobiography, and the same attraction to the occult is recorded in the lives of other young men of that era. The biography of G. Whitfield Guinness, for instance, tells of what happened when he, and others from a Christian background, attended a séance while students at Cambridge:

> For about twenty minutes nothing particular happened. The table round which they were seated gave no response to the questions put to it, and they were getting distinctly tired. 'Just two minutes more,' urged the medium. The table began to move a little, round and round, then rolled right over and across the room. Aroused to interest, the group began to ply it with questions – two bangs on the floor meant 'No', and three 'Yes'. One asked whether his brother had passed his examination (he had just received the news himself). The table gave the right answer. Another wanted to know the number of books on a bookshelf over which a curtain was hanging; it was not the medium's room. The table said forty-nine, which proved to be exactly right. For almost an hour they went on showering questions, all of which were correctly answered.

[7] I am quoting from a loose-leaf notebook of Pink's. It contains 109 pages of handwritten outlines of sermons and addresses (the first on 'Paul's estimate of Life and Death' from Philippians 1:21), and contains three entitled 'Spiritualism', 'Spiritism', and 'Theosophy'. My quotation is from the second of these outlines which, like the third, can be dated about 1913. The first of the three, on different paper and with different ink is earlier, when he still called the movement 'Spiritualism', not ' Spiritism' (its proper title, he later believed).

> Greatly intrigued, they now came to more serious matters, and asked how long it would take for them to become initiated – how many séances they would have to attend before they could be considered mediums? . . . [Whitfield Guinness was told 'thirteen or fourteen']. A strange consciousness of some unseen power was stealing over them, Whitfield began to be uneasy. Then he remembered the passage, 1 John 4:1–3, 'Try (or test) the spirits, whether they are of God . . . Every spirit which confesseth that Jesus Christ is come in the flesh is of God; and every spirit which confesseth not Jesus is not of God.' Quietly he put the question: 'Has Jesus Christ, the Son of God, come in the flesh?' The table rose right up, about two feet high, and crashed out an unmistakable 'No!' That broke up the atmosphere and, for Whitfield, put an end to tampering with Spiritualism. Some who went on with it had grave cause to regret the first steps by which they became enslaved.[8]

Arthur Pink's involvement led to no such early escape. From an initial interest it is clear that he moved to a thorough commitment. He addressed cult meetings and became so closely involved with the London headquarters of Theosophy – from whence *Lucifer* had originated – that in a photograph taken of some of the leaders at that period he was to be found seated in their midst.

When news of Pink's eloquent propagation of Theosophy reached Madame Besant in Madras she opened a correspondence with him, and subsequently

[8] Mrs Howard Taylor, *Guinness of Honan* (London: CIM, 1930), pp. 77–8. G. Whitfield Guinness (1869–1927), as a medical missionary in China, would later have more abundant evidence of the power of evil spirits.

proposed to confer a title upon him which would rank him among the cult's chiefs – a dignity which apparently would also entail his removal to India. One of Pink's closest friends, although a fellow theosophist, was not enamoured with the proposal. This man was an opera singer by profession and, having a high opinion of Pink's baritone voice, he urged him to study for the same career. But although the two men went together to Paris about this time, the appeal of Madame Besant's offer was stronger than that of music and Pink accepted it. It 'fed [his] ego', he later commented, and he characterized the whole system as one that 'appeals to the flesh, panders to pride, and exalts man'. C. S. Lewis has made the same point in speaking of how he was drawn to the occult at one time:

> The idea that if there were Occult knowledge it was known to very few and scorned by the very many became an added attraction . . . That the means should be Magic – the most exquisitely unorthodox thing in the world, unorthodox both by Christian and Rationalist standards – of course appealed to the rebel in me.[9]

The date when the Besant proposal came to Pink is not known. It was probably early in 1908, for we know that in that year he was still in Nottingham. He was now twenty-two years of age, and so deeply involved in the occult that he later recorded, 'Five years ago I was a medium,' practising 'clairvoyance, psychomancy, and magical healing.'[10] All this time Pink was earning a living in business. He also continued to live at home, which tells

[9] C. S. Lewis, *Surprised by Joy* (Glasgow: Collins/Fontana, 1977), p. 142.
[10] Notebook address on 'Spiritism'. As Pink was converted in 1908, 'five years ago' fixes 1913 as the date when the words were written.

us something about his patient parents. They grieved, prayed and were not altogether silent. His father always waited up until his son returned from meetings late in the evening and to Arthur's annoyance often accompanied his 'Good-night' with some brief but telling word of Scripture. One such evening, in the year 1908, as Pink hurriedly passed his father and dashed upstairs to his room, the text which he received was, 'There is a way which seemeth right unto a man, but the end thereof are the ways of death' (*Prov.*14:12). As he shut the bedroom door, intending to do some work on a speech for an important annual meeting of theosophists that was to take place on the Friday evening of that same week, the text remained with him and so disturbed his concentration that work was impossible. The story continues in the words of Charles and Elsie Pressel:

> A.W.P. decided he was fatigued, and would take a bath to relax, but during this process all he could see 'mentally' was 'There is a way that seemeth right, etc.' – Again he returned to work on his speech and all his mind brought forth was Proverbs 14:12. He, A.W.P., told us he could no longer reject the God of the Bible and began to cry unto the Lord in prayer, convicted by the Holy Spirit and his power to bring a soul to see his lost condition and believe in the Lord Jesus Christ as his Saviour. His early training taught him about our Lord, but now, like Paul of old, was the appointment with a Holy Sovereign God. For almost three days he did not leave his room to join the family, but his father and mother prayed, and in late afternoon on the third day A.W.P. made his appearance and his father said, 'Praise God, my son has been delivered.'

> A.W.P. kept his next appointment before the Society of Theosophists; the speech he was preparing was never completed but by God's grace he made known to them the God of the Bible. A 'groan' went up from the listeners. Many remarked that he had 'gone mad' and needed a rest, for they were aware of his plans to join Madame Besant.

This last address of Pink's among theosophists was a gospel message on the true God and Jesus Christ, his Son, in whom alone there is salvation. He must have told them what he recorded a few years later. He put the question, 'Why did I leave Spiritism and Theosophy?' and replied: 'Because it failed to satisfy my soul. I was trying to save myself. There was no peace for a burdened conscience, no assurance of sins forgiven, no power of sin broken, no satisfaction of heart. I found I could not save myself and came to the only One who could save me. "Thou, O Christ, art all I want, more than all in Thee I find."'[11]

No one, it appears, stood with him on that Friday night in 1908. Alone he confessed Jesus Christ and alone resigned his membership of the Society. Later he would write: 'I have yet to meet the first Spiritist who bows the knee to Christ and owns Him as Lord.'[12] His testimony, as quoted above, should not be interpreted as though a prolonged inner dissatisfaction preceded his conversion, for he speaks elsewhere of being suddenly struck down in the midst of rebellion. Christ 'apprehended him when he

[11] Notebook address on 'Spiritism'.

[12] The antipathy of Theosophy and of similar movements to biblical Christianity is long continued. At a conference on 'Religion and Cultural Diversity', at Melbourne, attended by leading Australian political and church leaders, it is reported that 'Christian fundamentalists came under the heaviest attack'. The same report called Madame Blavatsky, 'originator of Theosophy, the driving force behind the ecumenical movement'. *National Focus* (Nanango, Queensland, July 1998).

was altogether unconscious of his deep need, and had no desire whatever for a Saviour'. Pink had no doubt that his conversion, as every true conversion, was a deliverance from the power of Satan and now the nature of that Satanic power appeared to him as it had never done before. His eyes were opened to the real meaning of Spiritism. It was true some clairvoyants might be simply tricksters, but that had not been his position and he was sure 'the whole phenomenon cannot be accounted for on natural grounds'. Many of the spirit-communicated messages were real, but they came not from the dead but from demons impersonating the departed. God had called him from the deepest darkness and, if he dwelt on the subject in later years, something of the darkness could come back to him. In 1919 when he had a prolonged correspondence with a person caught in Spiritism, and seemingly seeking deliverance, he commented to a friend:

> This correspondence has weighed on me: Satan is trying hard to use it as a hindrance. It has always affected me detrimentally whenever I have turned my mind and attention back to Spiritism.[13]

For two years after this spiritual crisis Pink continued in his daily work but in his bedroom it was now his Bible that was ever open. Ten chapters of Scripture were read daily, plus one particular portion to which he would give particular study, 'ten minutes or more', through seven days. In addition, he would take one special verse each day for meditation, carrying it with him on a slip of paper to which he would turn in spare moments, 'asking God to open to me its spiritual meaning and to write it on my heart'. Recommending the practice to others, he was to

[13] A. W. Pink, *Letters from Spartanburg*, ed. Richard P. Belcher (Columbia, SC: Richbarry Press, 1993), p. 69.

say, 'The writer memorised the whole epistle of Ephesians on the street-car, a verse at a time.'[14] On days when he was free of business he could spend up to ten hours in his new delight with the Bible.

In part this intense study of Scripture was connected with a conviction that his lifework lay in the service of the gospel. In a brief summary of his early life, written in 1934, he said:

> I was born in England in 1886, and at the age of sixteen entered business, in which God granted me considerable success. In 1908 he saved me in my bedroom. I knew right then he had also called me to be his servant.

In that same year he had first addressed a Christian gathering. He recalled in 1948:

> Forty years have passed since the editor preached his first sermon. It was on the words, 'For I am not ashamed of the gospel of Christ' etc. (*Rom.* 1:16), and to a congregation of over 700 people. Though it was not the first time we had spoken in public, yet it was quite an ordeal, especially as it was in our home-town, Nottingham.[15]

There is no record of the church and denomination in which Pink had been brought up. As we shall see, his first pastorate was Congregational and that may well have been his own background. All we know of his church attendance after his conversion is in the brief sentence:

[14] See *Letters of Pink*, pp. 23–4, and *Gleanings in Exodus* (Chicago: Moody Press, n.d.), p. 128, quoted by Richard P. Belcher, *Arthur W. Pink: Born to Write* (Columbia, SC: Richbarry Press, 1982), p.27. Pink says that he maintained the same diet of Scripture for the first ten years of his Christian life.

[15] *Studies*, 1948, p. 285. See p. 29, footnote.

'Occasionally I attended the services of various men, but I was found much more frequently in one place, and that was where I received most profit for my soul.'[16] It is clear that he sought out like-minded friends and to the home of one of these (an elderly friend of his father's), six miles away, he would walk regularly to speak about Christ and the Word of God. These friends soon recognized that his career was not to lie in business and, as he discussed his future with them, the general advice he received was to enter a theological college in England. Herein lay a problem that, although a young Christian, Pink could recognize. A far-reaching change with respect to education for the Christian ministry was in process in England. It was the consequence of changed views of the authority of Scripture and it led, in turn, to a widespread weakening of commitment to evangelical and biblical Christianity. The main source of this change lay in the very institutions originally founded to train men for the gospel ministry.

All the denominations were affected by this change and, not least, Pink's own, if we are right to suppose that his family background in Nottingham was Congregational. At this date the Congregational churches were in the midst of what was called the 'New Theology Controversy', led by the Rev. R. J. Campbell of the City Temple, London. As a student at Oxford Campbell had been taught that Christianity does not depend on 'the infallibility of the Scriptural records', and he was now busy popularizing that teaching. At a meeting of Congregational leaders in London in 1910, where the issue was discussed, it was decided to take no action to stop what was happening; the truth was that 'Higher

[16] *Letters of Pink*, p. 120.

Criticism' was already too widely accepted to be effectively opposed.[17]

An exception to the prevailing sentiment among the Congregationalists was Dr Campbell Morgan, of Westminster Chapel, London, and it was noticeable that Morgan seemed to have more affinity with men on the other side of the Atlantic than he did with many of his English peers. The same had been increasingly true of C. H. Spurgeon in his later years. Pink's own thoughts now turned to the United States. The visits of D. L. Moody in the 1870s and 1880s were still well remembered and people spoke of the good done by his plain gospel message. So it was that Pink went not to Madras but to Chicago: 'As a young man of twenty-four, acting on the advice of those I respected, in June 1910 I sailed from England and entered the Moody Bible Institute for a two years' course.'[18]

On his reason for not proceeding into the ministry through the normal British channels Pink was very definite. Having already been trained in one school of unbelief he had no intention of entering another:

> I had to make my own choice regarding entering or not some theological seminary and against the advice and counsels of all my friends (my parents alone excepted) I determined to give them a wide berth, and I have never regretted that decision. One cannot handle doctrinal 'filth' without becoming defiled,

[17] See E. J. Poole-Connor, *Evangelicalism in England* (London: FIEC, 1951), p. 256. Also, for detail on the decline of orthodoxy among the Congregational churches, see John W. Grant, *Free Churchmanship in England, 1840–1940* (London: Independent Press, 1955).

[18] Letter to John C. Blackburn, March 12, 1940. Unless otherwise stated, all letters quoted in these pages are from the unpublished originals. Blackburn (1889–1959), was a minister of the Southern Presbyterian Church in the United States who maintained the faith of his grandfather, John L. Girardeau.

> though many think otherwise. It is not without reason that the statement 'evil communications corrupt good manners' is prefaced by, 'Be not deceived' (*1 Cor.* 15:33) – many are![19]

No records have survived of what Arthur Pink thought of his journey of more than three thousand miles. There is not a word on the Atlantic voyage, on his first sight of New York, with its horses, noise and dirt so often remarked on by travellers at that date, nothing of the long train journey to the Mid-West where Chicago stands as a great entrepôt on the shore of Lake Michigan. Another Britisher, a decade before, gave this first impression of the pulsating life of Chicago:

> In Chicago everyone wears his hat at the back of his head, everyone speaks at the rate of 200 words a minute, everyone gulps down a stodgy American meal in five minutes, everyone smokes and chews. What a paltry rheumatic Briton one feels in the midst of these electric batteries. Every man you meet down town has in his head a scheme that is to lick creation . . . is the pushfullest and roughest elbower in the world.[20]

Within the Bible Institute on Institute Place, Pink, no doubt, had a somewhat different view. His first business was with the daily lectures in which the leading teachers were Dr James M. Gray, then fifty-nine years of age, and the English-born Dr William Evans. Yet such was the Institute's emphasis upon 'practical Christian work' that after morning lectures Pink must also often have gone

[19] To John C. Blackburn, Feb. 14, 1945.
[20] David Marquand, *Ramsay MacDonald* (London: Jonathan Cape , 1977), p. 58.

on one of the Institute's 'open gospel wagons' to a street preaching, or a jail or hospital visit. On Sundays he would have found his way with other students to the great Moody Memorial Church where Dr A. C. Dixon was in the final year of his highly-acclaimed evangelistic ministry. The next year (1911) Dixon would leave for his next pastorate in Spurgeon's Tabernacle, London. 'In the course of each year,' Dixon's biographer writes of the Chicago period, 'from five hundred to a thousand professions of conversion had been noted on the books of the Moody Church.'[21]

Pink's days at Moody Bible Institute were short lived. 'After I had been there six weeks,' he recalled to John Blackburn, 'I interviewed Dr Howard Pope and stated I desired to enter the pastorate without further delay, that I felt I was "wasting my time" at the Institute.'[22] The conversation could hardly have been so precise as these few words suggest, for Dr Pope, instead of curtly dismissing the Englishman, proceeded to help him to find a pastoral charge. Thus at the end of July 1910, after less than two months in Chicago, Pink went to serve the Congregational church at Silverton, a small town situated at over 9000 feet, in the San Juan Mountains of Colorado. He arrived on Wednesday, August 2.

The explanation for Pink's abrupt change of plans does not appear to have been any disgruntlement with the teaching at Moody; we suspect it was rather the immature level at which that teaching was pitched. Another Moody student of the period tells us that Dr Gray, in Bostonian accents, would coax his youthful hearers to study with

[21] From a different standpoint I have described something of Dixon's ministry in *The Forgotten Spurgeon* (Edinburgh: Banner of Truth, 1978), pp. 217ff.
[22] Letter to Blackburn, March 12, 1940.

such aphorisms as, 'Do not ask the Lord to bring back to your mind that which never entered into your mind.'[23] Pink, long accustomed to hard study, and already well read in the English Bible, plainly did not need the degree of patience which was shown to his younger contemporaries. It may also have been clear to him that an important part of Dr Gray's thought was to be found in one of the Institute's key books, the Scofield Reference Bible. This was a book that went with him to Colorado where he expected to have ample time to master its many notes and interpretations.

In later years, in a passing reference to his first pastorate at Silverton, Pink was to mention the place as 'a mining camp'. As a description the term is somewhat misleading. Colorado, the fifth largest state in the Union and half the size of France, was the nation's foremost producer of silver and gold. It was from the widespread mining going on in the surrounding mountains that the community of Silverton on the Rio De Las Animas had grown up, but by the time Pink arrived it had been an established town for more than thirty years. The Congregationalists had built their church on the corner of Reese Street and 11th Street in 1880, adding a steeple in 1885. Other substantial buildings of similar date included a general store in 1876, another in 1880, and the Grand Imperial Hotel, finished in 1883. Buildings had multiplied in the first decade of the twentieth century and a showpiece Town Hall was finished the year before Pink arrived. Claiming to be the oldest continuous business in Western Colorado, the town had its own newspaper, the *Silverton Standard*. Under

[23] Quoted by Wilbur M. Smith, *Before I Forget* (Chicago: Moody Press, 1971), p. 35. Smith went to Moody as a student in 1913 and remained one year.

the heading 'New Congregational Pastor', in its edition of August 6, 1910, the paper welcomed the new arrival in these words:

> Rev. A. W. Pink, who was recently called from Chicago to fill the pastorate of the Congregational church, made vacant by the resignation of the former parson, Rev. A. C. Hacke, arrived last Wednesday evening and will conduct the usual services next Sunday. Mr Pink is a recent arrival in the United States from Nottingham, England. He is a young gentleman of pleasant address, manly bearing and impresses one with the thought that he is in every way most eminently fitted for the discharge of the duties of his new position.

Pink's new duties were soon upon him. Three days after his arrival, one of the town's oldest residents, George Hollingsworth, died, and the funeral the following Wednesday was in his hands. According to the *Silverton Standard* it proved to be 'one of the largest ever held in the city'. The new pastor had scarcely opportunity to know whether the same paper's description of the deceased as 'one of earth's noble men' was true to life. According to the editor of the *Silverton Standard*, Mr Hollingsworth had 'surrendered the cross of troubles in this life for the crown of glory in the realms of eternal happiness beyond the grave'.[24] The language suggests that the town was not without a good deal of religious sentiment, and many years later Pink wrote of the situation he found:

> During our first pastorate we were much engaged in combating the error of salvation by personal culture and reformation, and therefore we threw our main

[24] 'Another Pioneer Has Passed Away', *Silverton Standard*, August 13, 1910.

> emphasis on the truth contained in our Lord's words, 'Ye must be born again' (*John* 3:3, 5, 7), showing that something far more potent and radical than any efforts of our own was required in order to give admission into the kingdom of God; that no education, mortification, or religious adorning of the natural man could possibly fit him to dwell for ever in holy heaven.[25]

Probably the first notes that have survived of Pink's hand are from this date and consist of a one-page outline of a sermon prepared for the situation just described. Entitled 'Regeneration', it reads:[26]

> The new birth is the divine side of the application of salvation. It is a birth, resurrection, new creation; a transcendent wonder, supernatural, a miracle – no mere reformation; the divine [dividing?] line between heaven and hell: all on one side or the other.
>
> 1. *The nature of the new birth.*
> (i) Not a process of reformation, not a work of man attempting to eliminate evil.
> (ii) Not the purification of the heart, Jer. 17; John 3:6.
> (iii) It is the impartation of the divine nature. Birth in spiritual realm analogous to birth in natural. Everything that is born partakes of the nature of its parents, Gen.1.
>
> 2. *The need of the new birth.*
> It is an absolute necessity. Cannot be set aside: no substitute. 'Ye must'. 'Cannot'. Imperative necessity:

[25] *Studies*, 1947, pp. 19–20.

[26] Many words are abbreviated in the original and in a few instances the sense is so unclear that I have omitted them. Words in italics are words written in red ink.

(i) Because by nature man is spiritually dead; not merely weak or sick.

(ii) Because by nature outside God's kingdom John 3:5. All born out of Eden. Eph. 2:13.

(iii) Spiritual kingdom demands spiritual nature. Heaven is a prepared place for a prepared people. This follows a universal law. Illustration of fish in garden.

3. *It is an exclusive necessity. Nothing can take its place.* Education cannot – cultivation, reformation, religion cannot.

4. *It is a universal necessity.*
'Except a man be born again' – not 'except a thief, adulterer, murderer' etc. These words spoken to Nicodemus. On death bed all that matters is, Have I been born again?

The Author of the new birth John 1:13; 3:6.

The instrument John 3:5

The characteristics of the new birth

(i) A clinging to Jesus in helplessness – faith – analogy of baby.

(ii) Hatred and resistance of sin: God is holy and I have his nature in me.

(iii) *Love for God my 'Father'.* How is love manifested? By glad obedience. *A love for the brethren: 1John 3:14.* Bound by ties of affection, manifested by endeavours to assist one another – 1 John 3:17–18.

Application. Have you been born again? If not, day coming when wish never been born at all. Apply fourfold test.

Those who are born only once will die twice.

Those born twice will only die once and may not at all.

Another sermon from Silverton in 1911 was edited by Pink and printed at a later date. Entitled 'Beholding the Crucified Christ', it was a powerful proclamation both of human sin and of divine justice and grace. The believer, he declared, glories in the cross as he beholds Christ identified with those whose sins he bore: 'In the sight of God they are one. Christ took my place and faith appropriates that fact. In the person of my Substitute I satisfied every requirement of God's law. In the person of Christ I paid the full price which divine justice demanded. In the person of Christ I stand approved before God, for I am clothed with his meritorious perfections (Isa. 61:10).'[27]

From the first it is clear that Pink's aspirations as a Christian could be summed up by a verse which meant much to him,

> O fix our earnest gaze,
> So wholly, Lord, on thee,
> That with thy beauty occupied,
> We elsewhere none may see.

All that we know of Pink's weekly routine at Silverton is from a notice in the *Silverton Standard* the week after his arrival. Under the heading 'Congregational Church' there was announced:

[27] Pink printed this sermon, 'slightly revised', in *Studies*, 1943, pp. 114–19.

Saturday, Aug.13, 1910
7.30 p.m. Christian Endeavour Meeting.
Sunday, Aug.14, 1910
10.30 a.m. Morning worship and sermon.
11.15 a.m. Sunday School.
6.30 p.m. Evening worship and gospel sermon.
Monday, Aug. 15, 1910
At 8 p.m. Bible study meeting at Wilkinsons' residence.
Thursday, Aug.18, 1910
At 7.30 p.m. Prayer meeting and study of the Sunday School lesson.
You are cordially invited to all these services.
Rev. Pink, pastor.

Evidently the church had traditionally been evangelical for, less than two weeks after his arrival, Pink can hardly have introduced all these meetings.

Two other churches existed in Silverton, St John's Episcopal Church, which had no incumbent, and St Patrick's Catholic Church that had exchanged its frame building for brick in 1905. Speaking of the priest of the latter church, Pink says, 'We got acquainted.' Before long, spiritual issues became a matter of conversation between the two men but with a consequence which Pink did not anticipate: 'He volunteered to give us Scripture for every Popish dogma and practice, and when we put him to the test (as we did, again and again) we were amazed and awed by the subtle manner in which he misappropriated the Word.'[28] This demonstrated to Pink the uselessness of arguing about divine things and it also confirmed him in his view of the vital importance of possessing a deep and accurate knowledge of Scripture. He saw that it was 'a big mistake' to suppose that teachers of error are

[28] *Studies*, 1937, p. 31.

'incapable of making a Scriptural defence of their positions'. 'During our first pastorate,' he notes on another occasion, 'we wrote on the inside page of our Bible, "Ye shall not add unto the word which I command you, neither shall ye diminish ought from it" (Deut. 4:2). To which we then added Exodus 4: 12; Isaiah 51:16; 55:11 and for many years it was our practice to read them immediately before entering the pulpit.'[29]

Pink remained at Silverton for rather less than two years. We should like to know more but all that the *Silverton Standard* recorded in its edition of 20 April 1912 was as follows:

> A farewell reception will be tendered to Rev. A. W. Pink, at the Congregational Church on the evening of April 26th. Everyone is invited to attend and have a jolly good time.

[29] *Studies*, 1944, p. 284.

2

The Emerging Preacher

From the tone of the notice reporting the end of Pink's ministry at Silverton, it would appear that trouble or controversy was not the cause of his departure. The reason he left when he did is unknown. It could be that in the course of his studies he had come to Baptist convictions (a change which probably took place around this period). In this case he would have been too conscientious to remain in a Congregational church.[1] The explanation would be clearer if we were sure of all his locations in the three years after he left Colorado in April 1912. But his movements between that date and his settlement at Spartanburg, South Carolina, in the early summer of 1917 are the least known of all his life.

It appears that first he went from Silverton to California. Writing in January 1934, he gave notes of a sermon 'which was preached by the editor in Garden Grove, California, over twenty years ago' [that is, before 1914].[2] He also speaks of being 'in close touch' with the Bible Institute of Los Angeles (BIOLA) in California for over a year. There is no other time when a period of that length

[1] As there was no Baptist cause in Silverton at this date we cannot, however, be sure that the church insisted on a pastor of paedo-Baptist convictions.
[2] *Studies*, 1934, p. 23.

can be fitted into the chronology of his life. It may be that a consciousness of the need for further study entered into his decision to leave Silverton,[3] or, more probably, that he went to the West Coast because he was called to a pastoral charge there. One of his early friends, I. C. Herendeen, believed that Pink was in a Californian pastorate at this date. If the location was in the Garden Grove area it was only some twenty-five miles away from Los Angeles. Without telling us where precisely his second pastorate was, Pink does record this about it:

> Our second pastorate was located in a community where the teaching of 'entire sanctification' or sinless perfectionism was rife, and in combating it we stressed the fact that sin is not eradicated from any man's being in this life, that even after he is born again the 'old nature' still remains within him.[4]

We know that Pink was also studying at this date, for his first book *The Divine Inspiration of the Bible* was completed by 1914. In a letter of 1944 he was to write: 'My book on Inspiration was my first – over 30 years ago.'[5] The dedication page of the book read:

> I affectionately inscribe this book to my dear father and mother, in grateful appreciation of the fact that from a child I was taught to revere the Holy Scriptures.

Affection for his parents no doubt entered into the next change. Thomas and Agnes Pink had only anticipated the absence of their eldest son for two years when he went to

[3] Enquiries at the Bible Institute reveal that they possess no records as far back as this date.
[4] *Studies*, 1947, pp. 19–20.
[5] *Letters to a Young Pastor* (Grandville, Mich.: Grandville Protestant Reformed Church, 1993), p. 15. It is uncertain when Pink's title was first published.

Chicago in 1910. By 1913 it was time he saw them again. From fragments of information, I believe we can deduce that he returned to Britain in the closing months of 1913. In 1932, referring to England, he was to write of having spent 'less than two-and-a-half years there since 1910'. As we shall see, he was in England for just over eight months in 1928–29, and that leaves another eighteen months (to make up the two-and-a-half years) to be fitted into the 1913–15 period for his whereabouts in all the other years down to 1932 are known. Further, in 1928 he wrote of his not having been in Britain for 'thirteen years', which dates the end of a previous last visit to 1915. The date is confirmed by another letter written in America in 1929 in which he speaks of a friend he knew in London 'fourteen years ago'.

So from California Pink spent eighteen months back in England until the early half of the year 1915. It was the period that saw the outbreak of the Great War and all the excitement that it occasioned. There was no conscription of men into the British army until 1916 or at the age of twenty-eight he might have found himself at the Front in France. All that he tells us of the time in Britain was that he had opportunity to preach and speak in many places.

The next definite information we have on his movements is that in 1915 he began to serve 'a joint pastorate of two half-time churches' at Burkesville and Albany, in southern Kentucky, close to the border with Tennessee. 'It was so rural', he commented, 'that the nearest railway was forty miles away!'[6]

[6] This 'joint pastorate' in two places about fifteen miles away from each other raises questions that cannot presently be answered. We do not know whether Pink preached at each place every Sunday or on alternate Sundays, or it is possible one building was shared somewhere between the two locations.

At this point we gain additional light from the largest of the notebooks that Pink used to prepare his sermons in outline form, material that has happily survived. He numbered the blank pages, 594 pages in all, and divided his hand-written contents into two sections; the first with the heading 'Sermons to Saints' runs from p. 10 to p. 269. Blank pages follow to p. 290, where the untitled second section of the book begins and runs to p. 509. After that the remaining pages were never used. While the second section is untitled it is very clearly made up of evangelistic sermons, the first one being headed, 'Not Ashamed of the Gospel, Rom 1:16'.[7]

Internal evidence in this notebook fixes Pink's entrance into the ministry at Burkesville and Albany at about May 1915, and to allow for the prior eighteen months in England, we can assume he must have left California about the autumn of 1913.

The first sermon he prepared for his Kentucky charges is the first in this large sermon notebook. With the title 'An Evangelical Determination' he took for his text the words of 1 Corinthians 1:17, 'For I determined not to know anything among you save Jesus Christ and him crucified.' The opening notes read:

> Today I commence my official ministry among you and I know of no text in the Bible which more definitely sets forth my own aim and purpose. I began both my previous pastorates by preaching from this verse, and decided to do so again. I shall not discuss politics, philosophy, science, or social reform, nor treat of topics of the day, but Christ.

[7] The same title, it will be noticed, as the sermon he preached in Nottingham in 1908 (see p. 15). But the outline, included as Appendix 2, does not date from that time. Pink frequently revised and rewrote his sermon outlines.

His introduction then set out four reasons for the apostle's determination: '1. This is the theme which most honours God. 2. This is the theme which God honours the most. 3. This is the theme that is needed the most. 4. This is the theme which the people love the most.' Each of these points had some amplification before he proceeded to the main headings of the sermon. These were:

> 1. The apostle determined not to know anything save the Crucified as his dominating idea.
> 2. The apostle determined not to know anything save the Crucified as the ground of salvation.
> 3. The apostle determined not to know anything else save the Crucified as the centre of his religious life.
> 4. The apostle determined to know nothing else save the Crucified as the motive and end of Christian work.
> 5. The apostle determined not to know anything save the Crucified as the pattern of character.

Each of these divisions was given sub-heads which Pink obviously filled out in delivery. The whole sermon outline is on two compact pages, with the heads and sub-heads in red ink and other notes in black. No sermons were written in full, except, at times, the opening and closing words.

The sermons which follow in the notebook show that it was not Pink's usual method to preach consecutively on a passage or book of Scripture;[8] rather there is a considerable variety of theme, with the searching and the experimental pressed home after doctrinal teaching.

[8] An exception were expositions of the Gospel of John which he did in all his early pastorates, probably at the mid-week Bible Class.

His sermons to the 'saints' continued with these titles: 'The Divine Inspiration of the Scriptures'(*2 Tim.* 3:16); 'Sin - On & In' (*1 John* 1:7,8); 'The Preciousness of Christ' (*Song of Sol.* 2:16,17); 'The Hope of the Church' (*Titus* 2:13); 'Why we should pray – "Men ought always to pray"' (*Luke* 18:1); 'How we should pray' (*Luke* 18:1); 'The New Birth: its Author and Evidence' (*James* 1:18); 'A Noble View of Life' (*Job* 23:10).

Many other doctrinal and practical subjects were taken up before the end of 1915, with some preponderance on unfulfilled prophecy and on truths commonly called 'Calvinistic'. The truth of 'The Divine Government' is introduced from the text, 'Alleluia: for the Lord God omnipotent reigneth' (*Rev.* 19:6). 'The Doctrine of Election' (*John* 15:16) follows, then 'Sovereignty in Salvation' (*Jon.* 2:9). After four sermons on other subjects he returned to the same theme with 'The Evidences and Fruits of Election'(*2 Pet.* 1:10).

This notebook shows that it would be quite wrong to think that Pink saw his role chiefly as a teacher. The 'Sermons to Saints' that fill 259 pages in this notebook are not without frequent challenge and application to the unconverted. But concurrently (as the ink and writing show) he was preparing evangelistic sermons in the second section of the notebook. There are 219 pages taken up exclusively with sermons intended to awaken and convert the non-Christian. By any standard they constitute powerful evangelistic preaching on pointed texts. After eleven such sermons he introduced a series on the seven words of Christ from the cross.

Pink's notebook, thus begun with his third pastorate, tells us almost nothing of a personal nature. As to how he came to go to Kentucky we learn nothing. But there are some significant things about him to be learned from these neat, hand-written pages. They demonstrate that by the time he was thirty years old he was already an able speaker. The layout of his sermon outlines shows a man who could think exactly, and who had learned how to present Scripture in a lucid and memorable way. Every sermon reveals thorough preparation. Hard work had led him to master a form of sermon construction which left him free to speak without dependence upon notes, for the headings of his outlines could be easily carried in his mind or seen at a glance. In later life he was to tell a friend how he came to his convictions about the construction of sermons:

> As a young man, with a critical mind, I was much disappointed with most of the sermons I heard, mainly because the preacher wandered so much from his text, and even his general subject, bringing in much that was irrelevant, and (in order to fill up the time) wandering all over the place - some preachers apparently considering it their business to give a synopsis of nearly the whole range of theology in a single discourse. The result was that I carried away very little, and after twenty-four hours only a blurred impression remained. On questioning others who heard those sermons, I found the effect on them was the same as on myself. (As Spurgeon said in a homiletical lecture to his students: "Too many preachers aim at nothing - and succeed in hitting it."). I therefore decided to avoid this snare and strive after unity in every sermon, having a single object or aim in each. The style thus acquired in preaching has influenced my writing. Perhaps it is a matter of opinion, but were I to re-live my life, I should unhesitatingly adopt this method. Repeated blows of

the hammer on the head of the same nail are necessary if it is to be driven in deeply, and one nail securely fixed is better than three or four loosely attached. Many, many times did it come to my ears that those who listened to my preaching exclaimed, 'Whether you agreed with him or not, there was no mistaking his meaning.'[9]

* * * * *

Pink's first sermon for the New Year 1916, and the fortieth in the notebook, was 'A Call to Forget' from the words of Philippians 3:13,14, 'forgetting those things that are behind . . .'. 'The year 1915 is ended, 1916 just dawned,' he told his people. 'Our faces are set to the unknown future, to the ultimate goal. We are running and as we are running we are to forget. What? Four things - our blessings, sorrows, disagreements, sins of the past.' The elaboration of these points was the first 'head' for his sermon. The second head was on 'Why we are to forget.' '1. Because the past is with God and you cannot undo it. 2. Because the best is still to be: because God has higher things in store for us than we have yet seen. 3. Because everything of value in the past is included in the present, hence ought to forget past. 4. Because not to forget means a slackening of pace.' After amplification of all these points he proceeded to 'How are we to forget?' 1. By keeping the goal in view. 2. By strenuous action in the present.

For the 'application' of this sermon, he noted: 'Here then is my (God's) message to you for the New Year. Perhaps last year you slacked in running – what hindered

[9] Letter to H. J. Bradshaw, Sept. 5, 1943.

you? – a blessing, a sorrow, a disagreement, a sin? Forget it then and, setting your face toward God begin a new year of consecration, of effort, of growth.'

After his New Year sermon of 1916 six more sermons follow before, to our surprise, we find in his notebook a sermon which evidently concluded this third pastorate. The title was 'Commended to a Rich Inheritance', from the words of Acts 20:32. For his introduction to this last sermon he noted: 'Nine months ago I commenced my pastorate by preaching from 1 Corinthians 2:2 and as I have prepared my sermons week by week I have steadily sought to keep this before me . . . If I have deepened your love and reverence for God's Word and you heed this parting message, my ministry among you will not have been in vain.'

This sermon was preached about February 1916. Nine months back from that point gives us a starting date around May 1915.[10]

There is nothing in the notebook to suggest any reason why Pink's third pastorate concluded when it did. His sermon outlines give no hint of unhappiness in himself or dissatisfaction with his people. It is just possible that the explanation is connected to romance. In this third pastorate there was no provision of a house for a pastor and as a bachelor he boarded with a family in Burkesville. In a brief personal allusion he once wrote: 'In 1916 I was much in prayer that God would provide me with a spiritual and godly wife.' Rural Kentucky might seem an unlikely place to see an answer to that prayer but it was at hand in the person of another guest who also came to

[10] I deduce 'about February' from the fact that the farewell sermon was the seventh to saints after the New Year address, yet some of the seven might have been given at a mid-week service, or he might, as I have said above, have been preaching the same sermons on alternate Sundays.

board in the same home. She was Vera E. Russell, a slightly-built, vivacious Christian, who spoke with a rich Kentucky drawl that she would retain all her days. She came to Burkesville from Bowling Green, some sixty miles away where she had been brought up by grandparents after the early death of her own parents. Her father is said to have been a surgeon, perhaps somewhat of the frontier type for at her birth (January 8, 1893), when it was feared she was dead, he hopefully 'dipped her in a barrel of icy water outside the house and shocked her into action'. 'This', she smilingly maintained in later years, 'is why I always feel so cold!'

Pink tells us nothing of how they fell in love, but living together in the same house cannot have been the best situation. Perhaps Vera introduced her future husband to churches in her own part of Kentucky for the next thing we know for sure about Pink's movements was that he was at Scottsville, a little over twenty miles from Bowling Green. We know this from the Spartanburg *Herald Journal* of July 1, 1917, which had the following among its church notices:

> Northside Baptist Church – Rev. Arthur W. Pink, of Scottsville, Ky., who has recently been called to the pastorate of Northside Church, will conduct both morning and evening services. Rev. R. V. Miller, of Hendersonville, and others are expected to take part in the services. A special invitation is extended to the public to attend these services. Morning service at 11:15 and evening at 8.30 o'clock. Sunday school at 10 a.m.

The quotation does not of course prove that Pink was at Scottsville for the whole time between his departure from Burkesville and his going to Spartanburg in the summer of the following year. We know from words written in 1929 that he had become familiar at this time with Christians at Morton's Gap, some sixty miles west of Vera's home town of Bowling Green and in the opposite direction to Scottsville. But there are good reasons for thinking that he was in a pastoral charge for most of this period, whether in the Scottsville area or elsewhere. We know that he spent a total of twelve years in pastorates and that figure is only possible if most of the period between 1912 and 1917 found him so engaged. This belief gains confirmation from three other facts.

First, words of Vera's suggest that when she and Arthur married on November 16, 1916, she was at once in a pastorate situation. She recalled: 'I was young – twenty-three – and inexperienced when I married. I felt my responsibility in being the pastor's wife. But not one of the deacons' wives in the church Mr Pink was pastor of ever gave the slightest help or encouragement. An old woman, seventy-seven years of age, was the first person among the women who was able to counsel and advise me on things I needed help upon. I praise God for her faithful words.'

Second, in a Foreword to volume 1 of Pink's *Exposition of the Gospel of John* (1923), he said that he had 'taught this book to five different classes in the course of as many pastorates'. With three pastorates before 1916 and only one more before 1923, the fifth has to be located at this time.

Third, Pink's sermon notebook, started in his third pastorate, shows that he was again in a settled charge later in 1916. For the last sermon of that year he preached on 'A Call to Remembrance', from the words, 'Remember all the way that the Lord thy God led thee' (*Deut.* 8:2). The last 'head' of this sermon was on 'The Results of

Remembrance' and had these points:

1. Humiliation: as recall past failures and sins we are humbled and chastened.
2. Revelation of our weakness and frailty - need of Divine grace. This is the great lesson of history - man is frail and needs God.
3. Gratitude – Ps. 63:5,6. – no life is destitute of mercies.
4. Praise - 'When all thy mercies, O my God' etc. Then sing Ps. 103:1-3.
Application. Remember Jesus Christ. All remembrance leads to Him: every review of life demonstrates two things: Our Need, Christ's Sufficiency. Every remembrance of sin brings us back to the Cross.

Pink's New Year sermon for 1917 was the same sermon, 'A Call to Forget', that he had preached before, only written out again with minor changes and obviously for a different congregation. The second sermon prepared in 1917 surely sounds as though it was prepared for a people among whom he was settled. He introduced 'A Call to Godly Living' with the words: 'The merit by which a soul enters heaven is not its own, but the merits of Christ. Quite sure you'll all hold me guiltless of ever having spoken about this great doctrine in any but unmistakable language. If I have erred it is not in this direction. At the same time it is an equally dangerous state of affairs if doctrine is made to drive out precept, and faith is held up as making godly living a superfluity.'

Next to his own conversion Vera was to be the greatest blessing in Arthur Pink's life. Counselling others in later years, Pink wrote: 'The question of choosing a wife is not easily answered . . . personally, I acted very slowly, being thirty years of age before I entertained any serious thoughts on the matter. But God does not deal with all alike. "A prudent wife is from the Lord" (*Prov.* 19:14) is what guided me, and I begged him to direct me to such, and he did.'

As with all marriages it was not without some initial problems of a practical nature. Commenting on their first setting up house together Vera Pink recalled: 'I knew how to cook. I could prepare all sorts of dishes but I found my husband could not eat them.' The fact was that she had been trained to prepare the kind of rich food commonly served in a typical Southern home, a diet admirable for men who did long hours of work outdoors, but never intended for those whose day was spent largely in study. 'So I had to learn all over again,' she reports to the same friend, and the result was that henceforth they lived on 'plain food' and 'very simple menus'.[11]

After some twenty years of marriage Vera Pink was to write to a friend:

> It is blessed when the Lord brings two of his own together and unites them in wedlock. There is a double oneness between such, and it is little wonder that their ways, thoughts and perhaps features are so alike. Yes, undoubtedly the Lord did prepare us for each other. We have seen it from the first and praise him for his goodness unto us. My greatest longing is to be a help, and used of him in whatever sphere or place he has for me.

[11] Letter to Evelyn Green in 1936.

3

Spartanburg

With Pink's arrival at Northside Baptist Church we come to a much clearer knowledge of his life. This is due to a large number of letters that he wrote from Spartanburg that have survived. Beginning with one dated September 12, 1917, they were all written to I. C. Herendeen, the owner of a small publishing and book work called 'The Bible Truth Depot', situated at Swengel in Pennsylvania. It seems that Herendeen had visited Pink during the latter's time in Kentucky and he was the publisher of Pink's first book, *The Divine Inspiration of the Bible.*

As there was no house belonging to the Spartanburg congregation, the Pinks' accommodation was rented. It was barely comfortable and their first winter there proved remarkably cold for South Carolina: 'We were living in a small wooden house, built on piles (no foundations to it), some feet off the ground. Only a small fireplace in each room. For weeks we had it around or below zero. Pipes all frozen; drinking water had to be carried.'[1]

The inflation brought about by the First World War also hit them. While their salary remained stationary for two years, their rent was increased four times, and prices

[1] Letter to Mr and Mrs Lowell Green, Feb. 18, 1940.

rose dramatically until eggs were $1 a dozen, milk $1 a gallon, and sugar 30 cents a pound!

The church, he later remembered, met in 'a smallish wooden building, on an unfenced plot of ground, about half a mile from the railway depot. I was then just over thirty: dark, five foot eight inches tall.'[2]

Reading the correspondence between Pink and Herendeen it is clear that Pink was now a man with many more contacts than he had known in his first years in the States. In addition to his first book he had also begun to write tracts, and was being accepted as an up-and-coming figure in Fundamentalist circles.

The Fundamentalist movement had arisen in reaction to the downgrade in belief in the mainline denominations. A number of its leaders had withdrawn from denominational involvement and, by means of Bible Conferences and literature, they developed an influential network across the country. In twelve paperbacks, entitled *The Fundamentals* (1910–15), leaders of this movement had identified themselves with the position of historic Christianity on the authority of Scripture and other major doctrines. One of the main contributors to that series was Philip Mauro, attorney-at-law in New York, and a prolific writer. In a chapter entitled, 'A Personal Testimony', Mauro began, 'I came to a saving knowledge of the Lord Jesus Christ on May 24, 1903, being then in my forty-fifth year.'[3]

Another contributor to *The Fundamentals* was Arno C. Gaebelein who also edited the well-known magazine *Our Hope*.[4] But while the difference was unnoticed in *The*

[2] Letter to Blackburn, Jan. 22, 1939.
[3] *The Fundamentals* (Chicago: Testimony Publishing, n.d), vol. 4, p. 105.
[4] Established in 1894, *Our Hope* continued to 1957. See David A. Rausch, *Arno C. Gaebelein 1861–1945* (New York: Edwin Mellen Press, 1983).

Fundamentals, the Fundamentalist movement was not in every respect a continuation of historic, evangelical Christianity. A number of the leaders, such as H. A. (Harry) Ironside, as well as leaving denominations had embraced Brethren beliefs, and most prominent among those beliefs was the thinking that was being widely popularized in the notes of the Scofield Bible. According to this teaching the next coming of Christ would not be at the day of judgment, as had long been generally believed, but rather another 'dispensation' is to be expected before the final consummation of history. This would be introduced by Christ coming to 'rapture' the church, before a great tribulation, leading to the conversion of Israel and to the millennium. Premillennial Dispensationalism, as it was called, became so pervasive and popular in evangelical circles that it was often held as a fundamental article of faith, and the output of books on the subject was near endless. Gaebelein, it is said, 'ambitious and conscientious, provided the spark for the millenarian movement during the first two decades of the twentieth century'.[5]

It is probable that Pink was first introduced into this circle during his time in California in 1912–13. In 1918 he was to write: 'The Lord graciously inclined Mr Gaebelein's heart towards me six or seven years ago, and he has always been most friendly.'[6] This was the age of Bible Conferences, and Gaebelein and Ironside had met up in such a conference on the West Coast about 1911–12. Both men were itinerants in 'Bible ministry' and

[5] Ernest R. Sandeen, *The Roots of Fundamentalism: British and American Millenarianism 1800–1930* (Chicago: University of Chicago Press, 1970), p. 221.

[6] *Letters from Spartanburg*, p. 55. All further quotations from Pink's letters written during his Spartanburg years are from this source.

Ironside's biographer believed, 'There are no other men of this generation who have travelled more extensively as ambassadors for Christ or produced more material over a period of years.'[7] Ironside was based at Oakland, in northern California, where he organized the Western Book and Tract Company in 1914. In 1930 he was to become President of Moody Bible Institute.

Pink's first surviving letter to Herendeen of September 12, 1917, speaks of the latter's contact with Mauro, and reports that he had recently returned from a Bible Conference at Asheville, North Carolina. While at Asheville, Pink had been asked not to distribute any more copies of his tract 'Sins of the Saints', an event which proved a precursor of things to come. For the present, however, he was a welcome contributor to the pages of Gaebelein's *Our Hope*, and his second book *The Redeemer's Return*, published by Herendeen in 1918, was in full accord with the teaching which that magazine promoted. Pink believed that Gaebelein had been influenced by him on a point in the interpretation of the book of Daniel and was gratified when the Fundamentalist leader wished to print his own edition of one of Pink's booklets, previously published by Herendeen. Meanwhile Herendeen had increasing respect for Pink's judgment and even asked him to critique an item of Mauro's that he had been offered for publication.

While unfulfilled prophecy comes up periodically in the letters of Pink to Herendeen, it was another subject which majors in Pink's thinking in their correspondence during the year 1918. In his sympathies, it seems, Pink had always been inclined to Calvinistic belief. Early in his Christian

[7] E. Schuler English, *H. A. Ironside: Ordained of the Lord* (Grand Rapids: Zondervan, 1956), p. 133.

life he knew Robert Haldane's *Commentary on Romans* and soon after coming to the United States he was aware of some of the writings of Jonathan Edwards.[8] In preaching the gospel, while urging immediate repentance and faith, he had never used the method of bringing sinners to 'decide for Christ' by calling them to the front of a meeting, a practice widespread and popular in Fundamentalist circles. At the same time he may have regarded it as simply a difference over methods, and it would seem that at first he did not regard Calvinistic belief as the major issue it was to become for him. His first book made no mention of it, and the authors he quoted from in that work were not of that tradition.

By 1915, however, as we have seen from sermon titles preached during his pastorate at Burkesville and Albany, Pink's convictions were developing. He had come to see that the man-centredness of too much evangelical practice was due to a theological failure; it was the result of low views of the majesty and sovereignty of God. Instead of recognizing the New Testament's emphasis on grace, and on God's determining power in electing and calling men to salvation, the current emphasis was all on 'free will'. God was often presented as though he were unable to save anyone until he was 'allowed' to do so. Too much evangelism, instead of humbling men, thus gave the impression that everything depended upon man. Contemporary evangelical weakness, Pink became convinced, was weak at the point where they least expected it, the doctrine of God.

It has been said that 'writing is torn from a person. If you are going to say something worthwhile you're going

[8] In a letter of October 1936 he says: 'Jonathan Edwards' writings are very searching and they were much blest to me almost twenty-five years ago. His *Religious Affections* is one of his best.'

to burn'. In 1918 Pink was certainly burning as he wrote on the sovereignty of God. Instead of waiting till he had a complete manuscript ready to send to Herendeen, he sent the book to him in draft form, chapter by chapter, and these the publisher was expected to return with any comments. There was no lack of comment from the owner of the Bible Truth Depot and Pink found himself having to deal with his doubting friend. He wrote to Herendeen on April 23, 1918:

> Am also exceedingly joyed to know that you were all blessed by the reading of Chapter 5 of 'God's Sovereignty'– returned mss. received safely, with thanks. I have prayed several times after you left us that He would enlighten the eyes of your understanding and enlarge your heart to take in this most vital, important, and precious truth. I have been studying it diligently now for nine years and it has been the 'sheet anchor' of my soul. If He permits the completion and publication of this work, I doubt not that it will involve some bitter criticism . . . yet I am fully assured it will meet a real, present need among the Lord's dear people. I have now written out Chapter 6 and enclose mss. (Try and return within a *week* if possible.)[9]

On May 5, 1918 Pink told his friend, 'The Lord is giving me new light on the *meeting point* between God's Sovereignty and man's Responsibility.' But when Herendeen received the chapter on 'Reprobation' he was not at all sure that Pink had enough light. From Pink's letter to him of July 18 we gather that Herendeen had advised that the last chapter he had received should be excluded. Pink wrote:

[9] *Letters from Spartanburg*, pp. 13–14.

> Your looked-for letter of the 15th to hand yesterday afternoon. I must say I am disappointed at your brief remarks upon Chapter 9 . . . Having prayed long and earnestly to the Lord for light and guidance as to whether or not to include or exclude these pages, and feeling that *He would have me include* them, personally, I have no option; but as to whether or not *you* feel free to *publish* same is *your* responsibility and for *you* to decide before God . . . the passages that treat Reprobation are few in number, but plain and simple in their teaching. With you, dear brother, as with everyone else, it is simply a question of whether you will *believe* what God's Word says – you are not required to *understand* it in the first instance . . . God certainly *foreknew* and *foresaw* who would and who would not accept Christ (foresaw it before the foundation of the world), and therefore in giving being to (creating) those He knew *would not* accept Christ, He necessarily created them unto damnation.[10]

Herendeen remained unsure that it was a 'simple' matter of believing Scripture and evidently requested more scriptural evidence. Pink responded on July 21, 1918 with a detailed exposition of Romans 9:13–23. It reached Swengel the next day and his publisher declared himself 'satisfied'. By July 24 Pink was ready to send Herendeen the conclusion of the book, and he recommended a first printing of 500 copies. 'My opinion', he warned, 'is that my denial that God loves everybody will provoke the most criticism of anything in the book; but, as said therein, the fact that this is a favourite tenet of all false cults and isms of the day ought to be sufficient to show true believers it is false.' 'God does not love sinners,' he had written in an earlier letter. His case was

[10] I will defer comment on this and kindred points to later pages.

that God only loves those who are in Christ, that is, the elect. For Scripture says, 'Jacob have I loved, but Esau have I hated.' Corresponding with this thinking was his belief, stated in the published book, that the gospel is not an 'offer' of salvation to all; it is an announcement of 'the terms upon which men may be saved (namely, repentance and faith) and, indiscriminately, all are commanded to fulfil them'.[11]

The Sovereignty of God, which was in print before the end of November 1918, was a powerful treatment of many Scriptures which had too long received little attention in evangelical circles. It presented sin and man's fallen nature in a far more serious light than was customary, yet, as we shall consider later on, it was the work of a young man and some of his conclusions would need to be revised. The book did not arrive in the market as a bombshell; rather it seems scarcely to have been noticed, and for some months Pink heard little comment. A first review came from William Pettingill, Fundamentalist editor of *Serving and Waiting*. On reading it, Pink commented to Herendeen, 'I am thankful he does not condemn the book: but neither does he recommend it. If I knew nothing of its merits myself, his review would not encourage me to purchase a copy!' Meanwhile Gaebelein, for whom Pink was regularly contributing a Genesis series for *Our Hope*, said nothing; Pink suspected he had still to read it.

This muted reception for *The Sovereignty of God* hardly surprised the author. In the Foreword, dated June 1918, he had written:

[11] Pink, *The Sovereignty of God* (Swengel, PA: Bible Truth Depot, 1959), p. 257. There were three editions of this title, 1918, 1921, and 1929. The 1959 printing was a reissue of the 1929 edition. I have not had access to the first or second editions but it is certain that the sentence quoted represents his thinking in 1918.

> It would be foolish for us to expect that this work will meet with general approval. The trend of modern theology, if theology it can be called, is ever toward the deification of the creature rather than the glorification of the Creator. Even those who are clear, intellectually, upon other truths, are rarely sound in *doctrine*. Few, very few, today, really believe in the *complete* ruin and *total* depravity of man. Those who speak of man's 'free will', and insist upon his inherent power to either accept or reject the Saviour, do but voice their ignorance of the real condition of Adam's fallen children. And if there are few who believe that, so far as he is concerned, the condition of the sinner is entirely hopeless, there are fewer still who really believe in the absolute Sovereignty of God.

* * * * *

At first the prospects at Northside Baptist were hopeful and Pink gave himself energetically to the work. Besides two sermons Sunday, there was a Tuesday night prayer meeting and a Bible address on Friday nights.[12] In the expectation of more people being interested in the Bible addresses the venue was changed to a comfortable room in the 'uptown' YMCA and the night changed to Thursday. For a time this proved 'highly encouraging' but unexpected problems arose. The influenza epidemic that took so many lives elsewhere reached South Carolina. Suffering from flu himself, Pink was unable to take the class one week, and then for the next seven or eight weeks a quarantine was imposed on the town, with no public

[12] He gave a consecutive exposition of the Gospel of John at Spartanburg, probably on the Thursday nights.

meetings allowed. It was lifted, only to be reimposed, so that in fourteen weeks it was only possible to meet four times. All continuity of interest in the class was thus lost. When the class eventually resumed on January 2, 1919, 'It just poured down all day and continued all the evening: at class time it was not fit to turn a dog out, but I went uptown and addressed five people.' By the end of February 1919 Pink had to report, 'The Bible class at the YMCA has proved quite a failure: fewer attending than when we had it at "Northside". I announced last night it would be transferred back again to the church house next week.'

At Northside itself support weakened as a minority of opposition gathered round a certain 'Brother Metcalfe'. In part this had a doctrinal source and was connected with the contents of Pink's book on sovereignty which were preached at this period. In our view resistance from among his hearers was not without some justification yet to be fair to Pink it must be said that he was by no means a man of one theme. His letters to Herendeen could mislead us here for the subject of his controversial book necessarily took up space that it did not do in the course of his week-to-week ministry. The notebook of his sermon outlines shows that specifically Calvinistic themes were not the staple of his ministry. His doctrinal teaching was varied and there was a practical emphasis on holy living. Such words as the following were not infrequent:

> It is a very great fault in any ministry if the doctrine of justification by faith be not clearly taught. I am quite sure you will all hold me guiltless of ever having spoken about this great doctrine in any but unmistakeable language. If I have erred it is not in this direction. At the same time it is an equally

> dangerous state of affairs if doctrine is made to drive out precept, and faith is held up to make godly living a superfluity. It is not by personal holiness man shall enter heaven, yet without holiness no man shall be saved.[13]

The series on Elijah, which became one of his best-known books, belongs to these years, and he continued preparing many new evangelistic sermons on the way of salvation. Even so by the winter of 1918–19 the unfavourable reception of Pink's teaching on the sovereignty of grace on the part of some in his congregation had become a concern to him. When on some occasions he was away on Sundays the supply preacher who took his place patently contradicted what the people had been hearing on sovereignty from their pastor. 'I have decided to get no supplies when I am absent in the future', he wrote to Herendeen on 28 February 1919. In facing this situation Pink recognized that to build up a congregation with the truth would take time: 'I have felt I could do more for God by remaining with some company of His people, and systematically indoctrinating them by consecutive Bible study, rather than the butterfly method [of the itinerant preacher] of just delivering half a dozen addresses here and another half dozen there and leaving to do same in another place.'

But the dissatisfaction was not only about his preaching. Ominously this note appeared at the end of a lengthy letter to Herendeen: 'Our offerings have fallen off some of late and the deacons have waited on those of our members who are not contributing to support the work, and three or four fairly well-to-do brethren say they will

[13] From sermon notes on 'A Call to Godly Living' preached in 1917. This was a revision of a sermon first preached early in 1916 during his third pastorate.

not support an unsociable pastor who spends his time in the study and won't call on his members unless they are sick.'

There may be some weight to this criticism. To Pink's credit it has to be said that he was diligent in visiting the sick; one person in hospital, for instance, he visited twice in one day. When a person had an accident on the way to church he immediately went to see her as soon as the service was over. But Pink was hardly a 'people's person'. He had little if any 'small talk' and the culture of South Carolina was not his own. In a sermon he preached at this period on the words, 'A time to keep silence, and a time to speak' (*Eccles* 3:7), he gave a well-balanced biblical treatment of 'the noble gift of speech'. Introducing his subject he told his people that 'talkativeness is utterly ruinous to deep spirituality, a waste of time and it inevitably leads to the saying of unwise, unpleasant and unprofitable things . . . If I am to walk in the Spirit I must cease talking for talk's sake. We have two eyes and two ears but only one tongue as if to show we should see and hear twice as much as we say!' Nonetheless it is true that Pink's own nature was reserved. Writing to Herendeen after Christmas, 1918, he confessed:

> I am glad the holiday season is nearing its close. I always find it demoralising. This year we have been on the go every day, either entertaining kind friends in our home, or else visiting them in theirs. We are to go out and dine again tomorrow, D.V., and ditto again the day following, and then I hope there will be an end to these festivities. By natural temperament, I am a born recluse and unsociable, and since I was born again, I have shrunk from spending God's time in idle recreations. Unless I can help somebody

spiritually or get edified myself by going out, I much prefer to remain in my study.

Not too much weight should be placed on this passing admission. In later years we shall find him rejecting criticism that he was 'unsociable'. It is clear that he could and did enjoy fellowship with others, yet his temperament probably did not help him to establish warm relationships on a social level with his comparatively small congregation. Richard Belcher has expressed the opinion that Pink was not well suited for the pastorate and we shall return to this point later.[14] However, wherever he was there were those who were thankful for him, and who gave him constant support. One of this number at Spartanburg was an elderly lady of whom he wrote some years later:

> The most active worker in the last church of which I was pastor was seventy-seven years old when I went there, and during my stay of three and a half years she did more for the Lord, and was a greater stimulus to me, than any other member of that church.[15]

The main personal difficulty Pink faced in Spartanburg was connected with the programme he set for himself. The truth was that he was attempting to undertake three roles simultaneously, and any one of them would have been sufficient for the average man: he was a faithful pastor, a constant student, and an author. All three might have been combined if he had moderated his input, and

[14] *Arthur W. Pink: Born to Write*, pp. 43–6. Dr Belcher gives three main reasons for his opinion: 1. Lack of sociability. 2. Absence of tact and compassionate sensitivity. 3. The length of his sermons – permissible in a conference but not in the average congregation. If Pink failed in the second area, it was to lead to greater wisdom in the advice he gave to other pastors in later years.

[15] *Studies*, 1927, p. 167.

lowered his aims, but that was not in his nature. Certainly the pastorate came first. He allowed nothing to interfere with his preparation of three new addresses for his people every week and commented to Herendeen: 'I prepare for these as diligently as if they were to be delivered before 5,000 and three addresses on three different books [of Scripture] every week is no light task, I assure you.' To the encouragement of prayer among his people he also gave himself. If a general pastoral visitation was not his forté, there is no indication of failure in other respects.

But along with this routine Pink was engaged in an enormous amount of reading. Until about 1915 his reading may have been much in general and contemporary evangelical literature, with some special interest in unfulfilled prophecy. The latter remained a special interest but a whole new school of authors was now capturing his attention, namely the English Puritans. These were authors long out of print and virtually unknown in the contemporary Christian world. Perhaps it was Jonathan Edwards that drew his interest to the Puritans. In the summer of 1918 he was attempting to read through all four volumes of Edwards' *Works.*[16]

'Dipping into books' was not Pink's idea of reading. In January 1919 he notes that he had read forty-five books in the preceding three months. A letter to Herendeen on May 15, 1919, contains this astonishing sentence: 'Next week, DV, I shall complete Manton's 22 volumes, and then I expect to make a careful study of 12 large volumes by Thomas Goodwin.' By July 26, 1919, little over two months later, he told Herendeen, 'I have just finished volume 8 of Goodwin's 12 volumes.' As that particular volume of Goodwin's contains 600 pages it is

[16] This would be the Worcester edition of Edwards' *Works*, reprinted in four volumes by Robert Carter of New York in 1881.

scarcely conceivable that he was reading Goodwin's volumes consecutively. On August 23 he reported, 'Have just concluded Goodwin's last volume and am now ready to begin the 18 volumes by Owen.' Before the end of the same year (1919), he told his friend on December 9, 'Owen is wearisome. I am not half-way through the fifteen volumes of his works.'

That no Puritan would have commended such an intensity of reading does not seem to have occurred to Pink. We may admire his enthusiasm while questioning his wisdom. From painful experience he would give better advice to young men in later years.[17] My point, however, is to illustrate the extent of his studies, and, as if all that were not enough, he was also giving regular time both to correspondence and especially to writing for publication, completing *The Redeemer's Return*, *The Godhood of God* and *The Seven Sayings of the Saviour on the Cross* at this period. We are hardly surprised when, in one of his letters to Herendeen, Pink mentions that 'it is already well past midnight'.

Plainly Pink was carrying a load that could not be sustained. It is not that he utterly ignored his health; he notes, for instance, the importance of walking, but he certainly overestimated how much can be done without a breakdown. On July 24, 1918, he noted in a letter to Herendeen: 'I have been feeling far from well. I think it must be the reaction from over exertion while working on "God's Sovereignty". I have been threatened with congestion of the brain[18] – an inherited tendency – and

[17] For instance, he wrote to Robert Harbach in 1944: 'I would advise you to go slow in reading Owen . . . You are likely to find him more helpful in another ten years' time, if you are spared, when your own spiritual life has further matured.' *Letters to a Young Pastor*, p. 9.

[18] No such medical term is recognized today; 'stress' would be our more usual term.

my heart has troubled me too. I spent most of yesterday in bed.' A week later he added: 'I was almost worn out (you may remember) when I came here to Spartanburg, and for the last twelve months have worked at very high pressure.' By November of the same year he believed his health was back to normal, 'though I have not yet quite recovered weight and strength recently lost'. But before February 1919 severe headaches overtook him as the multiplicity of his labours continued, and at the end of March he was only working, in his estimate, 'half-time, feeling considerably below my normal'. In late June, after spending half the week in bed he got up to take the Thursday Bible Class, dressed, 'made a fight for a minute or two and then had to give in, tumbling onto the bed fully dressed and sent Mrs Pink to tell the folks I was utterly unable to lead the meeting'. Two days later the doctor had to be called: 'He found my heart and lungs perfectly sound, but my nerves badly disordered, my blood pressure considerably below normal, and my general condition run down. He said I must have several weeks of complete rest and prescribed no medicine but is making me almost double my amount of food per day.'

By this time it was clear to both Arthur and Vera Pink that his course of life would have to change, and that either the pastorate or the ministry of writing would have to be given up. While there were some encouragements in the work at Northside in 1919, with support for his ministry somewhere between a dozen and twenty-five people, his local friends expressed the opinion that his future work was not in their midst. That might have made it obvious that he was to give himself to writing but such a conclusion was confused by the fact that for much of the year 1919 there were indications that there were other, and much larger, churches interested in him.

Gaebelein had now read *The Sovereignty of God* and while the news was passed on to Pink that he regarded its publication as 'a big blunder . . . which he condemns *in toto*', yet he tried to get Pink called to a church in Idaho; earlier he had recommended A. J. Gordon's former congregation in Boston to consider him. Other churches from whom a call was possible included two in California and one in Tennessee ('too worldly', was Pink's estimate of the last after responding to a request that he visit it). The enquiries and possible openings that came to him in 1919 undoubtedly added to the strain on him when his health was already impaired. In the first surviving letter from Vera Pink, written to Herendeen on June 22, 1919 (and before he had Gaebelein's criticism of his book), she said:

> I am quite worried about my husband. The work here is so discouraging and the strain of waiting for something else to open up is telling upon him. He is quite despondent, nervous and irritable and unable to sleep. This last week has been the worst of any . . . The only thing that has come has been a letter from Mr F. C. Jennings . . . He advised Mr Pink to go back into business. Mr Pink had already told me he believed he could accomplish more by making money in business and giving it to the Lord's work than what he is doing here. Mr Jennings' letter, in the absence of one from Mr Gaebelein, has thoroughly unsettled him. I certainly do not believe the Lord wants him to go back into business. It seems to me the Lord would have him devote more and more of his time to writing books. The fact that he keeps receiving letters from those who have been blessed in reading his other writings is one of the things that leads me

> to this conclusion. But, I believe that if he writes heavy books, he ought to be clear of all pastoral duties and responsibilities and yet exactly what to do and where to go is a puzzle.

It was the week after this letter that the doctor had to be called in, and with rest Pink recovered from this low point. As the summer turned to autumn nothing materialized in the way of calls from other churches and, his health largely restored, he continued steadily in the work of the pastorate. But although his general reading was now 'reduced considerably (much against my will)', there was little time to write and the choice he had to make became clearer to them both. 'I am thoroughly convinced', he wrote on December 6, 1919, 'that the Lord would have me give myself to writing.' The question now was where that should be. Herendeen suggested that they might remain in their rented accommodation in Spartanburg but Pink rightly thought it unwise to remain so close to the people he had been serving (and who might continue to need his help). It occurred to Pink that the quiet village in rural Pennsylvania where Herendeen was based, and which he had already visited, would be a good location. But in response to an enquiry from Pink, Herendeen could find no neighbours who would be able to let two rooms to him and Vera. An alternative was to buy land and build, and in a letter of 12 November 1919 Pink spoke of a four-roomed house that could, hopefully, be built of wood for $500. The prospect from the house did not matter but Mrs Pink would like enough space behind to keep chickens.

Much correspondence ensued on the feasibility of the house-building proposal, and Pink looked to Herendeen to make the arrangements for the purchase of materials and the necessary land. A first estimate was obtained but Pink thought it 'very exorbitant'. All he wanted was four rooms, sized 10 feet by 12, with 'no fire-places or fire-grates, no plastering and no expensive "fittings"'. A later proposal increased the room size to 12 feet by 12. At length prices were decided but Herendeen was clearly nervous about the possibility of proceeding to build only to find the Pinks disappointed with the result. Pink assured him that would not happen yet his continued suggestions on changes for the plan of the house must have given his friend reason to be anxious. In the end it was determined that while Herendeen should obtain all the timber and materials required, and fix a lease on land belonging to the Bible Truth Depot, the actual building was to await their arrival. Pink reckoned that if they left Spartanburg 'a day or two before building began', they could be present to supervise and get it completed before their household effects would arrive by freight train, ten to twenty days later. 'Go ahead and order doors and windows now as per bill I sent you', Pink wrote on January 10, 1920. A few days later he announced his resignation to the church at Northside to take effect at the beginning of March. A letter to Swengel of February 16 confirmed that they expected to be there on the afternoon of March 2. The Herendeens had invited them to stay until the new home was ready.

There is no indication that Pink left Spartanburg downcast. In his last 'New Year's Message' that he preached there in 1920, from Psalm 63:1–3, he observed at the outset 'how his sorrow had brought David into a closer union with God'. Looking over the year that was past, he told his hearers, while 'failures and sins' were a cause for sadness, there were also reasons for thankfulness: 'Some have been snatched as brands from the burning and added to the family of God; the weak have been strengthened; the sorrowful comforted; the bereaved sustained. For the Christian what a bright hope is ours! How precious the thought that ere 1920 is closed you may be "for ever with the Lord"! The bud of promise may have burst into the full fruit of joy unspeakable. The springtime of faith may have given way to the summertime of triumphant joy.'[19]

[19] With this sermon, the 'Sermons to Saints' begun in the notebook of 1915 are nearing a conclusion. There are only fourteen more, all on Genesis chapters 1–17, except for the last which is on John 6:44, with the title 'What is Included and Involved in Coming to Christ?' Along with evangelistic sermons these probably constituted his ministry on Sundays and mid-week until the end of February 1920.

4

Tent Meetings in California

At this point the story temporarily ends in silence, for the correspondence with Herendeen, on which we are entirely reliant for this period, obviously ended with the Pinks' arrival in Pennsylvania. More than four months pass before we can pick up the course of events. On July 28, 1920, there is a letter from Pink to Herendeen written at Garden Grove, California (the place where we noted Pink preaching in 1913). He had been invited to preach until August 7, by a group who were awaiting their new pastor.[1] After that engagement there was to be a week of meetings at Orange and he anticipated other openings on the West Coast. While no more thinking in terms of another pastorate, Pink had clearly not closed his mind to occasional conference and evangelistic ministry. What savings the Pinks had possessed had probably all gone into the new house, and it was almost certainly to this journey to the West Coast in the summer of 1920 that Pink was referring to when he recalled some years later:

> I had a three-days' meeting in Brooklyn before me, and from what I would receive there I figured there

[1] While, in his letters to Herendeen at this time, Pink speaks of meeting 'old friends' at Garden Grove he does not give the impression of being in a location where once he had been the pastor. *Letters of an Itinerant Preacher, 1920–1*, ed. R. P. Belcher (Columbia, SC: Richbarry Press, 1994), pp. 7–12.

would be just enough for my fare to California ($75 'tourist'), but *nothing* left for my wife. I had to leave her behind when I went to Brooklyn: the last night there, after the meeting, a lady handed me an envelope to 'give to your wife when you get home'. When she opened it we found bills for $75, and we had not mentioned the matter to a human soul. On our way to California we had to break our journey at Chicago, where we changed trains and had a seven-hour wait. Vera had never been to Chicago. I asked her which she preferred: to look around the city or make for the Moody Bible Institute. She chose the latter. We dined with the student-body, plus a few visitors. A lady next to her asked her name and then enquired if she was related to A.W.P., saying his articles in *Our Hope* some years before had been much blest to her soul. This lady and her husband were 'visitors' at the Moody Bible Institute that week. They at once took charge of us. They supplied us with a bountiful 'supper', and took us down to the train. Neither of us had scarcely any money in our pockets to buy food with for the three days' journey to Los Angeles. The gentleman handed me $3 and then went into a store and bought a large $2 basket full of all kinds of fruit, nuts, crackers, etc.!

In the letter of Herendeen already mentioned, of July 28, 1920, Pink wrote:

We arrived safely Monday noon. I took a severe cold on the train – head full of it and so hoarse I could only just manage to speak last night – 1st of the meetings . . . My old friend Gwynne Lewis came over yesterday afternoon and remained till this morning:

> he has already fixed up 8 days' meetings for me at Riverside, California, in which most of the churches are uniting – A. C. Gaebelein is there end of this week. Lewis believes the Lord may keep me in Riverside two full weeks at least; the last week to counteract the teaching of my old friend Dr Mabie there (universal reconciliation), which, he tells me, is being widely accepted by the Lord's people in Riverside . . . Brother Lee is very anxious for me to spend a week at Bible Institute in Los Angeles – he can secure me an opening if I will say the word – am looking to the Lord for guidance. Believe I shall have the best sale of books in Riverside.
>
> Has the Chicago second-hand bookstore sent the Hebrew grammar yet?
>
> Will you please forward to me my own copy of *God's Sovereignty* – it is on the top shelf of the second book case counting from the front door – I feel I must make a start on it.[2]

Subsequent letters to Herendeen reported conditions in the part of California with which Pink had formerly been familiar. Christians, he commonly found, 'all mixed up and do not know what they believe. The confusion is terrible. Men like Hadden and Farr seem to preach only on Prophecy – man's ruin, and God's grace,

[2] *Letters of an Itinerant Preacher*, pp. 7–8. All Pink's letters from the West Coast at this period are from this source. Making 'a start' on *God's Sovereignty* refers to his revision of the book before it was reprinted in 1921. The incidental reference to the whereabouts of his copy seems to confirm that a house was built for them in Swengel. In later letters he asked for other things and was able to tell Herendeen where they were to be found, that is, 'either in the small file of letters hanging on the wall of little spare room, or else among the things I left on the dining table'. The 'little spare room' was the result of a change in the plan to have all rooms 12 feet by 12. The living room, which was also his study and library, was 14 feet by 14, with the small room cut down to 8 feet by 10.

indoctrination of believers is utterly neglected.' By mid-August Pink had moved north to San Francisco in response to an appeal from another friend who ran what was called the National Bible Institute. Support for the meetings did not live up to what the title might have suggested, but an unexpected opportunity arose with the appeal for his help from a 'Brother Thompson' of Seattle. Thompson was a travelling evangelist, with his own large tent, and he had been preaching for three months in Oakland, across the bay from San Francisco. He spoke of having seen 'over 150 genuine converts', and had the support of some four to five hundred local Christians. 'I am no teacher,' he pleaded with Pink, 'and they sorely need a teacher, for hundreds of them are but babes in Christ.' Unsure of how to respond, Pink went over to Oakland one Sunday night to Thompson's Tent. He wrote of it to Herendeen: 'I got there ten minutes before time to begin, and the place was packed out. Every one of the 1000 seats was occupied and scores standing. By the time to begin, one of the sides had to be raised. I spoke for 65 minutes along the lines of my tract "The Way of Salvation". The people listened with breathless interest throughout. O how I praise God for such an opportunity and privilege.'

Thompson was equally thankful and prevailed upon Pink to stay with him to give doctrinal expositions. Four days later Pink wrote to Herendeen again:

> Am having a glorious time here. The most wonderful opening and opportunity I have ever had: 700 people nightly; over a 1000 Saturday and Sunday – all deeply interested, hungry for the Word. Bro Thompson is anxious I should remain some time (indefinitely) and teach.

The following days confirmed these first impressions. On August 20, 1920, he wrote of 'scores of sinners seeking the Lord and hundreds of the saints being built up. Numbers steadily increasing.' And on September 8, 'I wish I could snatch half an hour to describe to you in some detail the "wonderful works of God" here in Oakland these last two weeks, but it is utterly impossible.' Included with these letters Herendeen at the Bible Truth Depot must have been astonished to see lengthy lists of the names and addresses of individuals ordering complete sets of Pink's writings.

In the second week in September, Pink had to return to the Los Angeles area to fulfil engagements he had promised earlier. As he did so there was a new buoyancy evident in his spirit and this was reflected in the increased numbers who came to hear him. Thompson meanwhile wanted Pink to continue with him, 'to follow him up after he has done the evangelizing and gotten the crowds together'. The teacher declined, believing that he must devote at least a third of his time to study and writing. He wrote to his friend at Swengel that his present labours were such that finishing the revising of *The Sovereignty of God* would have to await his return. There were also words of encouragement to Herendeen: 'You are having part in a blessed work, dear brother, as I am sure the day will show. Though I have been too busy to write much to you, nevertheless you have been much on my heart, and I have prayed for you frequently. Probably my English temperament does much to conceal it, but I assure you I love you much in the Lord.'

A last letter from California in 1920 told Herendeen that they would be back home with them on Saturday, October 30. The letter also showed Pink had a practical side: Could his friend please have a quart of milk strained for their return, reserve a dozen eggs and two loaves to be picked up by them, and buy 'a 3 lb. *roast* of beef from the butcher on Sat. morning, one with plenty of fat preferred'?

Back in Pennsylvania the last two months of the year were spent at Swengel and we have no more detail until the correspondence resumed after they left for more engagements early in 1921. Their destination was again Oakland, California, and Brother Thompson and his Tent meetings. 'We came on the Burlington line from Chicago,' Pink wrote to Herendeen on January 17, 1921, 'and on the Rio Grande from Denver to Ogden. This took us over high altitudes, varying from 7,000 to 10,000 feet. We both of us found it very trying.'

Different trials were to follow. 'When I got here, the attendance at the tent had dwindled down to about 300 a night, with 500 Saturday and Sundays.' Evidently Pink himself was partly responsible for the changed situation. Oakland, as was mentioned earlier in these pages, was the home base of the Fundamentalist leader, Harry Ironside, who had been away when Pink was last there. He had charge of the Western Book and Tract Company and exercised a major influence in the Brethren Assembly that met in the 'Gospel Auditorium'. When Ironside had returned and resumed his own ministry in Oakland, relationships with the Tent work had become strained. According to Pink, people would not come to hear Ironside but had preferred to hear Thompson at the Tent. To improve the situation, Thompson had invited Ironside to share in the Tent ministry and this he did for a while until there was a public disagreement one night over whether or not Thompson was 'living by faith'. Ironside said that he received support from the Brethren Assembly. All this was before Pink came back for another visit.

Almost certainly Ironside had heard various things about the Englishman's first visit. At that time, for instance, Pink had attended the Brethren meeting on one occasion but, when he was drawn into conversation with some of the men afterwards, 'they were simply "flabbergasted" when I told them I was a member of a Baptist Church because I considered they were more scriptural than those known as "the Brethren". I "took the bull by the horns" and told them they were unscriptural on a number of points.'[3] An account of this conversation was likely to have been passed on to Ironside. Then Pink's book on Sovereignty had come into the picture:

> Someone went round to see Bro. Ironside about Reprobation, taking him a marked copy of my book. Ironside seized on this and made the most possible out of it: said it was a bottle of deadly poison and so on: he warned all who belonged to the Assembly to burn my books and urged them to shun the Tent: most of the Assembly folk have done so, and quite a few of the young converts have been stumbled by the breach between Ironside and Thompson.

When Pink called at the Book Room (headquarters of Ironside's Book and Tract Company), shortly after his return to Oakland, 'Brother Ironside was in his office – only glass partition between, but took no notice of me.' A few days later one of the Brethren itinerant preachers, Alesor Marshall, who was in town, asked for a meeting with Pink and Thompson. This meeting confirmed that it was Pink's Calvinism which had become the main point of concern. In a conversation of 90 minutes, conducted evidently in a Christian spirit, many of the main points of

[3] Letter to Herendeen, 30 August, 1920, in *Letters of an Itinerant Preacher*, p.18.

difference were gone over, including the texts that speak of 'all' and 'world' with reference to the redemptive work of Christ. Particular time was spent on 1 Timothy 2:1–6. Pink wrote to Herendeen, 'His main point was this: God had commanded us to preach the gospel to every creature: if Christ died for the elect only, God is tantalizing non-elect sinners with an offer of salvation. On this point we first had a lengthy duel on whether or not the gospel is an "offer"; ultimately he agreed it was *not* and we got nowhere on that point.' Progress was not made on any other points of difference. At length Marshall 'sighed and groaned', and said to Thompson, 'Now you see where Mr Pink stands.' He then concluded, 'Further conversation is useless.' Pink ends the account, 'We shook hands and parted friendly.'

When Pink was in the Book Room a week later, and briefly met Ironside and one of his associates, the atmosphere was somewhat different: 'They are scarcely civil . . . Brother Ironside is the "pope" of the Assembly, and has succeeded in persuading about two thirds of its members to keep away from the Tent. But while this is deplorable, we are not greatly concerned: we are far more anxious to reach those of the Lord's people who are starving in the denominations than we are to preach to those who (think they) know as much or more than we do – I mean "The B" [Brethren].'[4]

As in all controversies between Christians, this disagreement was not helped by third parties passing on what others were reputed to have said or written. Without

[4] Ibid., p.44. Had Pink been an older man he might have better understood the difference from Ironside's perspective; he certainly would have agreed that 'there is a pope in us all'. Schuler English in his biography of Ironside makes no mention of these events. Pink was a nonentity when that biography was written in the early 1950s.

saying his source, Pink wrote to Herendeen on February 28, 1921:

> The opposition is getting stronger and stronger on the part of Mr Ironside. He took it upon himself to write Bro. A. C. G. [Gaebelein] a letter, when he heard that he had promised to come to the tent for 3 days in April, telling him that Mr Pink was teaching 'damnable heresy' . . . and further said A. C. G. was doing a great wrong to publish 'Gleanings in Genesis' in *Our Hope* and advised him strongly to cease having them printed. Personally, we feel Brother G. has too much sense to listen to H.A.I.

Meanwhile 'Brother Thompson' continued to stand by Pink although evidently perplexed by some of the points of difference. He was an easy-going, 'happy-go-lucky' individual, and for two men so different to have got on as well as they did, Pink cannot have been as angular as he is sometimes thought to have been. The previous September, Thompson had told Pink that he 'felt irresistibly drawn' to him. 'He is an exceptionally fine fellow,' was Pink's opinion of him, 'though, like us, has his defects, of course.'

Before the end of January 1921 the attendance at the Tent meetings had risen again, with between 600 and 700 on weeknights. Pink preached often, although not every night,[5] and he gives this description of a typical evening:

> 7:30 p.m. song service during which the crowd straggles in: usually Bro. Thompson is on the platform during this, and gives a 3 to 5 minute talk between hymns – his talk following the line of the

[5] On January 29 Thompson invited Alesor Marshall to preach at the Tent. Marshall was shortly to leave Oakland.

> last hymn; he is at his best here: very original, but nothing vulgar or cheap: 7.50 I arrive and go on platform: one more hymn, a prayer led by Bro. Thompson, brief announcements and at 8 sharp I begin speaking and continue till 9.15 or 9.20 and close in prayer. I am now expounding John 1. Occasionally someone in the audience asks if he may put a question to which I say, Yes, if relevant – in nearly every instance it is eager souls seeking light.[6]

With no lessening of numbers, the Pinks moved in February from the one room they were renting at $6 per week to a suite of rooms offered to them at the same price by Christians. This was an unexpected help in the hard times that existed on the West Coast at this date. That same month he noted: 'Industrial conditions are bad here: 1000s out of employment: 100s of men lounging on the streets.' While expounding John's Gospel, Pink had an evident concern to keep 'the simple gospel' foremost. About the beginning of March, he wrote Herendeen: 'Attendances are being maintained, many are being blessed and God's blessing is very manifest. I have now spent over 50 hours on John's Gospel, and am only half way through Chapter 4!' On Sunday he diverged from this expository approach and preached evangelistically on such texts as the Prodigal Son, Blind Bartimaeus and Zaccheus. 'Last night from Acts 17:30, 31, the Judgment Day,' he noted on March 7. 'About 1000 out, had great liberty and a most solemn time: a number appeared to be deeply affected.' Later in the

[6] *Letters of an Itinerant Preacher*, p. 50. One man, who Pink believed was 'primed beforehand', asked: 'Are those who are not born again damned because God did not work so mightily in them as in those who believe?' To which the preacher replied: 'No – they are damned because they have consciously and deliberately rejected Christ.'

month his subject at both Sunday services was the resurrection of Christians and he spoke of his joy in delivering the messages.

It has to be a reflection on Pink's ability as a speaker that numbers were maintained over such an extended period. In April 1921, after the tent had been eleven months in Oakland, Thompson believed that it was time to move on to Seattle at the end of the month. There was hope of a site for his tent in the centre of the town and he planned to add a gallery, so that 3,000 in all could be seated. Large crowds, he told Pink, were to be expected. 'I discount some of his big talk', Pink added, in reporting this news. With a deadline now before him, Pink speeded up on John's Gospel, and planned only two addresses on each chapter that remained.[7] During one week in April, as a Carnival took place immediately adjacent to the Tent, the plan was for evangelistic meetings only for the curious who might come in. 'Bro. Thompson said, "snappy and breezy talks" would be needed for such crowds. So I suggested *he* do this preaching – a type I am not cut out for.'

At this point, in April 1921, our close-up view of what Pink was doing is about to end, for no more correspondence to Herendeen survives beyond that month. Thompson had asked Pink to go with him to Seattle: 'Tells me I shall have the time of my life. Is willing for me to push sale of my literature but wants me to shut out Sovereignty.'[8] A few days after that invitation, Pink had

[7] On April 11 he noted: 'The week before last I spoke 7 times, and last week 8 times: have now given 77 addresses in all this trip.'

[8] While Thompson must have thought highly of Pink as a speaker, it is evident he remained unconvinced about some aspects of his Calvinism. 'One day,' wrote Pink, 'he will come out quite strong regarding God's Sovereignty – in favour of it – but next day, criticizes me for "riding a hobby horse", etc.'

[continued overleaf]

written to Herendeen, 'I still expect we *shall* leave here by end of April and go to Seattle but – cannot be certain, till we have actually started.' This uncertainty was related to a measure of the erratic that seemed to enter into Thompson's decisions. Evidently they did go to Seattle, for later on Pink referred to four months spent in Seattle, in the home of an older Christian couple by the name of Richards.

(18 March, 1921). 'The moment I lay down a premise and say "therefore" to draw a conclusion, he waves his hand and says, "Speculation". When I quote a Scripture, he answers, "Yes, I know, but there is this on the other side," and quotes another – often one that has no relevancy at all to what we were discussing . . . Concerning my book as a whole (which he has never read – says he hasn't read thro' a single book in his library) he says there must be something wrong with it as it divides God's people' (21 April 1921). As later pages of this book will reveal, there was more justification for Thompson's concerns than Pink could then recognize.

5

Author and Traveller

On the Pinks' return to their home in Swengel, probably in the late summer of 1921, we can have a fairly clear idea of what was to occupy his time. Despite the encouragement of the large meetings on the West Coast he remained convinced that writing and literature were the priority. He was confirmed in this conviction when the Moody Bible Institute took his large work *Gleanings in Genesis* for publication in 1922. He often discussed with Herendeen what might be taken up next, and one decision was the preparation of a first volume on John's Gospel for publication by the Bible Truth Depot. When it was ready in May 1923, Pink told his readers in the Foreword: 'This is no hasty production. The author has already devoted fifteen years of special study to John's Gospel.' Before this date, however, he had committed himself to a yet larger project. During 1921 Herendeen had proposed to him the need for a monthly magazine. Pink gave it much thought and prayer before deciding on what was to prove the most important ministry of his life:

> Having already written so much, that seemed no small order, but after spreading the matter before the Lord, and upon our publisher agreeing to look after

the clerical side of the work, together we launched forth.

Thus, in January 1922, there appeared in twenty pages and without covers the first issue of *Studies in the Scriptures, A Periodical (Monthly 'If the Lord will') Devoted to Bible Studies and Expositions.* A Preface 'To Our Readers', signed by I. C. Herendeen, declared: 'We shall "ride no hobbies" but seek to put before the Bible student faithful expositions of and studies in the Holy Scriptures from the pens of the Lord's servants of the past and present . . . we shall hope to have the hearty sympathy and co-operation of all lovers of "the deep things of God".' The pages which followed were made up of over fourteen from Pink's pen, including the start of a series on John's Gospel, plus extracts from older writers. Among the authors whom Pink was to draw upon during the first year of publication were Brethren writers (notably Charles Campbell), John Brown (the 19th-century Scots expositor), Andrew Fuller, Ralph Erskine, Jonathan Edwards, C. H. Spurgeon and Andrew Bonar. The editing was the work of Pink alone and in the June issue, in a Preface 'To Our Scripture Study Family', he wrote:

> Those who have given a careful reading to the first five issues will have discovered that *Studies in the Scriptures* differs, in several respects, from many other religious periodicals. There is little in this publication that will appeal to the popular reader.
> If this magazine be read as a newspaper is read, little profit to the soul will be obtained. What we solicit from our subscribers is this: First, that before taking up any article herein the reader will lift up his or her heart to God, and earnestly ask Him for a spirit of discernment to recognize His truth and an open

heart to receive it. Second, that to this end the reader will study each article with an open Bible before him, turning to each passage quoted to see whether or not the writer proves what he says by a "Thus saith the Lord". And a third, that he read slowly, critically and thoughtfully what is presented in these pages.

God has said in his Word, 'He that believeth shall not make haste' (*Isa.* 28:16), and if ever there was a time when his children needed to give special heed to this admonition it is now. The children of God are infected with the spirit of the world. The mad rush which characterizes everything around us, the awful hustle and bustle of the ungodly as they rush headlong to eternal death, has affected the members of the household of faith; and few, if any of us, are free from it. One of our most urgent needs is to be delivered from this feverish spirit, for it is rapidly sapping the spiritual vitality of many of God's people. The irreverent speed at which the Holy Scriptures are read in the average pulpit; the rate at which sacred songs are commonly sung; the unholy manner in which many rush into the presence of the Most High God, and gabble off the first words that come to their lips, are so many examples of this infection. And, alas, the same spirit possesses most of us when we read the Word of God and expositions of that Word. We earnestly ask our readers to make a prayerful study of the words 'stand', 'sit', 'wait', 'tarry', as they are found in Holy Writ.

The title of this magazine implies that it is designed not for lazy people, or for those who are so busily occupied with the things of this world, that they have no time (in reality, *no heart*) for the things of God. No, it is published for the benefit of those who are,

> or who wish to become, students of Scripture. The articles herein call for study, thoughtful perusal, prolonged meditation.
>
> Finally, let not this magazine become a substitute for your own daily study of God's Word: rather let it be an incentive for further search on *your* part to discover the priceless treasures hidden therein.

This was indeed a high standard to set and for Pink it meant a heavy load of work. All his articles had to be written by hand and finished for the printer at least two months before the date of publication. Herendeen undertook the typing and printing of the material and Pink was responsible to check for mistakes in the printer's proofs prior to the final printing.

Along with written ministry Pink took occasional services elsewhere. We read, for instance, of a ten-day Bible Conference at Spruce Street Baptist Church, Philadelphia, in 1921, which was to have particularly significant consequences. Among his hearers were a young couple, Charles Stanley Pressel and his wife Elsie, both nominal Christians of Methodist and Lutheran backgrounds respectively. Elsie Pressel, in later years recalling those meetings in the Spruce Street Church, wrote, 'We were awakened by the Holy Spirit as we listened to A.W.P.'s messages . We were "amazed" (that is too mild a statement) at the depth of his knowledge of the Scriptures and his God-given ability to present the precious truth of his blessed Word.'[1] Pink was at Spruce Street Baptist again in 1922 and in the summer of 1923 when he and Vera stayed with the Pressels. He left a copy of his book *The Seven Sayings of the Saviour on the Cross*

[1] All my quotations from the Pressels are from personal letters, written for us in the 1970s.

with them, inscribed, 'To Stanley and Elsie Pressel from the author and his wife as a little memento of three happy weeks, which we spent in their home. June 1923.' While Pink was thus used to bring new life to the Pressels, they, as we shall see, were shortly to be needed helpers for him.

Before the end of 1923, the second year of the publication of *Studies in the Scriptures*, the future of the magazine was in doubt. The first year had finished with just over 1,000 subscribers and with a small credit balance. On the strength of this, Herendeen and Pink increased the number of pages to thirty-two and adopted a larger and more attractive print, the price remaining the same, 10 cents per copy or $1.00 per year. But instead of a circulation increase, in October 1923, when the size was reduced to 24 pages, Pink had to report that the number of subscribers was 'slightly below what we had this time last year', and as November 15 was the deadline for the printing of the January 1924 issue he urged subscribers to send their renewals for the next year without delay, otherwise, he told them, 'we are quite in the dark as to how many of the January 1924 copies to have printed'.

Before 1924 had begun Pink was facing a greater crisis than he had anticipated. By the time the December 1923 issue of *Studies* appeared, Herendeen, his friend of at least eight years, and the Associate Editor and Publisher, resigned. Why he did so is not recorded. We know that some time in the 1920s, after eleven years at Swengel, Herendeen removed to Cleveland, Ohio, where he carried on his business as before. His removal was perhaps the cause of his resignation; certainly being left without his practical help Pink was confronted with a serious difficulty of which he wrote many years later:

> Toward the close of the second year [of the publication of *Studies in the Scriptures*] our partner resigned, at a time when we were much exercised over the virtual cessation of preaching engagements, for we were made to prove that 'he that increaseth knowledge increaseth sorrow' (*Eccles.* 1:18), our messages meeting with less acceptance by professing Christians.
>
> Neither myself nor my wife had any experience of typing, and living in a village where no typist could be hired, it looked as though the magazine would have to close down; and, shame upon himself, the writer had no hope to the contrary, and was in complete despair. But in his grace and mercy the Lord wrought faith and hope in his wife, and as the result of her noble efforts we moved from that village to the city of Philadelphia.[2]

It may be that the lack of opportunities to speak, to which Pink refers, had also been true in Swengel. We hear of no church in Swengel but there was a Brethren Assembly, to which the Herendeens seem to have been attached, and where a 'Brother Burd' appears to have been the leader. Burd had understandably entertained some apprehension before the Pinks moved from Spartanburg. In a letter from there of 7 December 1919 Pink had written to Herendeen:

> Glad to learn that apparently Brother C. Burd views the possibility of our coming more favourably. I hope you told him what I wrote re the meetings. I had thought that if the Lord brings us to Swengel (if agreeable to you) the weekly Bible class would be

[2] 'Our Semi-Jubilee Letter', a short autobiographical survey of his life (the only thing of its kind which he ever printed), in *Studies*, 1946, p. 283.

best held in your home, so that Sister Herendeen might get the advantage of them regularly.[3]

After his arrival at Swengel, Pink's disenchantment with the Brethren movement increased and it is possible that this entered into the lack of local opportunities for preaching. Be that as it may, the location at Swengel, that had seemed an ideal base, now lost all its attraction for him, and they saw no reason to remain. But the main cause of the 'despair' to which he refers above was surely his Elijah-like concern that the cause of God itself was failing in the land. While his resulting depression is not to be excused it would not have occurred if he had not, at the age of thirty-seven, loved the truth better than life.

It is at this point that Elsie Pressel of Philadelphia has to take up the story. One day towards the end of 1923 she received a phone call from Vera Pink, who, she was surprised to learn, had travelled alone to Philadelphia and was at the Reading railroad station. Mr Pink, she told her, was 'indisposed', and she needed advice on his condition from Elsie who had been a nurse during World War I. 'I insisted that she come to the house,' writes Elsie Pressel, 'and after her arrival by taxi, she told me of Arthur's symptoms. My suggestion to her was accepted and Vera returned home next day, and the following day Arthur and Vera arrived. He was suffering a nervous breakdown and needed a complete rest. Was it any wonder when he told us that he read about twenty to thirty thousand pages yearly!'

Elsie was already attracted to Mrs Pink. 'Vera was very gentle, warm, and open, and from the first meeting demonstrated her friendliness as only a "Southerner" is

[3] Ibid., p. 182. While Pink's *Sovereignty of God* was still at manuscript stage in July 1918, Burd had been critical of its teaching on reprobation (Ibid., p. 30).

capable.' But the young Pressels still stood somewhat in awe of the preacher. Elsie recalled his initial reserve that suggested he was 'sizing them up', and at first she did not find him an easy patient. 'He was', she writes, 'a man of strong determination: however, in a short period he seemed to permit me to take the reins and for a period I was as "stern" as to get him to follow the nursing programme, and he finally submitted graciously. The trouble was he resented being sort of "shackled" from reading, etc., and being told just how much he would be permitted to do – but aren't most of us similarly stubborn? The Lord gave us wisdom to help him back to health, having him with us for over three months.'

Through these months of closer acquaintance, the Pressels' love and respect for the man whom they had chiefly known only as a pulpit figure deepened. Stern and unsmiling as he might sometimes be, he was, above all else, a deeply exercised Christian. With returning health he was soon eager that the Pressels should invite people for Bible studies. This resulted in twice-weekly meetings, remembered by the Pressels as 'precious times', when about twenty to thirty people would gather in their Philadelphia home.

By this time Elsie Pressel knew that their guest was not without a sense of humour, as an incident one lunch-time illustrated. With Pink resuming a normal schedule it had become his habit to spend the morning studying upstairs until he was called for lunch with Elsie and Vera. When thanks had been given, and lunch was in progress, Mrs Pressel found that in Arthur's view her work was not yet done: 'Very suddenly he would address me and say, "Quote me 2 Chronicles 7: 14" or some other Scripture not commonly known. The first or second time this occurred I was absolutely blank: I did not know that the words he wished to hear were even in the Bible.' These failures Pink seemed to contemplate with a stern countenance until the hostess decided that a firm reply to such enquiries was the best policy. Thus when the next such question was put she responded: 'When I am preparing a meal, I have already asked God's help so the food will not be burned, nor the house for that matter, by some accident in the kitchen – and my job is to cook and serve, not to say the verse to which you refer. Now you say it for me!' 'He was flabbergasted, and truly laughed aloud at my reply. He did have a sense of humour.'

By 1924 the Pinks were ready to resume their own home life, first in temporary lodgings and then in a more suitable rented house, 222 N. Creighton Street (the address published in *Studies* from February 1924 to January 1925). Besides being a nurse, Elsie Pressel was also a typist and with her regular help the magazine went forward. 'Twice a week,' she writes, 'I went to Creighton Street for the day from 8.30 a.m. until supper, at times as late as 8.30 p.m., typing as A.W.P. dictated his articles from his own type of shorthand writing. Mr Pressel came after his day's work and we all had supper together.' Pink's own account of the Pressels' friendship continues immediately following his statement, already given, of their move to Philadelphia:

> There the Lord had moved a young couple, to whom we were almost strangers, to open their home to us until we could get suitably located, the wife typing our articles and giving Mrs Pink a few pointers, until after a while she was able to take over. It was a most signal interposition of the Lord on our behalf; such an evident token he would have us continue with this

printed ministry that from then until now the editor's faith has never wavered that God would supply all our need.

Before leaving this important episode in Pink's life, we must mention a comment of the Pressels on the fact that he was susceptible to depression. As they knew him well, both at this date and in later years, some weight has to be given to their judgment. They do not trace his lapse into darkness to any inherent instability in his temperament. In his general attitudes, Mrs Pressel writes, 'British was written all over him,' and he was not without his own 'idiosyncrasies'. 'But why dwell on these,' she continues, 'when most of us have our own share?'

Besides Pink's patent overwork,[4] the Pressels saw at least two contributing causes to his downcast state in the closing months of 1923. 'We often thought some of A.W.P.'s attitudes of low feelings (all of us are subject to such periods) were due to his memories of his days spent in the cult of Satan, feeling deep sorrow for his actions, but in these times he was brought out again as he saw he was forgiven solely and wholly in the provision provided for lost sinners, and as he reflected on the great miracle the Holy Spirit performed in bringing him from darkness into the marvellous light of God's great grace and mercy.'

A second reason which these early friends give for the sorrow which at this time temporarily overcame him, is

[4] This factor should not be minimized. Spurgeon, who was no stranger to depression, wrote: 'Sedentary habits have a tendency to create despondency in some constitutions . . . To sit long in one posture, poring over a book, or driving a quill, is in itself a taxing of nature; but add to this a badly-ventilated chamber, a body which has long been without muscular exercise, and a heart burdened with cares, and we have the elements for preparing a seething cauldron of despair.' 'The Minister's Fainting Fits', in *Lectures to My Students, First Series* (London: Passmore and Alabaster, 1887).

one to which I have already referred. It was the acuteness of his consciousness of the extent to which prevailing spiritual conditions were dishonouring to God. He felt something of that same grief known to the apostle Paul both over the unsaved and over defections in the church of Christ. Although he was no more immune than are other Christians from temptations to a sinful self-pity, his friends never doubted that his over-mastering concern was of a higher nature. 'A.W.P.'s aim in life was to honour his Blessed Lord.'

As with all Christians, Pink's 'fainting fit' was part of a God-given trial out of which he was to emerge a stronger Christian. *Studies in the Scriptures* for 1924 was to be the best of the three volumes thus far. It began a new series 'Gleanings in Exodus', and contained two articles, both entitled 'A Message of Comfort', which were clearly connected with his recent experiences, although he made no personal allusion. The first of these (on 2 Corinthians 4:17), published in May, concluded: 'What are years of toil, of sickness, of battling against poverty, of persecution, when weighed over against the pleasures at God's right hand, which are for evermore? One breath of paradise will extinguish all the adverse winds of earth. May God grant unto us that faith which will enable us to anticipatively lay hold of the future and live in the present enjoyment of it!' The second article enlarged upon a similar theme from Job 23: 10, 'But he knoweth the way that I take: when he hath tried me, I shall come forth as gold.'

Arthur Pink had never intended that *Studies in the Scriptures* should constitute the whole of his ministry and, with health and confidence restored in the spring and summer of 1924, he was ready for more public ministry. The question which concerned him was where that should be. The number of opportunities open to him was certainly restricted. Invitations arrived from a few places where he had formerly ministered, notably Colorado and California, but the appeal which particularly arrested him came in the form of two letters addressed to him from Sydney, New South Wales. Their writer was George Ardill, the manager of a Christian book depot in Sydney and Director of the Evangelization Society of New South Wales.[5] An eager reader of *Studies*, Ardill urged Pink to consider the good which might be done by a visit to Australia, and by October Pink had decided upon a 'Foreign Bible Conference tour'. But this was not an impetuous decision, for they were not to leave until the following spring. The intervening months of 1924 were crowded with preparations. No less than four months of *Studies* had to be prepared in advance and a number of items which the Pinks had accumulated in their days at Spartanburg, Swengel and in Creighton Street, Philadelphia, had to be parted with – including some of his prized library. Meanwhile, in November 1924, the Pressels had moved to York, Pennsylvania, and from their new home they undertook to maintain all the business involved in the monthly despatch of the magazine. Its printing was to continue in the States, Pink supplying the material and the Pressels doing the rest.

Thus on a cold winter's morning, January 5, 1925, the Pinks closed the door for the last time on their rented home in Creighton Street, and from Philadelphia began a journey which was to involve three thousand miles by land and six thousand five hundred by sea. The first stage was a three-

[5] G. E. Ardill (1857–1945) was a remarkable man, designated in the *Australian Dictionary of Evangelical Biography* (Sydney: Evangelical History Association, 1994), as 'Evangelist, welfare worker'. 'Ardill's significance lies in the multifarious enterprises he initiated, the varied programmes he undertook, and the energy with which he pursued them over a long life.'

days' train journey to Denver, Colorado, where Pink had to take a main part in the Rocky Mountains Bible Conference, 'speaking two and three times each day to appreciative congregations, the Lord granting us much liberty of utterance'. This was, in Pink's judgment, 'a wonderful season of blessing'. The meetings were held in Galilee Baptist Church, and, with both the pastor (Dr Gravett) and his people, the Pinks 'greatly enjoyed a week of Christian fellowship'. The same week he also addressed a gathering of Baptist pastors from the city and its suburbs on the subject of expository preaching.

Their next stop was to be at Oakland, California, where he comments, 'We had a royal welcome from our Christian friends.' In this place, for the next six weeks, he was to have 'the joy of ministering the Bread of Life to many hungry souls':

> The first meeting in the Swedish Mission Church greatly encouraged us; the earnestness, eagerness and joy of the congregations evidenced once more the satisfying power of the Word. The two weeks spent in the First Presbyterian Church will be long remembered. Its pastor, Dr Silsley, was in hearty accord, and his prayerful co-operation was a great help. We commend him to the prayers of our readers, that God will strengthen his hands and mightily use him to his glory. The three Sunday night services in his church were most blessed and solemn occasions. Well over a thousand people were present each time, and there was a holy hush over the congregations which could be felt. At the closing service, when we spoke on our Lord's return, extra seats had to be carried in. Only eternity will reveal the fruitage.'[6]

[6] *Studies*, 1925, p. 121.

During the same period Pink also spoke in San Francisco and gave a series of Bible expositions in the Friends' Meeting House in Berkeley. At these latter meetings he met two encouraging cases of people who owed much to his writings. The first was an ex-medium whose conversion, three years earlier, was occasioned by his article published in *Our Hope* and reprinted by Herendeen in pamphlet form, 'The Philosophy of Spiritualism'. It was not Pink alone whom God had intended to deliver from that evil cult. The second case was that of a person brought to Christ through his tract 'Not Saved'.

After such experiences we can well understand that the Pinks left San Francisco on March 3, 1925, 'with hearts full of praise'. Six days' sailing took their boat to Honolulu in the Hawaiian Islands where an eight-hour stop gave them welcome opportunity for exercise, along with a surprise at finding the place so full of Japanese and Chinese. The remainder of the journey deserves to be given in full from Pink's own account:

> From Honolulu we next sailed to the Samoan Islands, a journey which lasted exactly a week; this took us through the Tropics, but the fresh 'trade winds' supplied a refreshing breeze, which made the voyage comfortable and pleasant. One thing which impressed us deeply was the heavens by night. In the Southern Hemisphere the stars appear to be much closer and brighter, and more numerous, too. It made us think of the Psalmist's words, 'The heavens declare the glory of God, and the firmament showeth his handiwork.' The 'southern cross', which is not visible in the Northern Hemisphere, is very beautiful, composed of four stars all by themselves – each of

the first magnitude – they are so placed as to give a perfect outline of a cross.

The approach to the Samoan Islands is very pleasant, and we wound in and out between the smaller ones for a couple of hours before docking at Pango Pango [now known as Pago Pago]. Here is a small U.S.A. Naval Station, where some twenty or thirty American families are located, the rest of the population being made up of natives that are descended from cannibals. Two Mormon missionaries landed here to propagate their pernicious teachings. The scenery is indescribably grand. From a narrow beach, cliffs rise precipitously to a height of from seven hundred to a thousand feet. They are literally covered with luxuriant vegetation from base to summit; as showers of rain descend there almost daily, everything is beautifully fresh and green. The night before we landed a heathen chief had died, and we witnessed the natives marching to the funeral with palms in their hands, and chanting their weird lamentations as they passed. While standing by, we wondered how many of them had ever heard 'the Word of Life'. How thankful we were that it pleased our gracious God for us to be born in Christian homes!

Leaving Pango Pango on March 16 we began the last stage of our journey, sighting four hours out the Isle of Apia, where Robert Louis Stevenson lies buried. The weather was warm, though not unduly hot, as we crossed the equator. There we lost one whole day, jumping from Wednesday to Friday. On the Friday evening a sad incident happened that reminded us that 'in the midst of life we are in death', a fellow-passenger being washed overboard that evening through a sudden lurch of the vessel. She was an ardent 'Christian Scientist', and without a moment's warning was swept out of time into eternity. Oh, the vital importance of being prepared! As we neared Australia the sea was rougher than at any other part of the voyage due to the vernal equinox. The last two days we encountered high winds, the vessel pitched and tossed badly, it being so rough that the doctors and customs officers were unable to come on board until we were almost at the dock; but he who rules the waves and has given to the sea his decree brought us safely to Sydney on the morning of March twenty-four, after being on the ocean twenty-one days. Thus did our faithful God richly supply us with journeying mercies and bring us to our desired haven.[7]

[7] Ibid., p. 144.

6

Australia: A Mixed Reception

From the time that Pink landed at Circular Quay, Sydney, close to his thirty-ninth birthday, he was quietly exuberant. Although he did not know a single soul in Australia, and had no financial guarantee from any quarter, he believed that God had directed him. From the cold of a North American winter he had come to the late summer of the Antipodes. He was once more at home in a British culture. And, best of all, he was now among a number of earnest and prayerful Christians whose eagerness to give time to the Word of God delighted him. George Ardill fully answered the expectations which his letters had aroused, and he had preaching proposals arranged with various churches which would crowd the coming weeks. On April 22, 1925, as Pink posted the manuscript of the June issue of *Studies* to the United States for printing, he added a note for his readers: 'Most graciously has God wrought for us here, in giving us favour in the eyes of his people and in opening many doors of ministry. We are already reluctantly obliged to refuse numbers of invitations, being booked up for several months ahead. Everywhere we have been there are many really hungry for spiritual food. We fully expect a joyous season of heaven-sent blessing.'

The next month's issue of *Studies* contained a further note, written in Sydney on May 27, and addressed to 'Our Fellow-Christians in America'. Explaining his inability to write the personal letters which he would have wished to send, he explains:

> The truth is that we are now speaking ten times a week, and preparation for these services and the interviewing of different ones who are anxious to be shown the way of the Lord more perfectly is consuming almost all of our available time . . . The meetings here afford much ground for praise to our most gracious God. The attendances are steadily increasing, the interest is most manifest, and goodly numbers are being blest. Many here have been earnestly praying for months past that the Lord would send a teacher to open up to them some of the inexhaustible treasures of the Scriptures. Hundreds of eager souls are coming out five and six nights a week, with Bibles and notebooks; God is granting most blessed liberty of utterance and joy of heart in ministering his precious Word. We are receiving more invitations than we can accept. There is every indication that 'a great and effectual door is opened unto us'.

In the 1980s there were still those in Sydney who could confirm the measure of spiritual stirring which occurred under Pink's preaching nearly sixty years earlier. Alan McKerrell wrote: 'One now elderly lady told me recently that she used to walk miles each evening to sit under his ministry. She described him as an excellent teacher, very clear in his exposition of the Scriptures and most convincing. He seemed to draw people like a magnet. He was not what some might term a "fiery" preacher although he was very forthright, clear and uncompromising.'[1]

Others, who remembered Pink's ministry at this period, have noted how his sermons differed both in delivery and often in substance from those more commonly heard. He employed no gestures and did not shout. 'He stood before his hearers as a staunch warrior for God. He never deviated from his theme with stories or quip sayings. Everyone present knew that he had no time for levity for he spoke as a man whose one purpose was to honour the Blessed Trinity and to show what the Word of God requires of us.'

Sydney in the 1920s, with its million people, its electric trams, steam trains, and sprawling suburbs, was vastly different from the place of 675 houses that an early settler in 1804 described as more like a camp than a town. Thousands of Christians had joined the immigration movement of the 19th century, including men who had been trained at Spurgeon's Pastors' College in London. Among the evangelical churches of Sydney in the 1920s, one of the strongest was the Baptist Tabernacle at Ashfield, some six miles from the city centre, and perhaps it was the early invitation to take a 'Bible-teaching Campaign' at this church which induced the Pinks to make their first base at 5 Norton Street, Ashfield.

Supported by L. Sale-Harrison, whom he describes as 'its loyal and faithful Pastor', Pink was, in fact, to take two campaigns at the Ashfield Tabernacle before the end of June 1925. Many of the meetings were specifically

[1] 'The Early Life of A. W. Pink', in *Reformation Today*, Aug./Oct., 1977, p. 6. This was the first of a series of articles, the remainder coming from the pen of Ray Levick. *Reformation Today* was the first magazine to produce any biographical articles on Pink, and its editor, Erroll Hulse, when with the Banner of Truth Trust, played an important part in the first appearance of Pink titles in the U.K.

evangelistic, with addresses on such themes as the Prodigal Son, the Three Crosses, and the New Birth, but sermons primarily designed for believers were not excluded. Some of Pink's most frequently repeated sermons at this time in his life were entitled 'The Christian's Greatest Need' (an exposition of Luke 10:38–42), 'God's Food for His People' (Exodus 16) and 'The Sins of the Saints'.

As his time at Ashfield lengthened, Pink became convinced of the need for more doctrinal teaching and consequently he wrote:

> At the close of the second campaign in Ashfield we delivered a series of addresses on the much-neglected but most important truths of God's Sovereignty and Divine Election. The weather was wet and cold, yet from four to five hundred came out, Mondays to Fridays inclusive, and on Sundays the Tabernacle was packed, many extra seats having to be brought in. The Lord most signally honoured his Word, saints being edified and sinners saved.[2]

That Pink enjoyed much liberty in thus speaking more specifically on the doctrines of grace can be judged from the following. Concluding the first of three addresses on the Sovereignty of God on June 18, he declared:

> Now, my friends, I have been speaking almost an hour and a half and have only just got started, but let me wind up with this one point. What ought our attitude to be towards such a God? Let me give you four answers and I won't enlarge at all. One ought to *fear* him and *tremble* in his presence. The God of the Bible is a God to be feared and regarded with the utmost awe. Second, what ought our attitude to

[2] *Studies*, 1925, p. 216.

> be towards such a God as this? One of *implicit obedience*, for he is sovereign and we are simply his servants. He is sovereign and we are simply his subjects to do what he says and to obey his commands, however unreasonable they may seem to be to us. Third, what ought our attitude to be towards such a God as this? One of *abounding praise*, that he is able to make all things work together for our eternal good; and he is able to, because he is sovereign, supreme, and none can hinder him. He is a God to be praised! Finally, what ought our attitude to be towards such a God as this? One of *devout worship*. He is the Almighty King of kings and the Lord of lords, and our only suitable place is in the dust at his feet in adoration and in thanksgiving unto him.[3]

Again, in a fourth address on Election on June 26, he said:

> Now, then, I must draw to a close. In the last place – I wish the clock would stand still for about a couple of hours, I really do. Someone said to me this afternoon, 'Well, if Pastor Harrison wants you to come back here for another month, what are you going to do? You have preached to them fifty times already: isn't the barrel beginning to run dry?' Ah, my friends, listen, the preacher who relies on anecdotes and clippings from the newspaper, his barrel will soon run dry; of course it will; but the man who preaches the Word of God has an inexhaustible supply to draw from. My dear friends, the trouble is, I hardly know what to bring in and what to leave out. I would like to speak to you by

[3] *Studies*, 1925, p. 213.

> the Lord's help every night, for ten years, and then perhaps we would all of us know something of the Word – not much then, but a little.[4]

A man who spoke in this fashion clearly both loved the Scriptures and loved to preach! Without using the label, he delivered the old 'Calvinistic' doctrine of the Reformers, the Puritans and C. H. Spurgeon, whose name received a passing mention:

> Oh, that God would raise up some man today who could get the hearing that Mr Spurgeon had, and who would preach with like plainness and faithfulness . . . Of course, the preacher who is seeking the favour of the world, and who is looking for his support from worldlings, must necessarily be silent on this subject, but any preacher who is silent upon it – I mean entirely silent – is so for one of two reasons, and it proves one of two things: Either he is an incompetent servant of Christ, incompetent because he is ignorant of one of the cardinal truths of Scripture; or he is an unfaithful servant of Christ, because he shuns to declare all the counsel of God. Now I do not mean by that, that the preacher ought to be preaching on this subject all the time; far from it; but I mean that any true servant of God will believe that all Scripture is given by inspiration of God, and is profitable for doctrine, and therefore he will ignore no part of it.[5]

Along with such plain words Pink also made it clear that it was not with a view to provoking any doctrinal debate that he preached this truth of election, for it 'ought always to be preached and spoken about, not in a spirit of controversy, but in the spirit of reverence and

[4] *Studies*, 1926, p. 115.
[5] *Studies*, 1926, p. 39.

devotion'. He was equally emphatic that to hold these doctrines in no sense militated against evangelism, and he concludes one of his Election addresses in these words:

> Now my last word is this. You say that it is unjust of God to choose one and to pass by another. Listen, it is not. It is not unjust, because God never yet refused salvation to any man who really asked him for salvation, and asked from his heart. God never yet turned away one single sinner that sought him in true penitence. Oh, if there is a sinner here tonight, prove it for yourself. If there is a sinner here tonight, *test it out for yourself.* Christ has said, 'Come unto me, all ye that labour and are heavy laden, and I will give you rest,' and if you will *come to him* there is rest for *you*! Try him right now and see! Put him to the proof right now. Well but, you say, that contradicts what you have been saying all night. No, it doesn't, for no sinner will come to him unless he is drawn by God to come. It is his responsibility to come and he will be damned if he does not come. And listen, get this plainly, the sinner will be damned, not because God created him for that purpose, he will be damned because of his own sins. He will receive the just reward of his iniquities, but nevertheless it is the responsibility of the sinner to come, and if he will come there is salvation for him.[6]

Many who crowded the Ashfield Tabernacle, from various denominations, to hear Dr Pink (as he was then known) had rarely heard such plain preaching and not a few must have found his declaration of the doctrines of grace strangely new and unfamiliar. Evangelism of the Moody brand seemed to have all but captured the

[6] *Studies*, 1926, p. 94.

English-speaking world. But Pink's passion and depth were arresting and there was, at this stage, no falling away in numbers. In his remarkable early months in Australia he could write: 'In the hearts of many God is deepening an interest for and delight in his wondrous Word. Many doors are before us, and we are booked up for months to come. Invitations are to hand from Melbourne, but it will be some time yet before we can leave Sydney and its suburbs.'[7]

At the end of June 1925 the meetings at Ashfield had to be terminated so that Pink could keep a further engagement in Auburn, another suburb, where, to use his own words, he was to be for 'two very happy weeks enjoying the most hearty co-operation of its widely loved Pastor, Cleugh Black'. By August 21 he had completed six Bible-teaching Campaigns, each averaging three weeks, and was about to begin a seventh. Meanwhile the work of *Studies in the Scriptures* was increasing and widening, with its printing now transferred to Sydney where there was a good demand for copies: 'Several hundreds of new subscribers have been taken in this country.'[8] Pink's Australian sermons began appearing in its columns, the expositions of John's Gospel (begun in 1922) were still continuing, also 'Gleanings in Exodus', and the amount of material from other authors was commonly nothing more than short quotations. Among these John Owen's name was now appearing regularly.

At this date prudence was not a strong point in Pink's make-up, but, given the spiritual conditions which then existed in the Sydney churches, controversy over his ministry must sooner or later have been inevitable. He consciously faced the choice that he had either to endure

[7] *Studies*, 1925, p. 192.
[8] *Studies*, 1925, p. 217.

the disfavour of men or the disapprobation of Christ. In tmany of the churches there had long been little Bible teaching. The Presbyterians, once strong in the very truths which Pink was preaching, were mostly dominated by the liberal theology which Samuel Angus and others were then disseminating in New South Wales. The Brethren whom Pink met did not impress him, and the Baptists, as time was to show, were lacking the doctrinal backbone characteristic of Spurgeon. With the Anglicans, and the evangelical witness they had long maintained in Sydney, Pink appears to have had no contact.

Not until a breach had occurred with the Baptist pastors did Pink publish in *Studies* his views on conditions in Sydney. When he did give them, they were, as usual, clear-cut:

> So far as we can discover there is not another preacher in all Sydney who is proclaiming the sovereignty of God, eternal election, particular and efficacious redemption, and unconditional salvation.[9]
>
> General religious conditions here are very similar to those which obtain in the U.S.A. The vast majority of the churches are in a sorry state. Those that are out-and-out worldly are at their wits' end to invent new devices for drawing a crowd. Others which still preserve an outward form of godliness provide nothing substantial for the soul; there is little ministering of Christ to the heart and little preaching of 'sound doctrine', without which souls cannot be built up and established in the faith. The great majority of the 'pastors' summon to their aid some professional 'evangelist', who, for two to four weeks,

[9] *Studies*, 1926, p. 118. For a later comment on his addresses on Election given at this time see *Studies*, 1938, p. 26.

> puts on a high-pressure campaign and secures sufficient new 'converts' to take the place of those who have 'lapsed' since he was last with them. What a farce it all is! What an acknowledgement of their own failure! Imagine C. H. Spurgeon needing some evangelist to preach the gospel for him for a month each year! Why do not these well-paid 'pastors' heed 2 Timothy 4:5 and themselves 'do the work of an evangelist', and thus 'make full proof of their ministry'?
>
> The great need of Australia today is for God-sent and God-anointed men, who will not shun to declare all the counsel of God; men in whom the Word of Christ dwells richly, so that they can say with the apostle, 'Woe is me if I preach not the gospel'; men on whom rests the fear of God, so that they are delivered from the fear of man. Will Christian readers in distant lands join us in daily prayer that the Lord of the harvest will raise up and thrust forth more of his labourers into this portion of his vineyard.[10]

The cause of Pink's breach with the Baptists arose from his teaching in Ashfield Tabernacle in June 1925. Opposition was rising in some quarters before he finished his series on Sovereignty and Election. Consequently when he was asked to address the Monthly Meeting of the N.S.W. Baptist Ministers' Fraternal on August 4, he sought to meet criticism by taking 'Human Responsibility' for his subject. It proved to be a forceful statement of biblical doctrine, rightly distinguishing between spiritual 'ability' and 'responsibility' (the former having been lost in the Fall). 'Instead of denying man's responsibility (as I am accused of doing), I insist upon it,

[10] *Studies*, 1927, p. 120.

and probably believe in it to a greater degree and fuller extent than do some of my detractors.'[11] After the address, those present (reported in the press as 'an exceptionally large gathering') retired to the YMCA for a luncheon and a vote of thanks to the speaker was 'very heartily carried'. But the proceedings were not yet over. As *The Australian Baptist* of August 11, 1925, reported:

> At the close of the meal, an adjournment was made to the committee room where, for upwards of an hour, the doctor was submitted to a further series of questions, all of which he answered with unfailing courtesy. It was a fairly searching test, and one calculated to reveal any weak spots in his theological armour, supposing such to have existed; and whether in full agreement with him or otherwise, there was a consensus of opinion that a more profitable and thought-provoking session of the Fraternal had not been held.[12]

Another newspaper, under the heading 'N.S.Wales Ministers' Fraternal, Visit of Dr Pink', gave a full column to reporting the meeting:

> Dr Pink is a Bible teacher of marked qualifications, and his meetings at Ashfield, covering many weeks, have aroused widespread interest. Considerable divergence of opinion having arisen concerning the doctor's teaching on the subject of Divine Sovereignty and Human Responsibility, he took the latter for the subject of his address . . . 'I am not a hyper-Calvinist,' he said, 'but I am a strict and staunch Calvinist.'[13]

[11] The address is printed in full in *Studies*, 1926, pp. 159–63.
[12] *Studies*, 1926, p. 163. [13] The faded strip of newspaper, supplied by the Pressels, from which I here quote, has lost its name.

The writer of this not unsympathetic report acknowledged that 'the great themes brought into prominence by Dr Pink' had 'been overshadowed' in recent years, yet hoped for a consensus which would end further controversy.

It was not to be. Despite their 'vote of thanks' the same Fraternal at their September meeting 'unanimously resolved that they could not endorse Dr Pink' and the Chairman and Hon. Secretary sent a statement to that effect to be printed in *The Australian Baptist*.[14] Thus a door was shut on Pink's wider usefulness in Sydney. He must have felt it keenly although it was not his first experience of this kind. He knew that the truth divided men and he grieved that besides unfaithful, unregenerate ministers, there were others 'so afraid of the denominational heads, or so anxious to retain the goodwill of godless but wealthy men in their congregations, that only too often their mouths are muzzled'.

At this point in time it would be unprofitable to attempt to assess how far Pink was blameworthy for the Ashfield addresses and the resultant controversy. Certainly it is open to question whether he was wise to give such 'strong meat' so early in his stay to people evidently unused to doctrinal preaching. As he wrote himself in the June 1925 issue of *Studies in the Scriptures*, 'There has been very little Bible teaching here in Australia.' It is also easy to see that such a comment, expressed publicly, would be enough to aggravate the 'old Adam' in those evangelical preachers who considered that they were teaching their congregations. At the same time it has to be repeated in

[14] September 29, 1925, and given in *Studies*, 1926, p. 163, with this additional sentence from Pink, 'We refrain from any other comment on the above except to point out what a solemn and vivid illustration it furnishes of that declaration of Holy Writ: "The legs of the lame are not equal"' (*Prov.* 26:7).

Pink's defence, that the proclamation of those distinctive points of doctrine which have been labelled 'Calvinism' was by no means the chief characteristic of his ministry. His overriding concern was to be expository, evangelical and balanced.

That he was not yet as balanced as he would later become has to be conceded, as we shall see later. And he sometimes used a boldness of speech which exceeded the bounds of wisdom, yet this was not because he acted with the immaturity of a novice. He had counted the cost and the conviction burned in him that the churches were drifting, and grieving the Spirit by a superficiality which stemmed from ignorance of Scripture. He preached the doctrines of grace, not as some 'special study' for students but as truths vitally related both to God-honouring testimony and Christ-centred living. Though few others seemed to realize it, he was altogether persuaded that the low horizons of thought in the churches of evangelical profession were directly traceable to low views of God himself. Thus he told the congregation at Ashfield:

> Today it is true almost everywhere that we are far more concerned about the results of the gospel than we are about the purity of it! We are more concerned in the blessing of man than we are about the glory of Christ! Is not that true? Is it not true that the first great question asked everywhere today is, What are the 'results'? What is the fruitage? How many people have been saved in your church the last year? I am not saying that the question has no importance, but I do say that, if that is the first question that is asked, it only shows what a low level we are living on! The first question we ought to ask is, How scripturally is the gospel being preached in your church? Is the

preacher magnifying Christ? Is the preacher emphasizing the absolute sufficiency of his finished work? Does the preacher make it plain that God does not ask the sinner to do anything, that Christ has done it all for him? Ah, my friends, when the preachers today are tested by that, there are mighty few of them that will survive the test. How many there are today who tell the poor sinner that he has got to give his heart to God! Well, you say, isn't that right? Isn't that true? Must not the sinner give his heart to the Lord if he is going to be saved? Oh, the tragedy that such a question has to be asked! We talk about progress and advancing; why, we need indoctrinating in the ABC of Christianity, and the ABC of Christianity is the gospel! No, my friends, no sinner was ever saved by giving his heart to God. We are not saved by our giving, we are saved by God's giving . . .

A whole lot of our so-called Christian work today reminds me of little children when they first witness father or mother doing some gardening. The ground is prepared and then the seed is sown, and every day the child goes into the garden and he looks around to see if the seed is beginning to sprout, and if it doesn't show any signs and he wants to make sure that the seed is beginning to sprout, he just scratches around amongst the soil. He wants to see something. My friends, that is what a lot of us are doing in connection with so-called Christian work today! O we have so little confidence in the power and in the sufficiency of the Divine 'seed' to bring about the harvest that God has ordained it shall do![15]

[15] *Studies*, 1926, pp. 111–12.

It was this kind of assessment, and the doctrine upon which he based it, which was too much for many who first heard Pink enthusiastically. Undoubtedly it was the chief reason why the Baptist ministers of New South Wales reached their adverse decision in September 1925. 'Of course there has been opposition,' Pink wrote at that time, 'which has ever been the case where the doctrine [of election] has been scripturally presented . . . Some who stood by us while the crowds were in attendance have now deserted, but we read that when the Lord Jesus declared, "No man can come unto me except it were given unto him of my Father," then "from that time many of his disciples went back and walked no more with him" (*John* 6:65–66). Sufficient it is for the disciple to be as his Master.'[16] Later he was to write on the same subject, 'Most of those who were loudest in our praise at the beginning have proven the most fickle.'[17]

The same month that the door closed for Pink in the Baptist churches another door opened and that in a denomination with which he had no previous acquaintance. In England a denomination of Strict and Particular Baptists had long existed separately from those churches which went under the general designation of 'Baptist'. Their church order was distinguished by a more 'strict' attention to the concern for a spiritual church membership and their faith by the specific avowal of Calvinistic belief. While many Baptist churches had once held 'particular' over against 'general' redemption, the Strict and Particular Baptist churches maintained the old belief as a distinctive part of their denominational testimony. Three congregations of this denomination

[16] *Studies*, 1925, p. 265.
[17] *Studies*, 1926, p. 117. George Ardill was not among these but remained 'a staunch friend' and helper.

existed in Sydney in the 1920s, the largest of which, the Belvoir Street Church, in the down-town area, had been without a pastor for twelve months.

Not surprisingly the people at Belvoir Street rejoiced in the unexpected visitor to Sydney who had proclaimed the grace of God with such vigour and, setting aside the usual restriction which confined their pulpit to men of their own denomination, they invited Pink to preach to them. This he did at the end of September 1925. There followed an invitation for his services every Sunday and Wednesday for three months, and this was renewed for a further three months in December. Such was their enjoyment of his ministry that the only thing preventing the installation of Dr Pink as pastor at Belvoir Street was his lack of membership in the denomination. This rubicon was now crossed, as Pink reports in *Studies*: 'On the first Sabbath in March [1926] the Editor and his wife were received into membership and fellowship of the Strict and Particular Baptist Church in Sydney. Having carefully examined their Articles of Faith we found them in thorough accord with the Word of Truth.'

7

Australia: Two Pastorates

By the time Pink became pastor at Belvoir Street, Sydney, his first memorable summer in the Southern Hemisphere was drawing to a close.[1] He had never been busier. By December 1925 he had spoken over three hundred times during that year. Besides the services at Belvoir Street he had, to help 'the needy and starved sheep of Christ', commenced three 'Bible Study Classes' weekly in different parts of Sydney. These drew 'an average total attendance of over two hundred'.

In addition there was the full responsibility for the production, printing and circulation of *Studies in the Scriptures*: 'The magazine requires much time and attention, and were it not for the labours of Mrs Pink we could not very well continue. She types out all the articles, helps with the correspondence and other items of the office work.' In later years he recalled, 'To write so many articles for the *Studies* at that time and attend to all the correspondence necessitated our working most nights until 2 a.m., but the Lord sustained us and we suffered no ill effects.' On another occasion, in writing on the text, 'They that wait upon the LORD shall renew their strength'

[1] By March 1926, in Sydney's location in the Southern Hemisphere, summer would draw slowly into autumn.

(*Isa.* 40:31), he gave this illustration from his experience in Sydney: 'On many occasions has this writer – when preaching six times a week (rarely for less than an hour, usually seventy-five to ninety minutes) in the heat of Australia, journeying here and there to do so – returned home at 10 p.m., feeling worn and weary and pleading this promise expectantly and partaking of light refreshment, sat down for four hours' hard study and writing an article for this magazine.'[2]

Pink does not seem to have let up on this programme even in January and February when the temperatures could range between 85 and 105°F. In the States he had devised his own way of dealing with excessive heat when he wanted to study. Herendeen spoke of how he once found Pink on a very hot day, sitting with his feet in a tub of water and with a cloth around his head, to be comfortable enough to read his Bible! He was nevertheless troubled enough by Sydney's heat in high summer to rejoice when after two or three hot days a 'southerly' would bring the temperature down by 10°–25°, and 'the cool breezes at once acted as a tonic'.

Although six years had passed since Pink had last been in a pastoral charge he experienced no difficulty in settling to the regular routine of the work at Belvoir Street. In the May 1926 issue of *Studies in the Scriptures* he writes:

> Being in Sydney, this Church proved of most convenient location, the interested ones in the various suburbs (where we first ministered from May to September) making it their gathering centre. Goodly numbers of those whom we reached in the earlier meetings have continued to attend regularly and new ones are being gradually added. Never before, during

[2] *Studies*, 1943, p. 47.

> our sixteen years in the ministry, have we experienced such blessing and joy in our own souls, such liberty of utterance and such an encouraging response as we have done in this highly favoured portion of Christ's vineyard.

A year later, in May 1927, he reports the continuing happiness which he and his wife experienced in the Strict and Particular Baptist Church: 'Here we have enjoyed the Lord's continuous blessing, receiving many tokens of his gracious favour.' By this date, however, a serious difficulty had arisen which came to a head in September 1927 and resulted in his resignation. Once more the difficulty was occasioned by Pink's concern to be faithful to *all* Scripture, notwithstanding the prejudice of his hearers against some portions of the teaching which it contains. He did not court trouble, and to have ended his days as pastor at Belvoir Street he regarded as a satisfying prospect – 'The editor and his wife thought they had found a congenial church-home, and hoped to remain in it till the Lord came for them.' But it was not to be.

The trouble came from precisely the opposite direction to the controversy aroused at Ashfield Tabernacle. In their reaction against Arminianism he was to discover that a number at Belvoir Street had gone to another extreme. Some, hostile to the 'easy-believism' of the modern evangelicalism, professed no assurance at all and consequently declined membership in the congregation. To such hearers Pink spoke as follows:

> What the cause of Christ needs today is soldiers – brave men and women. We have too many of those half-hearted people who turn timorous when the world shrugs its shoulders at them. This is a generation that calls for Daniels and Esthers. May God give

> you holy boldness to follow Jesus in the way, to cast in your lot with a despised Saviour and to take your place with those who are seeking to honour him! What would become of the churches, and what would become of the preaching of the gospel, and what would become of the ministry of the Word, if everyone did as you do? I mean those of you who profess to be Christians and are on the outside. Supposing everyone followed your course – well, there would be no churches. And, my friends, if there had been no churches here I would not be in Sydney tonight. Had there been no Belvoir Street Church, I would not have been in Sydney this length of time. It is only by the grace of God that there was an open door and the people here that stood for the whole counsel of God.[3]

But the trouble went deeper than this and found expression in the thinking of not a few of those who were members. Pastors had for so long given emphasis to divine sovereignty that it was virtually believed that man has practically no part or duty in his conversion. Such thinking had become entrenched at Belvoir Street and Pink was soon convinced that opposition to it was an inescapable duty. Thus, in a powerful sermon on Luke 24:25 ('Then said he unto them, O fools, and slow of heart to believe all that the prophets have spoken'), preached in his congregation in 1926, Pink showed how both Arminians and hyper-Calvinists had erred in failing to believe 'all' the Scriptures and had thus distorted the proper proportions of the truth. 'The sad thing is that almost everywhere today there is just one feature of truth being disproportionately emphasized.' His point is so important that it is worth giving it at length:

[3] *Studies*, 1927, p. 166.

There are Arminians who have presented the 'free will' of man in such a way as to virtually dethrone God, and I have no sympathy whatever with their system. On the other hand, there have been some Calvinists who have presented a kind of fatalism (I know not what else to term it) reducing man to nothing more than a block of wood, exonerating him of all blame and excusing him for his unbelief. But they are both equally wrong, and I scarcely know which is the more mischievous of the two. When the Calvinist says, All things happen according to the predestination of God, I heartily say Amen, and I am willing to be called a Calvinist; but if the Arminian says that when a man sins, the sin is his own, and that if he continues sinning he will surely perish, and that if he perishes his blood is on his own head, then I believe the Arminian speaks according to God's truth; though I am not willing to be called an Arminian . . .

There are many Arminian preachers who are afraid to preach sermons on certain texts of the Bible. They would be afraid to stand up and preach from John 6:44: 'No man can come to me, except the Father which hath sent me draw him.' They would be afraid to stand up and preach from Romans 9:18 – 'Therefore hath he mercy on whom he will have mercy, and whom he will be hardeneth.' Yes, and it is also true that there are many Calvinist preachers who are equally afraid to preach from certain texts of the Scriptures lest their orthodoxy be challenged and lest they be called free-willers. They are afraid to stand up and preach, for example, on the words of the Lord Jesus: 'How often would I have gathered thy children together, even as a hen gathereth her

> chickens under her wings, and ye would not!' or on such a verse as this: 'The kingdom of heaven suffereth violence, and the violent take it by force'; or 'Strive (agonize) to enter in at the strait gate . . .'
> O may God help us to maintain the balance of truth! There is something more in this Book, brethren and sisters, beside election and particular redemption and the new birth. They are there, and I would not say one word to weaken or to repudiate them, but that is not all that is in this Book. There is a human side: there is man's responsibility: there is the sinner's repentance: there is the sinner's believing in Christ: there is the pressing of the gospel upon the unsaved: and I want to tell you frankly that if a church does not evangelize it will fossilize: and, if I am not much mistaken, that is what has happened in some of the Strict Baptist Churches in Australia. Numbers of them that once had a healthy existence are now no more; and some others are already dead, but they are not yet buried; and I believe one of the main reasons for that is this – they failed at the vital point of evangelism. If a church does not evangelize it will fossilize. That is God's method of perpetuating his work and of maintaining his churches. God uses means and the means that the Holy Spirit uses in his work is the preaching of the gospel to the unconverted, to every creature. True, the preaching will avail nothing without the Spirit's blessing and application. True, no sinner will or can believe until God has quickened him. Yet he ought to, and is commanded to.[4]

Preaching of this kind was astonishingly different from that to which the congregation had normally been

[4] *Studies*, 1927, p. 163.

accustomed. Equally unusual was the language of the evangelistic appeal with which Pink closed the same sermon:

> Why not believe in him for yourself? Why not trust his precious blood for yourself; and why not tonight? Why not tonight, my friend? God is ready, God is ready to save you now if you believe on him. The blood has been shed, the sacrifice has been offered, the atonement has been made, the feast has been spread. The call goes out to you tonight, 'Come, for all things are now ready.'

Another later sermon on Blind Bartimaeus was equally direct:

> In some quarters there is so much said about the inability of the natural man to perform acts of grace, there is such a disproportionate emphasis laid upon the helplessness of the creature, that a most deplorable and a tragic lethargy has been fostered and encouraged. And I am afraid there are some present tonight who are so obsessed with this do-nothing-ism that they sadly need to be shaken up and aroused to a sense of their responsibility.[5]

By this time the deacons were both understanding and disliking what they heard. The finale came when Pink discovered that the trust deeds of the two other Sydney congregations, at Ryde and Smithfield, who were linked with Belvoir Street, contained articles of faith which specifically approved the very errors against which he was contending. Sadly and regretfully the only course open to him was resignation, an event which came after he had been preaching for more than two years at Belvoir Street.

[5] *Studies*, 1927, p. 163.

This important turning point in Pink's life is fully explained in one of his letters which, on account of its importance, we now give in full. As well as the narrative which it contains it also supplies not a little insight into Pink's own character and spiritual sensitivity:

15 Hurlstone Avenue
Summer Hill
Dec. 27/1927

Dear Brother Brooks,

Greetings in Christ to you and yours: may he be magnified through and by you. Some months ago I wrote you mentioning the bare fact that I had felt compelled to resign from the Belvoir Street Church. In your reply you expressed the hope that I had not made a mistake or acted too hurriedly. Acting on the principle (which by grace has long governed me) that it is not for a servant of him who 'made himself of *no reputation*' to vindicate *himself* when his actions are misunderstood or misinterpreted, I attempted no self-defence, leaving it to the Lord to 'bring to light' the motives which had actuated me in the day to come, for 'we walk by faith and not by sight!' However, circumstances alter cases.

Last Sunday evening, when enquiring from dear Sister Coleman, your daughter, after your welfare, she said she feared you were worried over my leaving Belvoir Street, and handed me your letter of the 21st inst. After reading it, I felt it was nothing but a Christian duty for me to now seek to remove from your mind what has exercised you. I am now only able to supply a bare outline of the facts of the case.

For several years before coming to Australia, my dear wife and I had been on the outside of all church organizations, and declared we would never again enter one. After four or five months in Sydney, we were brought into touch with the 'Particular Baptists' of whose existence, creed, church polity, etc., I had never previously so much as heard.[6] I received from them an invitation to occupy their pulpit for four Sabbaths, and did so, the Lord unmistakably helping me and blessing the Word. They then invited me to preach for another three months, every other door being closed. After seeking the Lord's guidance, I did so, with no thought of uniting with them in church fellowship. God continued to grant 'seals' and many were blessed. A further invitation for three months followed, which I accepted. During this time, I prayerfully re-studied the New Testament re the local church and the responsibility of a Christian in relation thereto in 'the last days' of this dispensation. The Holy Spirit vouchsafed me further light and my course became clearer. I carefully studied the 'Articles of Faith', and 'Rules' of the Belvoir Street Church, and with the exception of two minor points, found them (so far as the light God had given me permitted) in accord with Holy Writ. I felt as this Church had faithfully maintained what are known as 'The Doctrines of Grace', and as they professedly stood for 'all the counsel of God', it was my duty to unite with them and so far as the Lord enabled, strengthen their hands.

[6] This statement is significant and it explains how Pink was taken by surprise at what had been a long-standing controversy among Baptists in England. I have written on this in *Spurgeon v. Hyper-Calvinism: The Battle for Gospel Preaching* (Edinburgh: Banner of Truth, 1995).

Accordingly I applied for membership, and when before the Church, expressed my dissent from two minor points, viz., their morning observance of the 'Lord's Supper' and the wording of their 'Article' under 'Justification' – that the gospel and not the law is the believer's rule of life. We were received in March 1926.

Having discovered that their views of human responsibility were very defective and that they were altogether lacking in evangelistic zeal, I sought by the Lord's help to remedy this. Seeking grace to be 'as wise as a serpent and harmless as a dove', I proceeded slowly and gently. From April to October 1926 I averaged one sermon out of five *to the unsaved*, the last of which you heard and endorsed – I discussed it with you on the way down to the station – on Bartimaeus. The deacons took me to task for this sermon. At the next church meeting, very soon after, the secretary denounced it as a 'free-will' sermon. Several of my friends resented this and rebuked Mr Miller for so unsparingly condemning a sermon which he had not personally heard.

Instead of 'siding in' with my friends, and expressing my own disapproval, I got up and said, 'Personally I am thankful to God that the officers of this Church have sufficient grace and backbone to challenge and condemn an occupant of their pulpit when they feel he is introducing false doctrine, and that they have sufficient love for the truth to take me to task, though they are fully aware that in doing so, they will render themselves unpopular with some of you.' I begged the entire membership to be patient, withhold their judgment and prayerfully seek the Lord's help. I then suggested I would be glad to set aside an evening for the purpose of meeting the deacons and discussing together the points on which we differed. Two long evenings were thus devoted and in a brotherly and friendly spirit we met. The outcome was that the secretary stated, 'There was no difference between us on fundamental doctrine; it was merely a matter of my method of *presenting* the truth' – i.e. confining myself to a *single* aspect of truth, instead of including a complete 'compendium of doctrine' in every sermon. For the next nine months I plodded along, slowly seeking to show them the way of the Lord more perfectly, during that time preaching two sermons on 'Man's Responsibility – Gospel Responsibility', as well as about a dozen on Election, Particular Redemption, and Effectual Calling. The Lord blessed these to the enlightenment of quite a number.

The climax came suddenly, and to me quite unexpectedly. Brethren from the churches at Ryde and Smithfield met our brethren to discuss united fellowship in Home Mission work. They stated they could only have fellowship if we worked together on a common basis. They then brought forward the fact that there were several 'Articles of Faith' included in what their churches used, not found in the Belvoir Street Church. These particular 'Articles' explicitly and emphatically *denied* human responsibility, categorically repudiating 'duty-repentance' and 'duty-faith'.[7] Had those 'Articles' been included in

[7] These Articles were those approved by the 'Gospel Standard' branch of the Strict Baptists. They declare: 'We reject the doctrine that man in a state of nature should be exhorted to believe in or turn to God'; and, 'For ministers in the present day to address unconverted persons, or indiscriminately all in a mixed congregation, calling upon them to savingly repent, believe, and receive Christ . . . is to imply creature power and to deny the doctrine of

the Belvoir Street Church's, I most certainly would never have 'joined' their membership. It was 'news' to me they were included in the Ryde and Smithfield Churches, for Belvoir Street had always referred to them as '*Sister* Churches of *like* faith and order'. The brethren from the other churches charged our brethren with departure from the faith, denounced me as a rank 'free willer', and demanded from our deacons a definite statement as to whether or not *they* 'endorsed' my pulpit utterances. The issue was clear-cut. The deacons dissented from my teachings on gospel responsibility. The brethren from Ryde and Smithfield then brought forward a motion that the 'united Home Missionary Department of the Particular Baptist Churches of N.S.W. adopt the Articles and Rules of Faith used by the Ryde and Smithfield Churches as their doctrinal basis'. A majority of the Belvoir Street delegates voted for it. It was then clear to me that I had, unconsciously, been 'sailing under false colours'. As a Church Belvoir Street denied 'duty-repentance and faith' though this is not formally stated in her own 'Articles of Faith'. Only one honest course was open to me: now I had learned what the Church really stood for doctrinally, I must resign. The deacons were unanimously and unmovably committed to a denial of human responsibility, though they had never been honest

special redemption' (Articles 26 and 33 in *Articles of Faith and Rules for the Government of Strict Baptist Churches*, London, 1907). It has subsequently been ascertained that the Trust Deeds of the Ryde and Smithfield Churches did not commit them to the 'Gospel Standard' Articles of Faith. In the case of Smithfield their original Articles were 'rescinded' in 1895 when the G. S. Articles were introduced – an action not warranted by their Trust Deed of 1857. The Smithfield Church today (2004), active and evangelical, would uphold Pink's position.

enough to tell me so. Further attempts to 'win' them to what I believe is the truth were useless. They had heard me preach for 22 months, we had discussed the matter together two whole evenings, they refused to bow to God's Word. God used the brethren from Ryde and Smithfield to expose their duplicity and unfaithfulness. Knowing my views on gospel responsibility, they did wrong in ever inviting me to occupy their pulpit.

Since coming out from them, the Lord has unmistakably and abundantly attested *his* approval. The Spirit is no longer 'quenched'.

One point in your letter: No, dear brother, there will be no '*perfect*' Church on earth 'before the Redeemer's return'. I am not expecting one. But there ought to be local assemblies whose outward ways, whose 'order' is regulated by and conformed to the Word in all things. If Luke 1:6 could be said of imperfect individuals, why not of imperfect churches? Philippians 2:16 sets before us the standard at which every church of Christ *should* aim and seek grace to reach!

To sum up. I believed that a decided majority of those who attended throughout my ministry at Belvoir Street would testify that so far from harping on one string, I endeavoured to preserve the balance of truth and declare all the counsel of God; that so far from pressing man's responsibility in a radical manner, I introduced it (for the most part) 'here a little and there a little'; that so far from hurriedly separating myself from the church on that ground, I bore patiently with them for almost two years. Humanly speaking, had not the issue been forced on me at that meeting with the brethren from Ryde and Smithfield

I would be with them now, still seeking to *lead* them into the truth. But when I discovered the church stood for what I am convinced is unscriptural, I should have been no better than one of these dishonest and traitorous Modernists who preaches *contrary* to what he is paid to defend, had I remained. Several of the deacons had led me to believe they *were* receiving added light, and the secretary that the only difference was merely one of form of presentation; but when I discovered that in reality and at the end of two years' ministry we were as far as the poles asunder in fundamental doctrine, I had no other alternative – a '*divided* house' could not stand! 'How can two walk together except they be agreed?' With heartiest Christian greetings to you all, I remain

Yours by God's wondrous grace,
Arthur W. Pink.

It is not easy to interpret Pink's thought in the ten months between the end of his Belvoir Street pastorate and his departure from Australia. Without pressure from him it appears that about forty per cent of the membership at Belvoir Street also resigned. On September 27, 1927, twenty-six of these former members met to form an independent church with Dr Pink as pastor. For a building they took a lease for six months of the Masonic Hall, Liverpool Road, in the Summer Hill district of Sydney, for use on Sundays. A Minute Book survives covering the period September 28, 1927, to April 15, 1928, and it gives a glimpse of the history of the congregation. Regular additions to their numbers during this period almost doubled their original number. A Mrs Ebbett was to be the first to experience the saving power of the gospel under Pink's preaching in the Masonic Hall. As the Minute Book records it:

> She said when the realization came to her that she was lost she did not know what to do, tried to do all sorts of things herself but soon discovered her own helplessness. When Dr Pink preached a sermon, the theme being 'Christ died for the ungodly', she then realized Christ died for her and was by grace enabled to tell the Lord all about her condition before him and ask him to accept her through Jesus Christ.

As a mid-week venue for prayer-meetings, George Ardill loaned them the Gospel Hall on Commonwealth and Reservoir Streets and this building was also used for baptisms. At a baptismal service, on November 2, 1927, it is recorded that the pastor was 'given remarkable liberty of utterance and the aid of the Divine Spirit of God in delivering a most impressive sermon on the subject of Believers' Baptism'. Other items of information in the Minutes include the facts that the church adopted 'Sankey's 1200 Songs and Solos' as their hymn book (buying 125), purchased a communion set and linen, decided to use unfermented wine for the Lord's Supper, and appointed two Sundays a year when the offerings would go to missionary work. There is also a record of clothes being sent to India and of help given to evangelism among the Jews. Regarding Pink's salary we read from the Minutes of a meeting on January 22, 1928:

> He had never accepted so much before and no one deplored the commercializing of the gospel more than he. For the past six months he had been receiving seven pounds per week and paying three pounds ten per week for a furnished cottage, the only reason being, the strain of composing the magazine was such that quiet was absolutely necessary. This could not be had in rooms as previously occupied.

The Minutes also record the pastor's request that he should no more be referred to as 'Dr Pink'.

Undoubtedly the most unusual entry in the Minutes reads as follows:

> The question was raised by the Pastor as to what the wishes of the members were in regard to the disposal of church property in the event of the Lord's near return to the earth to take his people home, or in the case of the church disbanding. It was decided that in either event the property should be sold and the money resulting from such sale (should be) handed over to the British and Foreign Bible Society.

At a subsequent meeting the church changed the name of the possible beneficiary to the Trinitarian Bible Society.

Although there were evidently no scruples in supporting Bible Societies, there were scruples with respect to Societies formed for missionary endeavour, and a certain 'Brother Dockaby', a worker among Aborigines, was told, 'It is unscriptural to work for a Society.'[8] The church therefore discussed whether they could provide him with the needed help.

When the present writer lived in Sydney in the 1980s there were several people who remembered the spiritual blessing which they received from Pink's ministry sixty years earlier. One of them, Vida McAulay, although never a member in his congregation, often went with her mother and sisters to hear him preach at mid-week

[8] Pink was wiser on this point when writing to R. Harbach in later years: 'I do not think you are wise in dwelling upon and making an issue of the extra-religious organizations . . . Suppose you are right in your contention, there is nothing you can do about it, except withhold support from such organizations . . . True, unqualifiedly true, the 'churches' are the only media appointed by God. But all denominations have departed in some things, and in varying degrees, from the Scriptural Rule.' Letter of 10 Nov. 1947, *Letters to a Young Pastor*, p. 35.

services. In a conversation with the present writer in 1980, Miss McAulay spoke of his ministry as doing more good for herself and her family than any other under which they had sat. At that date she was already a believer and had read such books as *M'Cheyne's Memoir and Remains* but, she recalled: 'Mr Pink came just at the right time for me. I will never forget it. He taught me more than anyone and made all the difference to me. A couple of my sisters said the same thing.' He did not read his sermons but spoke fluently and had 'a beautiful speaking and singing voice'. When we reminded Miss McAulay that Pink was a lengthy preacher to be listened to by young people and asked what it was, particularly, which held her attention, she replied, 'It was the Holy Spirit . . . he was a wonderful speaker.'

At the same time Miss McAulay also remembered that 'he was not popular out here. Two or three ministers were terribly opposed to him'. Stories were invented about his character, such as allegations that he beat his wife and was seen leaving licensed hotels. To the question, 'Was Pink eccentric?' she replied with an emphatic, 'Oh no! He was a most level-headed man.' On the occasions when she was invited with her mother to the hospitality of the Pinks' rented cottage she always found him 'very friendly', and among other human aspects she noticed his interest in sport. Perhaps, she conceded, there was sometimes a reserve in his dealings with people: 'I wouldn't say he wasn't friendly but he never made a fuss over people. He was quick to check anything that was wrong.' When a female pianist once left the piano before Pink began to preach and walked across the front of the platform in the style of a mannequin, to take another seat, Pink at once told her that there was to be no repetition! Miss McAulay did not doubt that the real source of opposition to Pink was the prevalent unpopularity of the Reformed teaching on salvation. She recalled how Pink had to face the objection, 'If you believe election, then why do you preach?' and his straight answer, 'Because I am commanded to do so!'

Another surviving hearer, Alan McKerrell, has written: 'It does certainly appear that the blessing of the Lord rested upon the newly-formed church which met at the Masonic Hall.' He continues:

> One of my present friends, who was converted through Mr Pink's ministry and baptized by him, still talks often of those times of blessing under his ministry.
>
> My father and our family commenced to attend the church at Summer Hill and it was here that we first came in contact with Mr Pink who preached twice each Lord's Day, with a Sunday School and Bible Class being held in the afternoon. We would spend the whole day there as it was too far to travel home and back for each service.
>
> It was during this time that I first came under conviction of sin, and being only a lad in those days, perhaps the only thing I can remember personally concerning Mr Pink's ministry is his preaching on the text Romans 6:23. Through this text in the providence of God, in His time, I was brought to see myself as a sinner deserving eternal death, and in due time was led by God's grace to true gospel repentance with contrition and tears, and to faith in our Lord Jesus Christ.[9]

But notwithstanding such encouragements as these, Pink had reached the conclusion by March 1928 that his

[9] *Reformation Today*, Aug./Oct. 1972, p. 8.

decision to be their pastor had been premature. Certain aspects of the formation of the new church troubled him, and on March 25, while promising them help with preaching if they so desired, he resigned. In an address to the members after his last evening service as pastor on March 25 he indicated his unease over the motives which, he now believed, had entered into the formation of the new church. The glory of God had not been paramount in their thinking. 'He felt', the Minute Book records, 'that the main onus of guilt rested on him.' But it is also clear that Pink's view of unfulfilled prophecy and particularly of the apostasy apparent in so many churches influenced his judgment. It was never his practice to hold any beliefs in a purely theoretical way. He regarded it as unmistakably clear that the same spiritual conditions which in 1920 had contributed to his withdrawal from his Baptist pastorate in South Carolina were established across the professing church. 'Seven years ago he had seen as plainly as now that the Ship was already broken,' the writer of the Minutes in the Masonic Hall noted, and 'that it was not in accord with the revealed will of God to set up a church. He had been influenced by human sentimentality and was swayed by affection at the prospect of those who came out from Belvoir Street being without a church home.'

In a cryptic sentence the Minutes also record that 'Referring to Acts 2, he said it was not possible to practise all things in common' – perhaps a reference to their desire that all procedure should be in thorough accord with the New Testament. We wonder if 'Brother Dockaby' heard that remark and pondered any relevance it might have to the counsel he had received.

There may well have been other factors influencing Pink's decision. Although he believed in independent church government, he disliked 'sectarianism', and he may have felt that the new congregation had not escaped that danger. Far from being a natural bulldog who enjoyed a fight, he increasingly wished to avoid 'the strife of tongues' and perhaps he felt that his presence would have contributed to further controversy in Sydney. Neither can considerations of physical tiredness and a desire to be home (where both parents were still alive and where he had not been since 1915) be excluded from the motives leading to his resignation.

It seems to us, however, that it may have been his doctrine of unfulfilled prophecy that was at the centre of his course of action. For some while he had, as indicated above, entertained fundamental doubts over the future of *any* organized church work. 'There seem to be many intimations that the present dispensation has almost run its course', he wrote in 1927, and in 1931 he was to speak of 'leaving Sydney, Australia, where a corporate testimony for Christ had become impossible'.

However we interpret the situation, Pink's own words assure us that 'God made it clear that the work for which he took us to Australia was finished'. Thus, on July 20, 1928, Arthur and Vera Pink sailed for England.

Alan McKerrell remembered the parting scene as the *Ormonde* left Circular Quay:

> To the sorrowing brethren and sisters, who had gathered to bid him farewell, Mr Pink called out a parting word from the ship – Acts 20:32, 'And now, brethren, I commend you to God, and to the word of his grace, which is able to build you up, and to give you an inheritance among all them which are sanctified.'
>
> As the ship broke moorings and commenced to glide down the harbour, the little company sang the

doxology. We never had the privilege of seeing Mr and Mrs Pink again in the flesh, but, praise God, in the glory-land we shall meet again and we shall know even as we are known, as we gather round the throne of God and sing the new song, 'Unto him that loved us, and washed us from our sins in his own blood, and hath made us kings and priests unto God and his Father; to him be glory and dominion for ever and ever. Amen.' Revelation 1:5–6.

Nine days later, approaching Fremantle, after 2,500 miles 'as calm as on a ferry boat in Sydney bay', Pink concluded a letter to two of his closest Australian friends, Mr and Mrs Horace Coleman:

> We shall never forget the many seasons of happy fellowship which God so graciously granted us with you all in Sydney – I doubt not they will be recalled on high, as the 'Book of Remembrance' (*Mal.* 3:16) more than hints. The Lord was wondrously good to us. *No* good thing did he withhold from us!

Eighteen years later Pink remembered the time in Australia as 'three and a half of our happiest and busiest years'.[10]

[10] *Studies*, 1946, p. 283.

8

An Unwanted Preacher 1928–1930

Remarkably the Pinks' 12,500 mile voyage, across the Indian Ocean to the Suez Canal, and through the Mediterranean to the Atlantic, was passed without 'so much as a squall'. After forty peaceful days spent largely in preparing articles for the magazine, and in letter writing, they arrived in London on August 30, 1928. Behind them, as we have noted, were 'three-and-a-half of our happiest and busiest years'. Ahead were eight years of trial. From the time of their arrival in England, until 1936, Arthur and Vera Pink were to reside at about a dozen different addresses. Thus between forty-two and fifty years of age, when most men are well settled in their occupations, Pink was to find himself in the undesirable position of seeking a more permanent calling than any of these changing locations were to offer.

Of course he believed that God had willed it, and in that confidence he was to emerge from the trial a more deeply exercised and humble Christian, but it was a very testing and, at times, dismaying experience. We shall, perhaps, understand it somewhat more clearly as the narrative proceeds, yet at the outset it is necessary to point out that the key to the interpretation of this period in his life lies in his view both of the church and of his own calling as a minister of the gospel.

At the Baptist Tabernacle in Ashfield in 1925 Pink had preached on the duty of separation from unfaithful ministers of the gospel. After his experiences in the two years which had followed he was practically convinced that existing denominations had reached such a condition that separation from them was fast becoming a Christian duty. Significantly his first sermon to the group which had withdrawn with him from the Strict and Particular Baptists was on Hebrews 13:13, 'Let us go forth therefore unto him without the camp, bearing his reproach.' The title 'Outside the Camp', which he gave to the sermon when it was published in *Studies*, was to be an oft-repeated phrase in the coming years.

Yet while, in some instances, Pink was prepared to say, 'Better stay at home and read God's Word', he was far from counselling the abandonment of church connections. 'Next to being saved,' he declared, 'the writer deems it his greatest privilege of all to belong to one of Christ's churches'[1] – that is to say, to a congregation possessing true New Testament characteristics. Writing on the text, 'Despise ye the church of God?' (*1 Cor.* 11: 22), he asserts, 'This is done by God's people who deem his churches as of such little importance and value that they never join them.'[2] Clearly he was not blind to the truth which John Calvin places at the head of the fourth book of his *Institutes*, namely, that the church in its organizational form is one of 'the external means or aids by which God calls us into communion with Christ, and retains us in it'. As he wrote in March 1929, 'Only by the daily use of means and through fellowship with the godly are we preserved.'[3]

[1] *Studies*, 1927, p. 281.
[2] *Studies*, 1928, p. 19.
[3] *Studies*, 1929, p. 52.

Pink's thinking with respect to the work of the ministry was similar. While warning against unfaithful men, and the denominations which supported them, he was far from discounting the pastoral office itself. The Brethren rejection of pastors and preachers authorized to teach never appealed to him. Writing at one time to a young man of Brethren background who was inclined to 'the every-man-ministry' view, Pink advised that, while he held no brief for unregenerate ministers, 'Counterfeits do not invalidate the genuine! The one question you should concentrate upon is, What does the New Testament teach? Was preaching and teaching in the hands of a responsible leader, or was any Dick, Tom or Harry free to get up and spout in their meetings?'[4]

Most certainly, while Pink in 1928 found himself on the outside of denominationalism, he had not resigned his God-given calling as a preacher of the gospel. Had he done so at that date, and been prepared to work quietly in some corner as a writer, he would undoubtedly have spared himself many of the hardships which followed. But, given his convictions as to his calling, that was not an option which was open to him. The often trying consequences of his preaching in Sydney had not robbed him of the joy of preaching Christ or of meeting with fellow believers.

Thus Pink's return to England in 1928 did not constitute a retirement from public ministry. While still on the voyage he wrote to the Colemans: 'I am beginning to look forward to our arrival in London, God willing, and to ask him to give us access to *many* of his hungry sheep, to grant us favour in their eyes, and to enable us

[4] Letter to William Naismith, May 21, 1950. His fuller convictions on this are given in *Studies*, 1937, pp. 354 ff. (reprinted in *An Exposition of Hebrews* (Grand Rapids: Baker,1954), vol. 3, 1954, pp. 334 ff.).

to feed them with "food convenient".' He was aware of some of the difficulties he would find in London. As he told the readers of *Studies*:

> We have received no human call or invitation; there is no 'open door' apparent in sight. We are acquainted with very few of the Lord's people in London, and most of them who have heard of us are likely to be prejudiced because we are on the outside of everything ecclesiastical.[5]

These words were written before he left Australia. In the event, he was later to report, 'Following six weeks' oral silence on ship (we encountered not a single Christian among our five hundred fellow passengers), a further period of four weeks' inactivity followed our landing.' At the end of September 1928, with no apparent opportunity for ministry in London (where they stayed at the home of his brother, Frank, in Surbiton) or in the Midlands, where he must have visited his now aged parents, he accepted the invitation of a reader of *Studies* in Seaton, Devon, to his home, the decisive factor being that there were 'opportunities to minister the Word in that neighbourhood'.

After a short time in Seaton, where he was able to speak with liberty and encouragement, an unsought invitation came from a pastorless church in Cheltenham which claimed to be 'built around the Scriptures' and to want 'a teacher of the Word' for their next pastor. 'We went there,' Pink reports in a letter to the Colemans, 'but at the close of the first week, the Committee informed me my services were required no longer.' The same letter continues:

[5] *Studies*, 1978, p. 215.

After earnestly crying to God for light and guidance, we felt he would have us return to Seaton, Devon; first, because this was the place he had first led us to. Second, because letters from there while we were in Cheltenham showed plainly that the Lord had been pleased to bless his Word there through us to quite a number – the 'leading brother' in the 'Brethren assembly' here wrote me that his recent apprehension of the blessed truth of God's absolute supremacy had been 'like a second conversion in his experience'. Third, because these saints in Seaton, though blessed with a number able to preach the gospel, had no teacher, and many longed for one. Fourth, because we must pitch our tent somewhere, for the sake of the magazine and as the Lord had not intimated any other place, Seaton seemed to be the only place. Fifth, because the cost of living is cheaper there than in London. So we returned here ten days ago. We were accorded a hearty welcome at their week-night service on the day of our arrival, and many rejoiced because the Lord had sent us back. But on the Saturday morning the 'leading brother' told me they were 'having trouble'. Three of the brethren had taken decided exception to my teaching on the sovereignty of God, and declared that if I were permitted to minister the Word any more in the assembly, they would walk out of the 'breaking of bread' meeting; that others were of the same mind as themselves, and that if those who agreed to my teaching insisted that I should be allowed to go on teaching, there would be a 'big split' in the assembly. Accordingly, an emergency meeting was called that Saturday evening (a week ago tonight) of the seven brethren on 'the oversight' (equivalent of deacons),

> two of the three objectors belonging to the oversight. The other five had greatly enjoyed and been much helped by what God had enabled me to teach; they were very grieved, but felt that they should seek to preserve peace (they have so far had practically no ructions in the seven years the Assembly has existed) and prevent a split. They therefore agreed that, for the time being, I should be silenced; and two of them called on me late Saturday evening to acquaint me with their decision.
>
> Thus, for the time being, the door for public ministry was closed fast against me! Sunday, Mrs Pink and I spent alone, but the Lord granted us refreshment from Psalm 25 and gave me full assurance that this was among the 'all things' of Romans 8:28, and that if we counted on him alone all would be well and come out right in the end.[6]

Despite some further discussion with the Brethren in Seaton the 'door' was not reopened. Five 'on the oversight' told him there were many, perhaps fifty to seventy, who like themselves desired to sit under his ministry but that further preaching would split the assembly in two. In a last-minute 'Personal Word', added to the January 1929 issue of *Studies in the Scriptures*, Pink wrote:

> During our four months here we have had only two comparatively brief speaking engagements, and at present everything seems to be fast closed against us . . . We have rented a small cottage in a little sea-side town for the winter, where we are devoting ourselves to the work of this magazine. We are looking to God

[6] Letter from Seaton, Nov. 24, 1928.

> to grant us access to companies of his hungry people, in his own good time and way . . . Entertaining preaching, bright and cheery evangelistic addresses, are still listened to; but solid teaching is, with very rare exceptions, no longer tolerated.

From their cottage in Sidmouth Road, Seaton, Pink wrote to the Colemans again on January 10, 1929. After rejoicing in the greatness and immutability of God – truths, which, he says, were 'staying' their hearts – he proceeded with some items of news:

> One wealthy professing Christian who has a large Mission Hall in Liverpool to whom a friend had recommended me, wrote us a patronizing letter (a 'feeler' to see if we would come and speak for him), in which he said he 'spoke to great crowds and always with acceptance'. In my reply, I pointed out how different was his experience from that of the prophets, the Lord himself, and his apostles. I have heard nothing further from him! Another mission-hall, undenominational, near Norwich, had my name given to them. They are seeking a pastor, and approached me. In my letter I stated that God's servants were called upon to 'contend earnestly for the faith once delivered unto the saints', and that a very important part of that faith was the grand truth of God's absolute supremacy and his discriminating grace in election; and that another vital part of that faith was the preaching of eternal punishment to the unsaved. In their reply they said, 'The call here is for a steady, peaceable, pastoral ministry': note, *not* 'for a God-honouring, Christ-exalting, faithful' one. Still another, in London, with whom I was intimately acquainted fourteen years ago, wrote and asked if I

was available for preaching. I wrote back stating honestly and frankly the kind of 'preaching' which I, by the infinite grace of God, sought to give out. I have heard nothing further from him! How true is 2 Timothy 4:3, 4!

As winter of 1928–29 turned to spring the situation remained unchanged. 'A little handful gather for the Bible-readings in our home; others would like to attend them, but they are afraid to.'[7] Slowly the Pinks' thoughts were turned back to the United States where friends urged their return and where invitations existed to conduct Bible Conferences in different places. By April 11, 1929, they had made their decision and on May 2 they sailed from Southampton. Despite all the constant work on the magazine they viewed the previous six months as the kind of interlude of rest in a 'desert place' such as Christ had afforded the disciples (*Mark* 6:31). 'When we left Australia last July, we thought the Lord was bringing us to England for active service. But he had other designs . . . since December 1 we have been in complete seclusion, and, from a spiritual viewpoint, in a "desert place". But O how wondrously and blessedly has the Lord manifested himself to us! He did not say "Go", but "Come" – We have been *with him*.'

The Pinks' destination was Vera's home state, Kentucky, where in the small country town of Morton's Gap they hoped to settle among the company who made up the Baptist Church 'to whom we are well known'. Arriving in New York, Pink enjoyed the exchange with the immigration officer who interviewed him: 'He enquired if we intended to pursue our calling as a minister of the gospel. To which we replied, "Yes, by the grace of God."

[7] *Studies*, 1929, p. 71.

Then he added, "You are coming here to mend broken souls?" To which we responded, "No, sir, instead, as an instrument in the Lord's hands, to bring life to those who are dead in sin." His face lit up, and he exclaimed, "Attaboy; that's the talk!""[8]

Their first stopping place was at York, Pennsylvania, with Charles and Elsie Pressel who had acted as the U.S. agents for the magazine in the four and a half years since they had last met. Then after a short visit to other friends at Altoona they reached Morton's Gap on May 30. For Vera it was 'home' and Arthur Pink also rejoiced in the new situation. They were able to rent a house ('three nice-sized rooms and a hall'), and also to find furniture for it 'second-hand, but clean and neat' for £40. Best of all was the Christian fellowship. The church had a pastor who, it seemed, welcomed 'a fellow-helper in the truth' and there were preaching opportunities in the neighbourhood. Writing to the Colemans on July 1, 1929, Pink reports:

> Yesterday I had the privilege of preaching twice in a little country church, in a farming section – to simple and unsophisticated people: in the a.m. on the Sabbath; in the p.m. on the Cross in the Christian life – Matthew 16:24. The Lord helped me, and I believe a number of his people were blessed. It is good to be in harness again. I am getting more 'calls' than I can respond to. Both of us are being kept in splendid health, and trust you are too.

Once again, however, these opportunities were not long continued. A further letter to the Colemans on August 19, 1929, is full of spiritual things but contains a note before it closes suggesting that their initial hopes of

[8] *Studies*, 1929, p. 163.

finding a spiritual home in the church at Morton's Gap were not being realized:

> I have been kept close at it since 7.45 this morning till almost suppertime correcting proofs of the October issue of *Studies*, copies of which I hope will be mailed at the beginning of next week. I am feeling somewhat tired, yet I must have a little talk with you on paper, in response to your very kind and ever-welcome letter of July 14, to hand this morning. And *what* shall be the subject of my 'talk'? Ah, rather, *who* shall be the subject, for I have good reason to hope that both of you (by sovereign and amazing grace) had far rather hear me say something concerning Him who is 'fairer than the children of men', than anything about *things or ourselves.*
>
> O how infinitely worthy of our constant thought, meditation, study and love, is the blessed One who died that we might live! The Lord of glory descending into unfathomable shame! The Giver of all blessing being made a curse for us! Well may we pause and wonder, marvel, worship. But blessed be his name, the cross did not end all: 'It was not possible *he* should be holden of death.' He rose in triumph from the tomb, ascending on high, and took his place at God's right hand. Why? For *his own* comfort, peace, or joy? No – 'Whither *for us* the forerunner hath entered'. We engage all his thoughts! Our interests are his one concern! Nor is *that* all. Heaven will not fully be Heaven to Christ till he has all his redeemed with himself. Not content with having gone to prepare a place for us, he is coming back to receive us unto himself, that where he is there may we be also. 'Father, I will', he says, 'that they

also whom thou hast given me, be *with* me where I am; that they may behold my glory' (*John* 17:24) . . . What a happy, praising, worshipping people we should be! We are too much occupied with ourselves, with our fellow-creatures, or with *things.* I am thoroughly convinced that one of the chief hindrances today to many of the Lord's dear people *enjoying* their inheritance is that they are in their *wrong place,* they are where Christ is not: he is on the *outside* of everything corporate. To be where he is not, is to miss the place of blessing, is to have our peace disturbed, and is to be corrupted by those who are not walking with him. I am *more* firmly convinced today than I was 14 months ago that our place is on the 'outside of the camp'. That is the place of 'reproach', of loneliness, and of testing; but as it is the place where *Christ* is, it is, necessarily, the place of blessing, peace, and joy. I will not defile your ears by describing conditions in these parts where the good providence of our unerring God has placed us, beyond saying they are neither better nor worse than everywhere we have been.

But, although thus speaking of his commitment to be 'outside the camp', Pink was still prepared to accept engagements in churches where, hopefully, the truth would be received. In October he reports again to the Colemans:

On Friday, 18th October [1929] I left for a little village 350 miles away, for a small rural Baptist Church. Its pastor had exchanged a number of letters with me during the past four months. He seemed to be an unusually spiritual man and assured me he had been seeking to build up a New Testament church,

> that there were twenty there who would value my teaching, etc. I hoped this church might prove the exception to the rule and be an oasis in the desert, for 'love thinketh no evil'. Alas, my hope was not realised! The pastor though having a wife and six children has no family worship. The 'church' had not celebrated the Lord's Supper for over four years. The one man in it evidencing any spirituality said to me, 'A few have sufficient natural sense to see it would be a mockery to have it under existing conditions.' I believe the Lord sent me there for that one lone sheep of his. He told me he had remained in the 'church'(?) with an uneasy conscience and at the loss of all peace and joy, but knew no other alternative. I went there for two weeks but concluded on the 8th. Unexpectedly the Lord opened another door where I spoke two afternoons and three nights – a city 'church' with rather well-to-do people in it. I was asked to address the Women's midweek service and spoke 45 minutes from 1 Peter 3:1–6. I had more liberty but there was much to sadden. I sought mainly to stress Matthew 16:24, 25 – am earnestly seeking grace to practise it more myself.[9]

Pink's friends in Sydney, who had known him preach six times a week and had seen the spiritual influence of that preaching, were clearly disturbed at this news of more closed doors. Writing again on December 11, 1929, Pink associates himself with those 'who, like ourselves, are virtually cut off from all visible fellowship with God's people', and yet he assures the Colemans: 'Do not be in anywise worried over our experiences and lot. We are not. By Divine grace we are quite content, never happier in our souls, never more conscious of the Lord's presence.'

[9] Quoted in *Reformation Today*, Nov./Dec. 1977, pp. 9–10.

On March 9, 1930, he writes again: 'We have less contact with people here in Morton's Gap than we had in Seaton. The common report is that much study has turned me mad. We neither of us ever go anywhere save to the post office and shops. Have not seen a newspaper for nearly a year so are quite ignorant of what is going on in the world. But the Lord is with us and that is all that matters. He continues to supply our every need.'[10]

At the time Pink gave no reason for his inability to resettle in Kentucky in 1929. Recalling the experience in 1946, he wrote, 'We found those who had run well twelve years previously did so no longer, and instead of enjoying happy fellowship with them, we were a thorn in their sides.' We wonder if there was not also a maturing in Pink which made him less acceptable to some former acquaintances. Calvinistic doctrine, which existed in the Morton's Gap Church, had never been enough for him and it was less now. There ought to be 'longings to see souls converted'. 'Have we declared *all* the counsel of God when we have expounded the "five points" of Calvinism? We trow not.'[11] It seems that the experimental side of Christianity was not prominent in the ministry he heard while for him that note had become increasingly important. 'As we grow older,' he wrote in 1931, 'we feel the great need of a deeper experimental acquaintance with God, and so of the Holy Spirit's applying his word in power to our hearts. More and more we are learning that there is a vast difference between a theoretical knowledge of the truth and inward experience of it.'[12] 'The general neglect of the heart is the root cause of the present sad state of Christendom.'[13]

[10] Ibid., p 11. His reference to newspapers does not mean that he disapproved of such reading; suitable papers had not been available in rural Kentucky.
[11] *Studies*, 1929, p. 144. [12] *Studies*, 1931, p. 286. [13] *Studies*, 1933, p. 278.

If Pink were to be judged simply by some of the extracts from letters given above, it might be supposed that all his work at this time was coloured by pessimism. But that was not the case, as can be illustrated by an additional enterprise he took on at this time. Pink had remained in contact with I. C. Herendeen and in 1929 the latter published another edition of *The Sovereignty of God* which Pink had revised. In the same year he proposed that Pink, in addition to *Studies* (which continued to appear monthly), should prepare another monthly magazine specifically for Sunday-School teachers. Pink agreed and the first issue, with the title *Help on the Sunday-School Lesson*, came out in January 1930, published by the Cleveland Bible Truth Depot. It consisted of eight pages of close print, in double columns, with lessons for each Sunday in the month. When the third issue came out in March, Herendeen noted in a 'Personal Word' that there were 133 subscribers, 'not a great many, but yet something; it is a start . . . Mr Pink is putting a great deal of study and hard work in the preparation of the lesson material.' With that issue the magazine became a Quarterly, and was enlarged to twenty-four pages. But the last issue for the year, for the months October–December 1930, contained a little note indicating that it was being 'discontinued for the present' and adding, 'We wish to thank all our readers who have done what they could to help us.'

Help on the Sunday-School Lesson was so short lived that it might hardly seem worth mentioning were it not for the fact that, besides demonstrating Pink's energy and his interest in helping children, its pages show how far he was from retreating into isolation. The small response cannot be blamed on the contents. Few such magazines can have contained an equal concentration of biblical teaching, carefully presented and with good application. Far from writing as a censor of others, his summary of his lesson on 'Judging our Brethren', Matthew 7:1–5, indicated the rule he sought to follow:

> What the Lord forbids is, first, the forming of an unfair and unrighteous judgment: ignoring the good, being occupied with only trifling evil. What He here reprimands is, second, forming the habit of going about looking for every spot and blemish which are to be found in our brethren. What he interdicts is, third, the hypocritical censuring of another's infirmities while failing to condemn my own glaring sins. In v. 2 He faithfully warns that we shall reap in this as we sow. The critic will in turn be criticised; he who is unmerciful to others will meet with a harsh verdict himself (*James* 2:13).

Perhaps one reason why Pink gave up the second magazine was that he was not persuaded that it was God's will they should spend the remainder of their days solely in a writing ministry in Kentucky. Early in April 1930, despite having the two magazines on hand, they moved a further three thousand miles to a northern suburb of Los Angeles on the West Coast. It was letters from that area which a year before had helped turn Pink's thoughts back to ministry in the States. On April 11, 1930, he reports to the Colemans from 1139 Alameda Avenue, Glendale, California:

> Once more the Lord has had us move our tent, and by his good hand we arrived at the above address safe and sound yesterday, receiving a most hearty welcome from a number of old and tried friends, most of whom we had not seen for ten years! What

the Lord has for us here I know not as yet. We are quietly waiting upon him. Glendale is a suburb of Los Angeles, which is now a city rather larger than Sydney. Conditions here are the same as everywhere else: ruin stares one in the face on every side. But in such a large place there are probably quite a few of 'his own'. Some of these we already know – sick at heart over existing conditions: yearning for fellowship with kindred minds, longing for spiritual teaching. I have *no* thought of attempting to 'organize' anything, or 'start something new'. But it may be in his will to have some Bible Classes 'on the outside'. In the meanwhile, 'he that believeth shall not make haste', is before me. We are staying with a Christian couple (quite a little older than ourselves) in whose home we once were for four months, nine years ago then in Seattle. Their name is Richards.[14]

Your good letter of March 4, with the enclosed money order for £3.4.0 has been forwarded from Morton's Gap and is safely to hand, for which I thank you cordially in the blessed name of him whom we are seeking to serve: may the Lord's blessing rest upon each giver and gift. It is almost two years since we sailed from Sydney, yet though I have done less than three weeks' preaching since then, the Lord has freely ministered to every need and we have lacked for nothing. Praise him! We appreciate the references to the Lord's dealing with you and your experiences and heart exercises. Each of us needs to pray daily that we may be enabled to walk by faith and not by sight.

Glendale, on the north side of Los Angeles, was an area familiar to Pink from earlier visits to the area but here,

[14] See above, p. 70.

too, he found a decline in conditions. Although he was able to start a Bible Class, a letter from Vera Pink to the Colemans on September 1, 1930, reported the result:

> We have given up the class which we started. Those who came are still mixed up with the religious views in this wicked city and refuse to separate from it. One who was, professedly, most interested in the class, the last Tuesday night was counting votes all night – a woman too – another said she did not at all agree on separation and so on, so once again Mr Pink is shut up to pen ministry. Things are in a most terrible state in all the churches and yet there are those who continue going and say they do so 'just to see friends whom they can't see during the week because of work'.[15]

Meanwhile the Pinks had moved to rented accommodation of their own at 1339 Bates Avenue, Los Angeles, and it was here as Mrs Pink narrates in another letter that they had a new experience:

> About 4.30 p.m. Sat., 1st September [1930], Mr Pink was sitting in our little living-room studying and I was in the kitchen cooking our Sunday meal and was standing leaning against the sink paring apples when I suddenly heard a rumbling noise, as if a huge lorry was coming up the drive, and right on top – so to speak – of this noise I felt the house rise as a ship at sea on a large wave. The sink left me. I was very unsteady and surprised. This was followed by two others, the second more pronounced than the first or last. The three quakes lasted, I should say, four seconds. It was the first earthquake either of us has

[15] Quoted by Ray Levick in *Reformation Today*, Mar./Apr. 1977, p. 20.

> experienced, but we both knew almost instantly what it was. I felt rather queer for a while physically – Mr Pink said I looked pale, but I was not frightened in the least. The suddenness of the shock and the rocking of the house like a ship made him a bit nauseated and head-achey. I thought afterwards what it must be when 'He ariseth to shake terribly the earth'. This was very slight and yet the hardest they have felt here in Los Angeles for ten years. Yet our godless neighbours were excited and frightened, but by his grace we could go right on with what we were doing.[16]

It seems that at Los Angeles, resulting from things which he heard or read in church bulletins, Pink (perhaps for the first time) declined to speak in some 'Fundamentalist' churches. We only note the fact now and defer a consideration of his reasons. He wrote to Horace Coleman on January 4, 1931, 'We have not been inside any "church" during 1930, and see very, very few people from one month to another.' Although this personal information was not communicated to the readers of *Studies in the Scriptures*, in an article entitled 'Sound the Alarm' written for the magazine during 1930 he wrote:

> In view of the appalling conditions now existing in almost all of the 'churches' what is the duty of the real child of God? Are you willing for Scripture to answer that question, my reader? If so, none need remain in any doubt as to the Divine will in the matter. 'Thou shalt not follow a multitude to do evil' (*Exod.* 23:2). 'Have no fellowship with the unfruitful works of darkness, but rather reprove them'

[16] Ibid., p. 21.

> (*Eph.* 5:11). 'Be ye not unequally yoked together with unbelievers' (*2 Cor.* 6:14).
>
> We do not say that it is the duty of every Christian to 'come out', for we are not personally acquainted with every 'church'. Yet this we do say, if there are any 'churches' which are scriptural in their membership, in their maintenance of discipline, in their preaching, and in all that concerns their public services, we do not know where to find them. We have travelled completely around the world, and ministered the Word in many places but there is no church known to us where we could hold membership. But if you are a member of a church where Scripture is followed in all its arrangements, and its pastor and officers are God-fearing men and honour him by their daily walk, then praise him with all your heart, and do everything in your power to strengthen their hands. This article is not intended as an attack upon the true servants of God. Nor is it designed as a brief for those known as the 'Plymouth Brethren'.[17]

Yet after all his experiences, Pink had no hesitation in writing in 1934, 'I entered the ministry in 1910, and I have never regretted it.'[18]

[17] *Studies*, 1931, pp. 46–7.
[18] Letter to Lowell Green, June 3, 1934.

9

The Mystery of Providence 1931–1936

On March 31, 1931, the Pinks left Los Angeles and the West Coast for the last time. It was the day before his forty-fifth birthday. Once more the reason for the change was the same. As he tells his friend John Blackburn, 'The Lord has opened a door for oral ministry to minister the Word to some small groups *outside* the camp.'[1]

The groups to which he refers were indeed small ones, centred in Pennsylvania, but their existence caused the Pinks to retrace their steps three thousand miles back to the eastern side of the United States. A brief reference to the anticipated 'happy privilege' of renewed ministry in *Studies in the Scriptures* was accompanied by a request for prayer 'that a "double portion" of our Master's Spirit may rest upon us'. The necessity for the Holy Spirit's indispensable aid to make preaching effective was certainly a subject much upon his heart. He writes:

> None will ever be drawn to Christ, savingly, by mere preaching; no, not by the most faithful and scriptural preaching . . . Most of us are in such a feverish rush

[1] March 30, 1931.

> to 'win souls', to do 'personal work', to preach, that we have no time for definite, reverent, importunate crying unto the Lord for his Spirit. O brethren, join the writer in contritely owning to God your sinful failure to give the Spirit his proper place![2]

Pink's faith in God as the hearer of prayer marked his life in a very practical way and many years later he was to record two instances of the intervention of God in answer to prayer which occurred during this period in 1931.

The first concerns the furnished bungalow at Bates Avenue, Glendale, which they had rented from a Jewish lady. When they gave notice of their departure the owner naturally placed a 'To Let' sign in front of the property and advertised in the local papers. But with the Pinks' earnest request that those making application should not be shown over the property on the Lord's Day she had not the least sympathy. 'Though she knew we kept the Lord's Day holy and held a small service in our room each Sabbath evening,' writes Pink, 'she insisted it was her right to show over the house those who answered the advertisement. We protested strongly, but she would not heed, saying "Sunday" was always her best letting day. We then told her that our God would keep away all applicants on the coming Sabbath, which she heard with derisive scorn. That Saturday evening my wife and I spread the matter before the Lord and begged him to cause his angel to encamp round about us, and protect us by keeping away all intruders. During the Sabbath, which was a cloudless day, we continued seeking God's face, confident he would not put us to confusion before our landlady. Not a single caller came to look over the house, and that night we had our little meeting as usual,

[2] *Studies*, 1935, p. 31.

undisturbed! Next day our landlady, who owned two similar bungalows, stated it was the first time in her ten years' experience of letting that she had ever failed to let on a Sunday.'[3]

The second incident occurred during the latter part of their long train journey to Pennsylvania. Pink recalled it in *Studies* in 1950:

> When entering our train from Chicago to Pittsburgh [April 1931] we encountered a Christian lady in distress. The porter had wrongly put her into an *express*, which would carry her hundreds of miles beyond her destination; and the ticket collector informed her that there was no possibility of the train halting at her village. The writer and his wife reminded her that nothing is too hard for God. We had special prayer, and were able to assure her that the Lord would *stop the train*. Some hours later she was told to get ready, and it stopped for a few seconds. Some of our readers in Pennsylvania will recall this incident, for they saw the letter of thanks which Mrs Pink received, telling of how the experience had brought her to trust more fully in a miracle-working God.[4]

One reason why Pink never disclosed such incidents until long after the event was that he did not believe in advising others 'how' to pray. 'One cannot "pray to order",' he wrote to a friend. 'Real prayer is in-breathed by the Holy Spirit, laying a burden on the heart. I have no sympathy with this modern method of keeping a "prayer list", nor have I ever attempted to pray by the clock! I have often been struck with how often preachers

[3] *Studies*, 1946, p. 156, or *Gleanings in Joshua*, p. 60.
[4] *Studies*, 1950, p. 179, or *Gleanings in Joshua*, p. 283.

and others misquote, "Lord, teach us to pray," by inserting, "teach us *how* to pray". Man is occupied with "how", but God with the "pray" – which is often an inarticulated *groan*!'[5]

The Pinks' first stopping place after they continued from Pittsburgh on their long journey at the beginning of April 1931 was at Altoona at the home of old friends, the Hunters. 'We remained there ten days,' he writes to the Colemans, 'and had a truly glorious time, sharing the kind hospitality of a Christian home which was a veritable "Bethel". We had a service each night and three each Sabbath.'[6] From there they proceeded a further 170 miles to the Pressels' new home in York where they were to stay for eight weeks, giving 'two or three Bible readings' each week on Hebrews 11 to a 'handful' who gathered with them. 'I am also counting on the Lord opening the way for me to spend one weekend each month in Philadelphia,' he told the Colemans in the letter already quoted, 'a city as large as greater Sydney, where we sojourned for the last eighteen months prior to our coming to Australia.'

The Pinks were always considerate guests in a home, and even with their closest friends they never stayed longer than was strictly necessary. He did not believe that two families should attempt to live together in one home. The question now before them was the location of their own future home. In June 1931 they decided to move to an unpainted wooden house at Millmont, Union County, somewhat less than a hundred miles from York and only one mile from Swengel, which they had left in 1923. It was probably Herendeen who had informed them of the availability of this house for he had himself returned to Swengel from Cleveland in 1930.

[5] Letter to Lowell Green, March 24, 1935. [6] April 19, 1931.

For a·while it seemed that the Pinks had at last reached a resting place where there would also be opportunity for spoken ministry. July 11, 1931, Pink could write to the Colemans that as many as seventeen people (including the Hunters and the Pressels) gathered some weekends: 'We have had some precious seasons together before the throne and around the Word.' Two nights a week about this period he was also ministering to 'a little group' in Glenholden. The Pinks enjoyed the peaceful isolation of their rented home 'right out in the country', even though it meant a walk of a mile each way every day to obtain milk. 'We can pray, study and write without disturbance. The only sounds we hear are the singing of the birds and an occasional car driving by.'

When the winter of 1931–32 came it brought problems, yet these did not deter them. The house had no electricity, and as temperatures fell below zero they had no option but to go to bed leaving a fire burning beneath them in the kitchen stove. The fear of a fire in their wooden dwelling they countered by a nightly trust in God: 'When we lie down in the arms of a "faithful Creator" and covenant God, fear is removed and sleep is sweet', he writes, and he quotes Spurgeon to the same effect, 'No pillow so soft as a Divine promise, no coverlet so warm as an assured interest in Christ.'[7] Speaking again of the severity of winter at Millmont, he also recalled in later years, 'I had to plough my way through 6 to 8 inches of snow with two large buckets and carry our water over half a mile uphill!'[8]

Towards the end of 1932, when again there was a bitter winter, Pink wrote in his Annual Letter:

[7] *Studies*, 1950, p. 167.
[8] Letter to Lowell Green, Feb. 18, 1940.

> For another year the editor and his wife have been spared a single day's sickness. What mercy is this! Though the editor spends at least twelve hours every day in his study, engaged in heavy mental work, yet this close confinement, year after year, has not impaired his health to the slightest degree. Though he has now read the Bible through over fifty times, and upwards of one million pages of theological literature, he has no glasses, and reads the finest print as comfortably as he did twenty-five years ago. Though the editor's wife does all her own housework, making of bread and her own clothes, looks after a garden, and has canned and preserved, jellied and pickled between two hundred and fifty and three hundred pints of fruit and vegetables; and though she does all the typing and addressing of envelopes for this magazine, yet, in spite of a frail body, God has graciously sustained and granted all needed strength.[9]

The opportunities for speaking were undoubtedly a part of Pink's pleasure at this period. He writes to the Colemans on July 21, 1932:

> Your most welcome letter of June 20 to hand yesterday. As I take up my pen to answer, I am reminded that it is exactly four years ago today since we sailed from Sydney. They have been blessed years, crowned with the Lord's abounding goodness. I trust they have been profitable ones, and that the Lord has been pruning and refining us amid the blessed solitude, apart from 'the strife of tongues' . . . You will rejoice

[9] *Studies*, 1932, p. 286. From the December 1925 issue of *Studies* Pink commonly gave some brief personal news annually in *Studies*. From 1932 this became an Annual Letter in each December issue.

to know that He is also owning our occasional oral work. During June two families drove five hundred miles to spend a couple of weeks in our humble abode, for fellowship around the Word and before the throne. One of them brought a niece of fifteen and the Lord, in his sovereign grace, was pleased to meet with her: her letters since returning home contain very clear and definite evidence that another brand was plucked from the burning. Hallelujah!

After more than two years at Millmont this comparatively peaceful period came to an end in the early autumn of 1933. The landlord of their rented home wished to sell it and the Pinks were confronted with the necessity of another move. About the time they received this news, he inserted a favourite verse in a space in the magazine:

> Ill that he blesses is our good,
> And unblest good is ill,
> And all is right that seems most wrong
> If it be his sweet will.

The Pinks moved back to York, where their friends the Pressels lived, about October 1933. Here they rented another home, 531 Thomas Street, and he hung on his study wall the painted motto, 'Thou Remainest'. These were still days of the great economic depression as is illustrated by the fact that he could tell a friend, 'We paid only $18 a month for an eight-roomed house (the third storey of which we never used) in a nice locality.' This address was to be their last home in the United States. In 1934 his only opportunities for spoken ministry were at the Pressels' home, and in meeting with one or two others once a week. Hoped-for openings in Philadelphia had never materialized. He came to believe that a return to Britain was the way forward. In a letter to Lowell Green of August 19, 1934, he wrote:

> God's blessing has been and now is upon my written ministry in a most unmistakable and gracious way; but my personal ministry through direct contact is almost a complete failure. As I sat alone in my room this morning, reviewing the past few years, and then realizing how soon I shall have left the States for ever, I hardly felt in the mood for writing a formal letter.[10]

If his ministry were only to be by the pen then he could do that as well in England, but he still entertained the hope that he might be led in his own country to some sphere of public ministry. Accordingly he asked for the prayer help of his readers, 'that God may be pleased to make his way very plain before our face, and mercifully preserve us from being deceived by Satan, or acting from any Self Will'.[11]

After a final stay with the Pressels, the Pinks with all their belongings in three trunks and six boxes (containing his books) set off by rail for New York. They sailed on R.M.S. *Majestic* on September 5, 1934: 'We remained on deck while we sailed down the river and passed the Statue of Liberty. It was with mingled feelings I watched the fading shore for, although born and educated in England, I have spent less than two and a half years there since 1910.'[12]

* * * * *

Their destination in England was Cheltenham, a comfortable spa resort of some 50,000 people in

[10] *Letters of A. W. Pink*, pp. 43 –5.
[11] *Studies*, 1934, p. 215.
[12] *Letters*, p. 49.

Gloucestershire. The Winstones, who had been the honorary agents for the magazine in the United Kingdom, lived there, and were the 'kind loyal friends' whom the Pinks had probably first met on their short visit to the town in 1928. From his new address at 31 North Place, Cheltenham, where they had arranged to lease rooms for six months, Pink briefly related his recent voyage to the readers of the magazine and continued:

> Our daily prayer is that the Lord of the harvest will graciously open doors where we may minister his Word orally. There are few places where we would feel free to enter, for we dare not, even by our presence, sanction much which is now going on under the cloak of Christ's holy name. Yet it seems almost impossible to get a hearing on the outside. We have hired a room where we teach every Wednesday evening, but only a handful have assembled thus far.
>
> The prayers of God's children are earnestly solicited. Our main work, by God's enabling, will still be the continued publication of this little monthly messenger, which reaches many of the scattered children of God whom we never expect to meet down here. Nevertheless, it is our fervent longing that we may have opportunity to preach and teach by lip as well as by pen.
>
> Surely there are still left somewhere in these British Isles congregations or groups which would welcome an oral ministry along the lines of our articles; places where 'all the counsel of God' would be welcomed. Pray that the Lord will bring us into touch with such, give us favour in their eyes, and use us to bring them into a closer walking with himself and into the fullness

of his rich blessing. As of old, it is largely true today that God's people 'are destroyed for lack of knowledge' (*Hos.* 4:6) – lack of faithful gospel preaching, lack of sound doctrinal instruction, lack of practical teaching as to how they may enter into God's best for them in this life. The need is indeed great, the situation is urgent – a challenge to faith, to prayer, to believing effort!

In the ensuing weeks during the mid-winter of 1934–35 Pink himself temporarily failed to rise to the 'challenge'. No prospect had developed from the small meetings in the hired hall in Cheltenham. Thirteen came one week and, in the hope of better attendance the night was changed to Monday, but it made no difference. Usually untroubled by weather conditions, England's 'raw, damp weather and sunless dark days' seemed to add to his oppression. His enquiry in the magazine about possible openings had brought no response, and even his usual mail from readers of the magazine was falling off. For a while his language was that of the Psalmist, 'My soul refused to be comforted.' In a letter to a friend, Wallace Nicolson, who was then studying for the ministry of the Free Presbyterian Church of Scotland, he opened his heart:

31 North Place
Cheltenham
Sabbath-day December 30, 1934

Our dear Brother in Christ
Greetings in the blessed name of him whose Holy Word instructs us to pray, 'So teach us to number our days that we may apply our hearts unto wisdom'

(*Psa.* 90:12). This is an appropriate verse to meditate upon at this season. Our responsibility is not measured in the term of 'years' but of days. As each new day dawns, we need to apply our hearts unto wisdom as the labouring man applies his hands to his manual tasks definitely, diligently, perseveringly. Yet for this we are not sufficient in and of ourselves: we need to be divinely 'taught'.

I thank you for your kind letter of the 27th and the enclosed New Year's card. I knew that my last would distress you, and am sorry I have no more cheering news to communicate this time. At present, I am a burden to myself and a grief to my friends. The past two weeks are the worst ones spiritually I have passed through for many years. I seem in a torpor and quite unable to arouse myself. The attempt of anyone to reason with or counsel me, only leaves me worse; so that my dear wife is not allowing anyone to come in and talk with me. Nothing will be of any avail unless the Lord is pleased to show himself strong on my behalf in a providential way: unless he does so, I shall pine away – a heart-broken man. Nothing I read makes any impression on me. The mails are very discouraging too: both new names and gifts for the magazine have fallen off 50% from the corresponding month last year. The smile of the Lord seems to have left us. I have heard nothing further from the Strict Baptist preacher in Lancashire.

Yes, my brother, I long since learned that the words and promises of men were of little worth. But I had hoped that the Lord would move others to mete out to me as I have measured to others. During the past 25 years I have gone out of my way to do not a little to help many preachers, but none of them will help me. The tragic thing is that those of my friends who would dearly like to help me are powerless to do so; while those who could, will not. And in a very few years at most it will be too late. What I have gone through the last seven years is so reacting on my physical and mental constitution, that ere long I shall be incapacitated even if doors should be opened unto me. However, I can see nothing else than to attempt to seek grace to bow to the Lord's sovereign pleasure, and say, 'Not my will, but thine be done.'

It is a mercy, then, you did not come to us for the New Year: I should only have depressed you and in my present state of mind am unable to help anyone. Nor can anyone help me: unless the Lord works for me despondency will possess me.

Don't worry, my brother, because now you are not suffering anything for Christ's sake: you will have plenty later on!

Re God's love not being limited by moral imperfection or change of the creature. This is true: but you need to distinguish carefully between God's love and the manifestation of it – as also our enjoyment of it.

The Song [of Solomon] is high above me these days, and I feel I shall never be spiritual enough to take up such a theme.

Well, I had better bring my dismal ramblings to an end, for you have sufficient cares enough of your own, without being burdened by mine. It may be the clouds will break soon and the sun shine through again for me. I know not, and neither faith nor hope are operative. Satan is sifting me, and I can see nothing through the cloud of dust and dirt he has raised in me. In a mechanical and lifeless way I am still able to thank God for his blessings; my lot might be far worse than it is. May it please the Lord to undertake for each of us and all his dear people!

Yours by his abounding mercy,

Arthur W. Pink.

You need to prepare one or two sermons more directly on the Person of Christ: try your hand on Psalm 45:2!

As the postscript to the above letter shows, faith was there, even in the gloom, but it would be an injustice to Pink to leave the above letter standing on its own. Such low points were not the pattern of his life. He was again passing through a major struggle with discouragement and was for a time without the comfort to which he directed others. In a letter to the Colemans of September 16, 1933, he had written: 'Many of God's dear children experience seasons of depression and despondency. In some cases it is due to temperament – a naturally gloomy disposition; with others, it comes from a physical condition. But this is part of the trying of their faith which God has ordained for them – to trust Him amid the shadows.'

The pages of the *Studies* for this period show that, instead of depressing his readers, Pink was giving them truths where he knew relief lay. His Annual Letter for 1934, published in the very month of the letter sent to Wallace Nicolson, was on the words, 'Rejoice in the Lord always: again I say, Rejoice.' 'It is true,' he wrote, 'that a gloomy disposition may affect the mind with doleful thoughts, that unpleasant surroundings are apt to dampen the natural spirits, that trying circumstances tend to harass, and that lack of fellowship with happy saints may sadden the heart. Nevertheless, the Holy Spirit is not limited by such things as those, and when He takes the things of Christ and shows them unto us we cannot but rejoice.'

Pink never wrote in *Studies* as he did in his personal letter to Nicolson. Instead of ever presenting moroseness as spirituality, he taught, 'It is a Christian duty to preserve a cheerful countenance . . . few things have done more injury to the cause of the gospel than the sourness, sadness and moroseness of a large class of its professors.'[13] At the same time he wanted his readers to know that he also was only a learner. Writing on the words in Hebrews 12:5, 'My son, despise not thou the chastening of the Lord, nor faint when thou art rebuked of him,' in the March issue of 1935, he spoke of the sinfulness of despair: 'Fight hard, my brother, against this attitude of despair, lest your complaining or gloominess stumble others. Despise not; faint not!' To which he added, 'May Divine grace preserve both writer and reader.'[14] The next year there was a more personal reference: 'We are very diffident from writing about ourselves, lest in appearing to magnify the grace and patience of God we are but seeking to gain a reputation for being very humble. Spiritually our experience is an up and down, in and out one, with faith and unbelief ever alternating. Not a day passes that we do not have to go to the throne of grace for *mercy*.'[15]

Pink's 'fainting fits', instead of keeping him permanently, as he feared, on a low level, actually led to greater usefulness

[13] *Exposition of the Sermon on the Mount* (Darlington: Evangelical Press, 1977), p. 184.
[14] *Studies*, March 1935, pp. 71–2. Also in his *Exposition of Hebrews* (Grand Rapids: Baker, 1954), vol. 3, pp.18–79.
[15] *Studies*, December 1936, p. 382. In his *Life of Elijah* (Edinburgh: Banner of Truth, 1976), p. 212, 'Though we cannot vindicate Elijah's peevishness and petulance, yet this writer can certainly sympathise with him under the juniper tree, for he has often been there himself.'

in his ministry to others. Thus at the time when he despaired of himself, he was producing (as *Studies* shows) some of his most helpful writings. The series on 'Union and Communion', which Martyn Lloyd-Jones regarded as one of his best series, was started in 1935.

Submission under trials did not, however, mean for Pink a passive acceptance of events and circumstances. The degree to which he was isolated from the church fellowship he had known in former years troubled him, and when Nicolson responded to the despairing letter of December 30, 1934, by urging him to move north to Scotland, Pink took the recommendation seriously. Historic Christianity had hopefully survived more in that land than it had in England, and there were several readers of *Studies* there, including, it seems, a few ministers who belonged to the Free Presbyterian Church. Nicolson was sure that Pink would be at home among the people of a denomination with which he had much in common.

In March 1935 Pink acted on Nicolson's suggestion and took lodgings at 386 Great Western Road, Glasgow (the home of a Free Presbyterian lady). Nicolson had arranged this for them, and was himself living not far away. Before travelling north, Pink is not without a touch of humour in a letter to this Scots friend, explaining that a screw-driver and steel bar would be needed to get into the various boxes they were bringing with them: 'My wrist is not strong enough to unfasten the thick wire, so may have to fall back on the Samson-like wrists of some Scot to help.'

They would need shelves, he wrote, for his 750 books, and, anticipating colder weather than at Cheltenham, he wished coal to be ordered for them in advance. Also among their luggage would be 'Dicky', their pet bird in his cage. He concludes his letter:

> I expect to give you a complete outline of our experiences of the last years, and when you have heard it, I don't think you will be surprised at my viewing the future gloomily . . . However, 'it may be' (*Amos* 5:15) that things will be brighter for us all round once we get settled in Glasgow: I wish I felt more confident, but 'hope deferred maketh the heart sick'. At any rate, I hope the experiences through which our all-wise God has taken us will at least make us more patient and gentle with other souls who are cast down – if so, it won't have been altogether in vain.

After a visit to Surbiton (to the home of his younger brother, Frank, whom he had not seen for six years), the Pinks left London by train at 10 a.m. on April 1, 1935, and arrived in Glasgow about 6 p.m. the same evening. In a brief 'personal word' to readers of the magazine he wrote:

> The Lord, we believe, has called us to pitch our tent next in Scotland. O that it may prove a case of 'they went to their own company' (*Acts* 4:23). Will Christian friends kindly pray that God will make his people of the land of Knox a blessing to our needy souls, and that it may please him to make us of some service to them. We hope to feel more at home in a land where the Sabbath is more strictly observed, and where the doctrines of the Reformers and Puritans are more widely held, than any country we have yet sojourned in.[16]

No further words appeared in the magazine about their time in Scotland and Pink drew a veil of silence over it.

[16] *Studies*, 1935, p. 19.

Not since he had been in Sydney had he published any statement which involved criticism of persons. The facts, however, can be pieced together from his correspondence. Although he had never been in Scotland before, so far as is known, he understood enough about the Scots to realize that his immediate acceptance in Glasgow was improbable: 'No doubt it will take some months before we gain their confidence, for the Scots are proverbially "canny" or conservative and slow to "lay hands" on any man.'[17]

On their arrival in the city, Arthur and Vera Pink attached themselves to the Free Presbyterian congregation and attended all services for the next two months, where they were warmly welcomed by the minister, the Rev. Roderick MacKenzie. One of the senior elders of this congregation had been an appreciative reader of *Studies*. Thankful for this new fellowship, Pink even travelled north at the beginning of May to visit another congregation in the denomination. He writes to Evelyn Sorrells on May 10, 1935:

> I only returned last night from attending a week's special meetings in the 'Highlands', so have to be briefer than I would like as I am rather behind with my work – this is already my tenth letter today. I was somewhat disappointed with the preaching: though sound in doctrine (for which I was thankful), it was lacking in power. But I attended two prayer-meetings, one on Saturday night and one on Sabbath morning at 8 o'clock, which were a real tonic to my soul. I had the privilege of meeting a number of very godly souls.[18]

[17] Letter to Lowell Green, March 24, 1935.
[18] Letter to Evelyn Sorrells, May 10, 1935.

Pink had let it be known that he was available to preach *gratis* in any of the denomination's vacant charges although, in view of the fact that he felt unable to join the Free Presbyterians formally, he realized that, humanly speaking, it was doubtful whether any invitations would be forthcoming.

He was soon to know the worst. When the Free Presbyterian Synod met at Inverness in mid-May 1935 it was proposed that 'their men be prohibited from calling on those of other denominations to lead in prayer or otherwise assist in their services'. One minister, seconding the motion, declared, 'We do not wish to hobnob with people of other denominations.' Regretfully Mr MacKenzie, for whom both the Pinks had come to have an affectionate regard, had to confess to him on his return from the Synod, 'We are a very exclusive people.'[19] Confronted by a situation in which he had either to give a full endorsement to the Free Presbyterian position or accept that he would not even be free to engage in public prayer, Pink, understandably, chose to withdraw quietly from his new association. 'I had hoped,' he writes to the Colemans on June 6, 1935, '(for there are "many devices in a man's heart") the Lord might be pleased to use me in some humble capacity among the Free Presbyterians – supplying their pulpits occasionally as I am more with them doctrinally than anyone else I know of, as they are more unworldly in their walk and because they are very

[19] *Letters of Pink*, p. 72. How different this procedure was from Scottish Presbyterianism in a brighter period can be seen in M'Cheyne's 'Letter on Communion with Brethren of Other Denominations', *Memoir and Remains of R. M. M'Cheyne*, Andrew Bonar, 1966, pp. 605 ff. In 1944 Robert MacKenzie was himself obliged to leave the Free Presbyterian denomination. 'O poor Christendom: what a state it is in!' Pink wrote to the Pressels on June 24, 1935: 'If it is not false doctrine on the one hand, or worldliness on the other, then it is sectarianism, which is just as effectual in grieving or quenching the Spirit as either of the others.'

short-handed. But God willed otherwise. The pastor of their church here in Glasgow has been very kind to us and several times called on me to lead in public prayer.'

Having returned from America in the hope of 'oral ministry', Pink had to tell John Blackburn on August 25, 1935, that he had 'not preached a single time this year'. Conveying the same information to the Pressels, in a letter of August 18, Pink concludes with this item of household news: 'Dicky is now moulting freely: six weeks earlier than last year. He sure is a game little fellow – succeeds in singing a bit each day. He puts me to shame.'

Pink's last *cri de coeur* on the subject of public ministry, written in the autumn of 1935, appeared in his Annual Letter published as usual in the December issue of *Studies in the Scriptures*:

> Do any of our readers know of any undenominational cause or 'independent' church anywhere in Great Britain where a man of truth would be welcome, or any 'mission', conducted on Scriptural lines, where there would be openings for Bible Conference addresses? Our preaching is along the same lines as our magazine articles. Some readers have a wide acquaintance and may know of suitable openings, and God may use them to give us contact with places that would welcome an uncompromising and soul-edifying message. Please pray over this, and write us.[20]

By the time these words appeared in print a few openings were, in fact, appearing in Scotland. A reader of the magazine who belonged to the Christian Brethren visited Glasgow in October 1935 and was the means of introducing Pink to local leaders among the Brethren. Probably it was through this means that Pink came to

[20] *Studies*, 1935, p. 382.

give his first address in Scotland, at Bethany Hall, Camelon, Falkirk (a town half-way between Glasgow and Edinburgh) when he took for his subject 'The Divine Inspiration of the Scriptures'.[21] On December 22, 1935, he preached his first sermon in Glasgow at one of the main Brethren Assemblies. It was earnest, searching, biblical preaching from the text, 'Blessed are they that mourn: for they shall be comforted' (*Matt.* 5:4). He was not asked to preach there again. The sermon, printed in *Studies in the Scriptures* was spiritual rather than controversial in tone, although some statements may well have been unexpected on that 'Christmas Sunday'. Mourning and poverty of spirit, he told them, are a necessary part of the moral portrait of those who have been born again. Joy alone is no sure mark of a Christian, for it was the stony-ground hearer of whom Jesus said that he received the word 'with *joy*', 'yet hath he not root in himself' (*Matt.* 13:21). 'And it is greatly to be feared there are many such today in orthodox circles of Christendom: the product of a superficial evangelism which is so eager to secure quick and visible "results" – their conversion was not preceded by conviction and contrition.'[22]

Pink himself believed that the door was closed at this Assembly not so much by the sermon as by something which happened beforehand. Noticing in the newspaper announcements that at the service where he was expected there would also be a solo by Miss B. and harp selections

[21] *Studies*, 1936, pp. 28–30. Originally Pink was asked to speak on 'The Antichrist' at Falkirk. 'I declined with thanks,' he tells the Pressels, 'after they firmly refused anything but Prophecy.' This is an illustration of Pink's unwillingness to be drawn into controversy on secondary issues. The Assembly at Falkirk evidently reconsidered their attitude in subsequently asking him to speak on Scripture.
[22] *Studies*, 1936, p. 87.

by another woman, he asked the head of the Assembly if he would, as a personal favour, forgo these items on that Sunday. After discussion the leader agreed to do so but with the protest that Pink was 'very stiff'. A luncheon meeting was arranged by the two men for January 7, 1936, when Pink was to meet 'another brother who had the arranging of speakers for a Bible class'. In the event Pink had to eat his lunch alone for no one else turned up. When Pink reminded the brother of the broken engagement at a mid-week meeting of the Assembly, he promised to write and to make another appointment. 'I have heard no more,' Pink wrote to Lowell Green in the United States on February 2, 1936.

In the early months of 1936 a few occasions for Pink to speak did continue in and around Glasgow. Probably it was due to the reputation of some of his early books that he was invited to speak at Berkeley Hall in the city – an opportunity which he used, not to speak on unfulfilled prophecy, but on 'Grace Preparing for Glory'.[23] Yet there was no prospect of an increase of such opportunities in Glasgow, and sympathizers with his ministry among the Brethren assured him that London was the place where there was the best hope for 'enlarged opportunities'.[24]

After just under a year in Scotland, the Pinks removed to Hove, on the south coast of England, on March 23, 1936. Their home was to be rented accommodation in the upstairs floor of a house in this quiet sea-side town and here they were hopeful that their wanderings of virtually eight years were at an end.

[23] Printed in *Studies*, 1936, pp. 141–5.

[24] Reporting this to John Blackburn on March 1, he wrote, 'By coming here, I have been brought into contact with some influential men who are giving me letters of commendation to others in London. How strangely the Lord works!'

It was still not Pink's intention to retreat from all public work, for before they took the train south he wrote to Lowell Green, 'We shall be within an hour's run of London, for occasional preaching engagements, D.V.' In the weeks that followed, however, he reached what was to be one of the principal decisions in his life. Whether he had further experiences of disappointment among Christian Brethren in London we do not know, but by June 1936 he believed that God had so ordered his way that all thoughts of further public ministry must be laid aside.

On June 11, 1936, he wrote to the Colemans:

> I believe our journeyings are now over. After eight years of moving from place to place vainly seeking some company with whom we could have fellowship, or who would at best care to make some use of me, I have at last definitely abandoned all hope and efforts (by prayer or otherwise) for openings for oral ministry and have (most reluctantly I can assure you) retired from all public life. I was really compelled, in the end, to take this drastic step for 'hope deferred maketh the heart sick', and one bitter disappointment after another was unfitting me for literary work – which is a heavy tax in itself. I am now devoting all my energies to the happy work of the magazine and the correspondence it entails.

In one brief sentence in the Annual Letter for 1936 Pink told his readers, 'We do not expect to engage again in any oral ministry.' At the end of 1937 he noted that his expectation had been confirmed: 'We have not opened our mouth in public a single time during 1937: this is a great grief, but we seek grace to bow to God's sovereign will.'

This was indeed a strange conclusion to the public ministry of a man who had once rejoiced to preach 300 times in a year. But as Matthew Henry wrote: 'God's dearest servants are not always gratified in everything they have a mind to. Yet all who delight in God have "the desire of their hearts" fulfilled (*Psa.* 27:4), though all the desires in their heart be not humoured.'

In his earlier years Pink had once preached on 'Illumined Clouds' from Job 37:21. He now understood more of what he had said then on the mysteries of Christian experience. 'Many a life', he wrote in his notes of that sermon, 'seems to consist of unrealised ideals, broken expectations, crushed hopes. But one day we shall view its strange and bewildering events from another point of view and everything will be seen in its true perspective and proportions. "Not now but in the coming years, It may be in the Better Land."'

10

Interpreting Pink's Isolation

In the last two chapters we have seen how the doors closed on Pink's public preaching ministry. The problem persisted from the time of his return from Australia to his final acceptance in 1936 that his spoken ministry was at an end. It was indeed an extraordinary experience for a man who, through most of the eighteen years down to 1928, had been a gifted and influential evangelist and teacher.

As we now turn to the interpretation of these later years an explanation immediately presents itself. Might it not be that Pink was too critical, too ready to judge the many with whom he was out of step, and too angular in temperament? In his failure to identify with any one branch of the church he lost the opportunity to work patiently with others for an improvement. Instead, his frequent moves and his detachment from the usual forms of evangelical witness led him into an individualism that inevitably made his ministry unacceptable to his contemporaries. In other words, it could be said, his isolation was largely self-imposed.

It would be foolish to say that there is no truth in these criticisms. According to Scripture every Christian ought to regard a local congregation as a primary sphere of life and service. Pink's degree of independence is not to be defended, and there were no doubt failures on his side that sometimes led to his not being received. Faithfulness does not require immediate plainness of speech on every issue (*Prov.* 29:11), and it takes time for a teacher to win the confidence of those whose practice he wants to see changed.

In another part of Britain, at this same period, Dr Martyn Lloyd-Jones was preaching what was fundamentally the same message as Pink's, and that in congregations unfamiliar with such teaching. But his policy varied from Pink's, as he was to say some years later:

> If I had behaved as Pink did, I would have achieved nothing. Nothing at all. I could see that the only hope was to let the weight of truth convince the people. So I had to be very patient and take a very long-term look at things. Otherwise I would have been dismissed and the whole thing would have been finished.[1]

At the same time it has to be said that Lloyd-Jones, working initially in the denomination in which he had been brought up, had advantages that Pink did not possess. We know too little about Pink's twelve years[2] in pastoral charges to say that his lack of continuance in one place was his own fault. As already noted, in his first charge at Silverton, Colorado, it could well have been his change from the Congregational belief in infant baptism that required him, in conscience, to move on. In the case

[1] Iain H.Murray, *D. Martyn Lloyd-Jones: The Fight of Faith, 1939–1981* (Edinburgh: Banner of Truth, 1990), p. 232.

[2] This is the figure Pink gives in *The Life of David* (Swengel, Pa.: Reiner Publications), vol. 1, p. 43, and elsewhere.

of his Belvoir Street pastorate in Sydney it was the church's formal adoption of hyper-Calvinistic Articles of Faith that necessitated his resignation.[3]

Back in England in 1928, after his years in Australia, he was virtually reduced to a choice between ministry among the Baptists or among the Brethren. Preaching engagements among the former would have meant joining a denomination. In so far as his convictions on baptism were concerned he had no difficulty, but his commitment to historic Calvinism would, in all probability, have excluded him, for different reasons, from both Baptist Union churches and from the 'Gospel Standard' Strict Baptists.

For a while, there seemed more hope for him among the Brethren, yet it proved impossible. He had moved too far from teaching that prevailed in Brethren assemblies. Yet Pink was not insisting on a narrow creed before there could be any association with others. In the June 1929 issue of *Studies* he wrote, as already quoted, that preaching '*all* the counsel of God' did not mean merely expounding 'the five points of Calvinism', and he went on: 'Surely we have need to pray earnestly for more devotion to Christ, more love to souls, more fervour and power in preaching the gospel.'

Richard Belcher, a sympathetic biographer of Pink, raised the question whether he was ever suited to the pastoral office in a local church. Pink, he wrote, was not sufficiently sociable. 'He did not seem to enjoy being with and fellowshipping with people.' In addition, Dr Belcher continued, he was unnecessarily blunt, witness the opening words of an address on election he gave in Australia, 'I am going to speak tonight on one of the

[3] See above, pp. 109–116.

most hated doctrines in the Bible, namely, that of God's sovereign election.'[4]

I do not find it easy to evaluate Dr Belcher's opinion. That Pink was by temperament reserved, and not given to small talk, has to be true. On the other hand, there is evidence enough – some of which we will look at later – that he had a true pastor's heart. He cared for people. Long after he left places, his letters show the keen interest he maintained in the welfare of the various individuals he had sought to help. Writing, for instance, to the Colemans in Sydney, he would enquire after a whole series of people by name. Further, it was not his habit to leave broken friendships behind him. George Ardill, the man who had invited him to Australia in 1924, was still supporting him in 1932. The Pressels, with whom he and Vera lived on several occasions, remained lifelong friends, as did others. He was undoubtedly genuinely interested in people and repeatedly gained their affection. A passing incident well illustrates this. On one occasion, when the Pinks were leaving a certain area in the United States, many friends were at the station to bid them farewell. They loaded them with gifts for the journey, mainly fruit. Pink, however, was not long on the train before he offered part of the fruit to a coloured worker. The man was almost overcome with emotion at the unexpected kindness, for he had just resumed work after a prolonged illness that had left his family in considerable need. Love and consideration for people were not missing in Pink's make-up.

* * * * *

The point at which most readers today are most likely to be incredulous in reading Pink's life has to do with his

[4] Belcher, *Arthur W. Pink*, pp. 43–5.

assessment of the prevailing spiritual conditions. Each generation of Christians is liable to regard their own time as worse than what has gone before, and it may be supposed Pink erred radically in that regard. This is a crucial consideration, for if Pink were quite wrong in his strictures on the 'professing' churches it would certainly justify the criticism that his isolation was entirely self-imposed.

Before commenting further on this point, it has to be agreed that if Pink had been able to spend more time in personal contact with other preachers of definite evangelical convictions it could have made him more cautious in his generalizations. In Sydney, for instance, although he lived in the Ashfield area, there is no indication that he ever met the Rev. R. J. H. McGowan, the strongly conservative minister of the local Presbyterian church; nor does he appear to have had contact with Anglicans of the same outlook. Among Baptist Union preachers in Sydney there were earnest men such as the Rev John G. Ridley whose spirit breathed devotion to Christ, yet Pink does not seem to have known them. Words written by Ridley, with reference to his experience, could well have been written by Pink himself.

Quoting the text, 'But to him that soweth righteousness shall be a sure reward' (*Prov.* 11:18), Ridley recalled how he had often been forced to return to that promise in the 1920s

> for courage to press on 'sowing in hope' for a distant day of the Master's praise. It was so different from what I had desired – the thrill of preaching; the eager attention of convicted congregations; the ready response of souls yielding to Christ. Now there was little preaching, little response, much silent sowing

by tracts, and much seeming rejection by the carefree people of the country.[5]

If Pink had enjoyed more fellowship with such men his pathway would not have seemed so lonely. He was so intensely given to the work before him that he does not seem to have recognized the importance of giving time to making contact with others. And yet, while conceding that his relative isolation entered into his sweeping judgments on contemporary conditions, I think there is evidence enough to say that the 1920s and 30s were a very low trough in the Christian history of the English-speaking world. In Britain, and to a considerable extent in the United States, the pulpits of the mainline denominations were reaping the whirlwind of doubt that had been allowed to enter through theological colleges in the previous century. There were leaders intent on the demolition of biblical faith, and there were others unprepared to do anything to oppose their influence. In these churches honours were often showered upon unbelievers, and those who held firmly to Scripture were likely to be described as 'obscurantists'. Dr T. R. Glover, a Baptist Union leader in England, gloried in the disappearance of men of Spurgeon's convictions, and declared in 1932, 'Today if you want a real old obscurantist college, you have to found one.'[6] This was precisely the condition of things that such men as Spurgeon and Ryle had seen coming before their deaths in 1892 and 1900 respectively.

[5] John G. Ridley, *Milestones of Mercy* (Sydney: Christian Press, 1957), p.183. In the case of Ridley (1896–1976) his 'little preaching' at this date was due to ill health.
[6] Writing in *The Times*, quoted by E.J.Poole-Connor, *Evangelicalism in England* (London: FIEC, 1951), p. 251.

Among other witnesses that may be cited to confirm Pink's reading of the low state of the churches at this date is B. B. Warfield of Princeton who died in 1921. A short time before his death a colleague, J. Gresham Machen, gained this impression of Warfield's reading of the situation: 'His expectation seemed to be that the organized Church, dominated by naturalism, would become so cold and dead, that people would come to see that spiritual life could be found only outside it, and that thus there might be a new beginning.'[7]

Whatever else may be said, the main reason Pink worked in a backwater was because the current of religious life was away from the truths he had been brought to love. For many preachers at this period the only alternatives seemed to be, either go with the popular current – then in full flood – or be a non-entity, bereft of influence. Thus a preacher from New Zealand, whom Pink happened to meet at Hove in 1936, told him, 'Had I preached what I was taught in the Glasgow Bible Institute thirty years ago, my wife and I had starved to death.' Pink did not lightly make the other choice. Vera Pink in that same year, commenting in a letter on their failure to find like-minded associates, spoke poignantly when she wrote to a friend: 'Mr Pink is a Puritan in reality and often says to me that he is 200 or 300 years out of his time.'[8] To believe that for balanced scriptural teaching

[7] N. B. Stonehouse, *J. Gresham Machen* (Grand Rapids: Eerdmans, 1955), p. 310. Speaking of their own denomination, the Presbyterian Church in the USA, Warfield told Machen, 'You can't split rotten wood.' More recently a professor of Princeton Seminary, with a different understanding of what constitutes the Christian Faith, said critically of Warfield: 'With all his erudition and learning, far outranking most of his contemporaries, he seemed in deadly fear that things biblical, theological, and ecclesiastical, within the restricted boundaries he set, would collapse, disintegrate, and perish.' Hugh Thomson Kerr, 'Warfield: the Person Behind the Theology', *Princeton Seminary Bulletin*, xxv, 1, New Series 2004.

[8] Letter to Evelyn Green, Sept. 6, 1936.

the Puritans 'were more used of God than any since the days of the apostles to the present hour' was a costly lesson to learn forty years after Puritan doctrine was supposed to have expired with Spurgeon. There was good reason why Pink often referred to the words in Ecclesiastes 1:18, 'He that increaseth knowledge increaseth sorrow.'

'God *is* still working', Pink wrote in 1935, but in his description of his days we think he had cause to write as follows:

> Our lot is also cast in a 'day of small things'. When present spiritual conditions are compared with those of fifty years ago, the difference is most marked: in the number of faithful preachers of the truth, in the number of homes where the family altar is maintained, in the demand for really helpful literature. The *cause* for this contrast may be looked for in two directions. First, in the *sovereignty* of God, for He does not act uniformly. Some seasons enjoy a much more bountiful supply of rain and sunshine than others: as it is in the natural realm, so it is in the spiritual. Second, the *unfaithfulness* of the Lord's people. Where light is given and it be not walked in, where great privileges are granted and there be no corresponding fruit, the Holy Spirit is grieved and quenched, and further blessings are withheld. Both of these factors explain the present situation.[9]

That Pink was unwilling to find a home in denominations where liberal belief was condoned is understandable. What may be less comprehensible is why the Fundamentalist churches in America, who did not repudiate Scripture, became as closed to him as they did.

[9] *Studies*, December 1935, p. 381.

It was here that Pink's most painful break occurred, for once he had been welcomed in many of these churches, spoken at their conferences, and been an author favoured in their circles. Some of his thinking that led to this situation will already be clear but I will now try to summarize it.

Pink was convinced that Fundamentalism seriously erred in its presentation of the gospel. Instead of preaching that a man must come to Christ in repentance and faith in order to be saved, it represented redemption as having been obtained already for every man, and that 'acceptance' of this 'fact' was what made a man a Christian. But this form of Arminian belief was altogether more dangerous than the Wesleyan form of evangelical Arminianism, for it treated 'accepting Christ' as virtually synonymous with an outward profession or 'decision'. Consequently, solely on the grounds of the performance of some physical act (such as walking to the front or raising a hand), multitudes were taught to regard themselves as 'born again'.

Even before Pink came to a fuller understanding of the doctrines of grace, he never accepted the 'decisionism' which he had seen A. C. Dixon employing in Chicago and which was popular throughout Fundamentalism. In a personal letter to Lowell Green he wrote:

> In preaching to the unsaved I never did anything more than I do in my articles: presented the truth of God so far as I knew it, and left the Holy Spirit to apply and bless it as he saw well. I never held any 'after meetings', never asked sinners to signify by any outward sign they had accepted Christ or desired to be prayed for. If any waited behind to speak with me, I told them frankly I could not help them, and urged

them to go home and read *God's* Word. Nor did Spurgeon use any of these Arminian methods of 'casting out the net', 'penitent forms', etc., for the simple but sufficient reason that neither Christ nor his apostles ever did so! Needless to say I was often criticized: yet God was pleased to honour my faith as the Day to come will show.[10]

As Pink surveyed the condition of the Fundamentalist churches at the beginning of the 1930s he believed that decisionist evangelism was responsible for large numbers of unregenerate church members: 'Christendom is reaping today the evil sowings of the last two or three generations, particularly the unscriptural "evangelistic" methods that have been employed – the demand for visible "results", the lusting after *numbers.* Thousands have been pressed into "making a profession" and rushed into "joining the church".'[11]

[10] March 19, 1939. [11] *Studies*, 1931, p. 188. More than forty years before, R. L. Dabney had repeatedly warned of the same evil. Answering the claim that 'altar calls', or public invitations for decisions, were justified by results, he said that the plea assumed two things both of which are untrue. 'One is that the majority, who prove to be spurious fruits of these excitements, are no worse off than before; the other is that the small minority of genuine fruits would not have been gathered in without these means.' Speaking of the former, he writes, 'What shall we say of that large number, who having entered the church with a counterfeit conversion, continue there as formal and dead professors, blinded by habit, pride of consistency, and self-righteousness, to their real condition?' (*Discussions*, vol. 1, 1890, reprinted 1967, pp. 571–3). Again: 'The ulterior evils of these rash measures are immense. A standard and type of religious experience are propagated by them in America, as utterly unscriptural and false as those prevalent in Popish lands . . . We believe that they are the chief cause, under the prime source, original sin, which has deteriorated the average standard of holy living, principles, and morality, and the church discipline of our religion, until it has nearly lost its practical power over the public conscience' (*Discussions*, vol. 3, 1892, pp. 468–74). Many professing Calvinists disagreed with Dabney and saw little danger. David R. Breed, for instance (in *The Princeton Theological Review*, 1903, pp. 227ff.) spoke of 'Moodyism' – which he distinguished from Moody – as 'a thing of the past'. By the 1930s the evils of this type of evangelism were at their height.

Again he writes on the same theme:

> The religion of vast multitudes consists in little more than a firm confidence that their sins are forgiven and that their souls are eternally secure. They consider it a serious fault to doubt their salvation, and the whole of their experience is made up of 'faith' and 'joy': faith that their sins are blotted out, joy in the sure prospect of eternal bliss. But there is no conformity to God's holy law, no mourning before him because of self-love and self-seeking, no humility and brokenness of heart. Let one bid them 'examine themselves,' test their foundations, take upon them the yoke of Christ, and they at once raise the howl of 'Legalism, Dangerous teaching'! O what a rude awakening awaits all such the first five minutes after death![12]

Further, he saw that this teaching as well as affecting the eternal destinies of individuals was changing the life of the church itself. Church services had now to be adjusted to accommodate the unscriptural tastes of unregenerate members, hence the levity of preachers with audiences needing 'entertainment', and the introduction in place of the simple music necessary for the solemn praise of God, of 'musical attractions' designed to please the ears of men. 'Almost everywhere', he noted in California in 1930, 'the Sunday night Gospel meeting starts with a thirty-minute "song service", instead of a united waiting upon God.'[13]

Fundamentalism had in many instances changed the worship of God from the 'vertical' to the 'horizontal', so that it was often little more than an adjunct to more 'soul-

[12] *Studies*, 1934, p. 37.
[13] *Studies*, 1931, p. 46.

-mont Terrace, Nottingham, where Pink was born.

-e-drawn bus crossing Trent Bridge, Nottingham c. 1908 (the year of Pink's conversion).

Silverton, Colorado, where Pink ministered 1910-12.
(Photograph from the 1980s when the population had fallen to about 800).

First Congregational Church and Parsonage, Silverton.

in 1910.

Pink in characteristic pose; a photograph from around 1920.

Arthur and Vera Pink, January 1925.

George Street, Sydney, in the late 1920s.

Arthur and Vera Pink at Circular Quay, Sydney, on their departure for England, July 20, 1928.

The Pinks' last home in the United States, 531 Thomas Street, York, Pennsylvania

In Pennsylvania, c. 1931-34.

An aerial view of Stornoway harbour.

29 Lewis Street, Stornoway, where the Pinks lived on the upper floor from early 1944 until . Pink's death, July 15, 1952. Their first years in Stornoway were spent next door at number .

winning'. As Pink now gave his attention more closely to the subject of worship, he reached the conclusion which he implemented in California in 1930, 'There are many "churches" which we dare not enter (*Eph.* 5:11) and though some are offended because of this, yet we are comforted by the realization that the Lord knows our heart.'[14]

Another issue entered into Pink's divergence from Fundamentalist churches. Contrary to the old Arminian teaching that a believer may finally be lost, the popular teaching, and one almost universally accepted, upheld 'eternal security'. This was interpreted to mean that once anyone 'accepts Christ' his salvation ought never to be in doubt. He is saved by 'faith' irrespective of his walk or conduct as a professing Christian. On the subject of good works and salvation Pink argued that there are two principal errors, 'salvation *by works* and salvation *without works*'. The former is the teaching of Roman Catholicism, the latter had been spread in the nineteenth century by those who 'assumed the garb of the orthodox and thereby obtained a hearing from many . . . They teach that while good works from Christians are certainly desirable, yet they are not imperative, the absence of them involving merely the loss of certain "millennial" honours and not the missing of heaven itself.'[15]

By 1930 Pink had come to regard this preaching as a chief source of the low standards of piety and Christian life that had become so commonplace in the churches.

[14] *Studies*, 1931, p. 191. Articles appeared in *Studies* on Worship in 1928, the first of which began: 'One of the most solemn and soul-destroying fallacies of the day is that unregenerate souls are capable of worshipping God' (p. 252).

[15] *Sermon on the Mount* (Welwyn, Herts: Evangelical Press, 1977), pp. 341–2. While insisting that good works are not necessary to justification, Pink gives many scriptural reasons why they are necessary, including 'the glorifying of God and the magnifying of his grace' (p. 348).

'We have no sympathy whatever', he writes, 'with the bald and unqualified declaration, "Once saved always saved".' To illustrate the reason for his disagreement he quotes 'a publication by a widely-known Bible institute' in which the writer speaks of his visit to a murderer in prison awaiting execution, in the following words: 'I had no right to offer him a pardon from the State . . . but I could tell him of the One who took his place on Calvary's cross. Thank God! I found that man clear on the plan of salvation, for years ago under the ministry of . . . he had accepted Jesus as his personal Saviour. But through the years he had grown cold and indifferent: he had lost his fellowship with his Lord, not his salvation. And the result was a life of sin.'[16]

Such a statement, Pink argued, was a flat contradiction in terms. 'The Saviour is the Holy One of God who saves his people "*from* their sins" (*Matt.* 1:21) and not *in* their sins: who saves them from the love and dominion of their sins. "If any man be in Christ, he is a new creature: old things are passed away; behold, all things are become new" (*2 Cor.* 5:17). Divine salvation is a supernatural work which produces supernatural effects. It is a miracle of grace that causes the wilderness to blossom as the rose. It is known by its fruits. It is a lie to call a tree good if it bears evil fruit. Justification is evidenced by sanctification. The new birth is made manifest by a new life.'

One of the few teachers of this era who spoke as Pink did on this subject was A. W. Tozer (1897–1963). Surveying the scene in Fundamentalism, Tozer wrote:

> The doctrine of justification by faith – a biblical truth, and a blessed relief from sterile legalism and unavailing self-effort – has in our time fallen into evil

[16] 'Doctrine of Saints' Perseverance' in *Studies*, 1947, p. 61.

> company and been interpreted by many in such a manner as actually to bar men and women from the knowledge of God.
>
> The whole transaction of religious conversion has been made mechanical and spiritless. Faith may now be exercised without a jar to the moral life and without embarrassment to the Adamic ego. Christ may now be 'received' without creating any special love for Him in the soul of the receiver. The man is 'saved' but he is not hungry and thirsty after God.[17]

Historic Christianity had taught that the saints persevere to the end *through* holiness and sanctification. But not only did Fundamentalism undermine this truth by separating justification (the Christian's standing before God) from regeneration (his inward *state* as renewed by the Holy Spirit); it also rejected the law of God as a rule by which holiness is to be judged. The moral law, and Christ's interpretation of its spiritual meaning in his Sermon on the Mount, is not, it was claimed, a rule for *Christians.* The moral law was thus set *against* the gospel as though the gospel was not intended to restore the very holiness which the law represents. Instead of the Christian being presented as one who, through grace, can now say, 'I delight in the law of God' (*Rom.* 7:22), men were being taught that the law is irrelevant for Christians. And so, given the inadequate definition of a Christian already introduced by Arminian evangelism, this further error of Antinomianism gave vast support to the toleration of unspiritual living within the church itself. In Pink's words:

[17] A. W. Tozer, *Renewed Day by Day* (Harrisburg, PA: Christian Publications, 1980), December 12. This material was spoken and written many years earlier.

> One of the most disastrous errors and follies of many preachers and 'Bible teachers' fifty years ago, the terrible effects of which are now spread before those who have eyes to see, was their idea that during the Old Testament era God's people were under the stern régime of law unrelieved by Divine grace, and that Christ came here to set aside that harsh régime and bring in a much milder dispensation.[18]

In a letter to the Colemans, in which he touches on the subject of the Ten Commandments, he urges them to 'avoid as you would a deadly snake any man who denies the law of God is the Christian's rule of life'.[19] And in another letter, after quoting the alleged words of a head of Moody Bible Institute to professing Christians, 'No matter what you may do, from stealing to murder, you will be saved for ever,' he writes: 'Thousands of "Fundamentalists" applaud such Satanic error, blindly imagining that such teaching magnifies the grace of God in the eternal security of his saints. But God does *not* preserve his people in the ways of sin: he preserves by working in them a hatred of such sins!'[20]

The rejection of the moral law, as a rule of life for the Christian, brings us to a final subject that made Pink's alienation from Fundamentalism complete. We have already noted that through his early ministry Pink had been largely in sympathy with what was a great rallying point for Fundamentalists, namely their teaching on unfulfilled prophecy commonly known as Dispensationalism. This was an elaboration of the Premillennial belief that Christ is to come again a thousand years *before* the end of the world: in the usual dispensational

[18] *Studies*, 1942, p. 27 (or *Exposition of the Sermon on the Mount*, ch. 20).
[19] August 10, 1941.
[20] To Lowell Green, Dec. 2, 1934, in *Letters*, p. 58.

understanding of events there is first to be an invisible coming of Christ – a 'secret rapture'– when the church remaining on earth will be removed before the 'great tribulation', then national Israel will be converted to become the means of evangelizing the nations. Seven years after 'the rapture', when the supposed 'seventieth week' of Daniel 9 will have ended, the church will return with Christ to earth. That will usher in the millennial reign, which will end in a further appearing of Christ, to end all history. This is known as 'the day of the Lord'.

But Dispensationalism had a new view of past as well as of future history. It held that God's saving purposes have differed according to the different ages or 'dispensations' into which, they said, history is to be divided. Thus the 'kingdom of God' was offered to the Jews on condition of their obedience. This was a 'legal dispensation', and with this dispensation Christ's own teaching was in accord until his death. But when the Jews rejected Christ and 'the kingdom', God, before renewing his saving intentions towards Israel, interposed the 'church age' during which all those who are to make up 'the body of Christ' will be saved.

That Pink should change his mind on unfulfilled prophecy in the early 1930s might seem to be of no great consequence. And, after all, it had been his policy for many years to keep controversial matters of a theoretical nature out of his magazine. He wrote to Blackburn in 1929, 'Personally, I do not believe polemical preaching or writing helps the saints at all. "Feed my sheep" is the pastor's commission.' But he was now convinced that Dispensationalism was no matter of theory only. His eyes were opened to far-reaching spiritual implications, and in a series of eighteen articles, which ran from January 1933 to June 1934, he set out what he believed they were.

He saw that if God's dealings with Israel were a 'dispensation of law', so that 'grace' and the 'church' only came in at Pentecost, then promises and commands in the Old Testament, and even in our Lord's teaching prior to Pentecost, must refer exclusively to the *Jew*. The Lord's Prayer, declared Isaac M. Haldeman, a leading dispensationalist, 'is a prayer that has no more place in the Christian Church than the thunders of Sinai, or the offerings of Leviticus'.[21] Against making such a division in the application of Scripture Pink wrote:

> Knowing that he is unable to shake the faith of the regenerate in the Divine inspiration and veracity of the promises recorded in Holy Writ, Satan has employed the subtler attack (which is equally effective if yielded to) of seeking to persuade us that the great majority of God's promises do not belong unto Christians at all, for, seeing they are recorded in the Old Testament, they are the property of the Jews only.
>
> Cleverly indeed has the Devil pushed this campaign of enervating the importance and value of the larger half of God's Word. The agents whom he has employed in this evil work have not been open atheists and avowed infidels, but instead, men who posed as the champions of orthodoxy, acknowledging their faith in the full inspiration of the Scriptures. Thereby the confidence of the unwary was gained.

[21] Haldeman (1845–1933), an associate of C. I. Scofield and J. M. Gray, is described by George Dollar as 'a careful student and writer on prophecy' (*A History of Fundamentalism in America*, Greenville, SC, Bob Jones University Press, 1973, p. 326). It is said that Haldeman, in his later ministry in New York, preached on some aspect of Christ's return every Sunday evening, and when repairs were needed for the church building, for which there were insufficient funds, he urged that they should go ahead with the work on the grounds that Christ would come before the bill had to be paid!

Though at first the radical and revolutionary postulates of the teachers of 'dispensational truth' may have awakened a measure of uneasiness in simple-minded souls, only too often they quenched their fears by reassuring themselves that such teachers – so faithful to the 'fundamentals', so loyal to Christ, so well-versed in the Scriptures – '*must* be right'. Moreover, the claims made by these men that God had given them much more 'light on his Word than all who had preceded them', made an attractive appeal to the pride of their hearers – for who wants to be 'behind the times'? In Jeremiah 36:23 we are told that when Jehoiakim, king of Judah, heard the prophet read a message from God, 'he cut it with the penknife'. This incident has often been referred to by teachers of 'dispensational truth' who have applied or accommodated it to the pernicious methods employed by the 'higher critics'. This too has served to quieten any fears that might exist in the hearer, for supposing that his teachers 'stood for the whole Word of God', and impressed by their fervent denunciations of 'modernism' and 'evolutionism' he thinks that they are to be safely followed in all their assertions. How wily the Devil is! Nevertheless, the fact remains that *in the effects produced* the labours of the 'dispensationalists' have been as subversive of faith as those of the 'higher critics': the latter affirming much of the Old Testament to be spurious, the former insisting that it belongs not unto us. In either case, the greater part of God's Word is reduced to a dead letter, so far as faith's receiving of its present validity and virtue is concerned.[22]

[22] *Studies*, 1933, p. 39.

Pink's last article on the subject summarised the ten 'indictments' of dispensationalist teachers that he had covered. They included: 'They repudiate the moral Law of God as a rule of life for the Christian today. They invidiously seek to pit Scripture against Scripture, instead of showing their perfect unity and lovely harmony.'[23]

To reach such a conclusion in the 1930s was far more stunning than anyone can well imagine today. For Dispensationalism was pervasive throughout Fundamentalism. Initiated by Brethren teachers in the 1830s, it had been endorsed by later evangelists, such as D. L. Moody, and gained authority across the world when Oxford University Press published a Bible, with a full apparatus of dispensational notes by C. I. Scofield, in 1909.

By 1945 more than two million copies of the Scofield Bible had been printed. Scofield's notes were followed in virtually every Bible school, and evangelical publishers almost fell over one another in promoting authors who followed the same interpretation. It is extraordinary that such a system of interpretation, resting as it did on an almost wholly new exegesis of Scripture, could have spread so far and wide through both American and British Protestantism. But that it did so is an unquestionable fact. Unfulfilled prophecy was *the* subject of the hour, and a sure gatherer of crowds wherever it was announced as the subject.[24]

[23] *Studies*, June 1943, p. 134.

[24] It was probably in the late 1930s that Dr Campbell Morgan, about to preach, said to Dr Lloyd-Jones in the Westminster Chapel vestry beforehand, 'Keep your eye on the increase in the congregation tonight.' When his colleague asked why, the response was, 'I'm announced to speak on a prophetic subject and I never deal with the question of prophecy but there's always a marked increase in the size of the congregation.' D. M. Lloyd-Jones, *The Church and the Last Things* (Wheaton: Crossway, 1998), p. 95.

What shocked Pink was not only that the teaching was wrong: it was distracting Christians with ideas that could do nothing to meet the real spiritual needs of the churches. The early 1930s saw the Great Depression, then the rise of new dictators in Europe, but instead of encouraging Christians concerning how to live in difficult days, the Fundamentalists' diet majored on 'prophetic questions' and interpretations of 'the signs of the times'.

'Alas,' Pink wrote in 1932, 'that so many of God's dear children have rather been instructed to puzzle their brains over whether the parable of the ten virgins treats of "Christendom", or the Jews in the "Tribulation period", or whether the battle of Armageddon is to be fought in a valley or on a mountain. Occupation with such questions these days makes us think of Nero fiddling while Rome was burning! It is the practical side of Christianity, that which pertains to our present welfare, both spiritually and temporally, which needs to be chiefly pondered.'

Recalling the same mania to which Pink here referred, Dr Lloyd-Jones said: 'When Molotov and Ribbentrop signed their pact in 1939, some people were absolutely certain that they were seeing the fulfilment of Ezekiel's prophecy about Gog and Magog and the great northern confederacy.'[25]

When Lloyd-Jones also spoke against Dispensationalism in 1954–55 the shock felt by many of his hearers was another confirmation of how pervasive the teaching had long been in evangelical circles. Twenty years earlier Pink was almost alone in his criticism. When Oswald T. Allis published his influential book *Prophecy and the Church* in

[25] Ibid., p. 108. The two men named, it was said, represented Soviet Russia and Germany. Of course, the interpretation 'did not seem quite so clear when Germany attacked Russia in 1941!'

1945, the only two active opponents of Dispensationalism that he could name were Philip Mauro and A. W. Pink.[26]

It is no wonder, then, that Pink was lonely, and we do not need to resort to any supposed eccentricities of temperament to explain it. He wrote in 1934: 'Real servants of God, sound teachers, have now almost disappeared from the earth. 2 Timothy 4:3 is now fulfilled before our eyes: men "will not endure sound doctrine".[27] There is at least partial confirmation of this from another contemporary preacher who found his appeals for seriousness, self-denial, and experimental godliness were unwelcome. A. W. Tozer was to say, 'I preached myself off every Bible Conference platform in the country.' And the reason that happened was that, like Pink, his evaluation of the Fundamentalist scene had shut the doors against him. In his own words:

> The voice of the prophet was silenced and the scribe captured the minds of the faithful . . . An unofficial hierarchy decided what Christians were to believe. Not the Scriptures, but what the scribe thought the Scriptures meant, became the Christian creed . . . The system of extreme dispensationalism which was devised, relieved the Christian of repentance, obedience and cross-carrying in any other than the most formal sense. Whole sections of the New Testament were taken from the Church and disposed of after a rigid system of 'dividing the Word of truth'. All this resulted in a religious mentality inimical to the true faith of Christ . . . Grace has become not free, but cheap. We are busy these days proving to

[26] O. T. Allis, *Prophecy and the Church* (Philadelphia: Presbyterian and Reformed, 1945), p. 15.
[27] *Letters of A. W. Pink*, p. 40.

> the world that they can have all the benefits of the Gospel without any inconvenience to their customary way of life. It's 'all this, and heaven too'. This description of modern Christianity, while not universally applicable, is yet true of an overwhelming majority of the present-day Christians.[28]

There is evidence that Pink was not the kind of man who enjoyed controversy, and in the case of his critique of dispensational teaching there was added reason why it was painful for him to write as he did. In a real sense he was criticizing himself. His early notebooks show how thoroughly he had studied and taught what he now had to deny.[29] Two of his books had majored on unfulfilled prophecy, *The Redeemer's Return* (1918) and *The Antichrist* (1923). How far these books were wrong on Premillennialism he was not entirely sure, but he now knew that he had taught error and he was too conscience-bound to Scripture not to feel this deeply. His former ignorance and misplaced confidence humbled him. He wrote to a friend on March 17, 1934, 'It seems to me that God has placed not a little in "prophecy" to stain the pride of man!' In the next month's issue of *Studies*, he confessed: 'In his youth the writer was taught by men

[28] A. W. Tozer, *Keys to the Deeper Life* (Grand Rapids: Zondervan, 1957), pp. 13–17.

[29] In his early writings Pink certainly accepted the dispensationalist division between 'kingdom' and 'church', e.g., 'It is in the Old Testament that the millennium receives the fullest consideration, whereas the Church is the subject of New Testament revelation. Moreover, we must remember that the millennium is the time when God's Kingdom is revealed on earth, whereas the Church is a heavenly creation, and has a heavenly citizenship and destiny' (*The Redeemer's Return*, 1918, p. 362). But the logic of this position, namely, that those in the 'Kingdom' do not belong to the church, and that the church does not have the law as a rule of life, he opposed from the early issues of *Studies* (e.g. 1924, p. 3, p. 43; 1925, p. 142, etc.) He never accepted the idea that the Old and the New Testaments presented different ways of salvation.

he looked up to, that law and grace could no more be united than oil and water: may the Lord forgive him for inserting this error in some of his earlier writings . . . Instead of being contradictory, they are complementary. Both shine forth in their full glory at the cross: both are published in the true gospel.'

In a letter to John Blackburn on February 3, 1934, Pink commented on what had led him into the revision of his earlier teaching on prophecy:

> It is the pre-mill. *doctrine* which I am now considerably out of love with. As a man is known by the company he keeps, so it is with a doctrine! As I have studied the *lives* of early 'pre's' and observed those of the present day – comparing most unfavourably with the godly Puritans – my suspicions became more and more aroused, and I decided to make a fresh examination of their foundations. Knowing how easy it is to swing from one extreme to another, and how difficult it is to really approach a subject free from bias, I have sought to proceed the more slowly and cautiously. This has been going on for upwards of five years, and I have now arrived at some positive (probably 'settled') conclusions. I have not yet definitely committed myself in print.[30]

Pink's long exposure to dispensational teaching may have hardened the opinion he formed in the 1920s on being 'outside the camp'. Dispensationalism offered no hope for any brighter conditions in the churches before

[30] 'Not yet committed myself'; the reference is to any exposition of another understanding of unfulfilled prophecy. He had already, as indicated above, been writing against Dispensationalism. In another letter to Blackburn he said: 'I am finding quite a little help in Patrick Fairbairn's two volumes on *Typology* and one on *Prophecy*.' Pink did not take up the subject of prophecy any further in *Studies*.

the millennium. It made pessimism virtually a point of orthodoxy for evangelicals. We have noted earlier his conviction in 1927 'that the present dispensation has almost run its course'. This teaching undoubtedly coalesced at times with the days of depression that Pink knew and, as he came to entertain doubts over its accuracy, so greater hopes seem to have dawned for the effectiveness of present witness.

One thing is clear. The trials through which Pink passed in the 1930s did not leave him a sour and disappointed Christian. There was a purpose in them. Instead of his becoming more narrow and sectarian, the pages of *Studies* show an increasing emphasis on need for balance, for brotherly love and for Christian catholicity. There is a deepening spirituality and a carefulness that was to make his later writings much more valuable than those of earlier years. At the age of fifty he was a gentler man with a broader vision than he had been when pulpits *were* open to him.

He wrote in the magazine in March 1935:

> Instead of dwelling so much upon minor things – concerning which God's children, most probably, never will all see eye to eye down here – we should be occupied with the major things which we all enjoy in common.
>
> The present writer is not prepared to hold a brief in defence of every peccadillo in any denomination, system, or company of professing Christians; on the other hand, he desires to freely recognize and gladly own whatever is of God in all of them. Though himself unattached ecclesiastically, and a partisan of no single group, he wishes to have Christian fellowship with any and all who love the Lord and

> whose daily walk evidences desire to please him. We have lived long enough and travelled sufficiently, to discover that no one 'church', company, or man, has all the truth, and as we grow older we have less patience with those who demand that others must adopt their interpretation of Scripture on all points.[31]

It is an illustration of this attitude that, while Pink gave up the Premillennial belief, to our knowledge he never attacked it. He saw that views on prophecy – provided they do not, as Dispensationalism did, overthrow foundation truths – 'ought never to alienate the affections of saints',[32] and he eschewed being a party to controversy on secondary issues. In his Annual Letter for 1937 he wrote:

> We know from experience how hard it is to break away from early ideas, while we are not unmindful of the danger of grasping at (without thoroughly weighing) what is novel. Our own views upon Prophecy have been considerably modified during the last few years. We are now satisfied that there has been a great deal of carnal speculation upon future events. Pride, curiosity, love of the sensational, and fondness of the limelight are native products of the flesh; but it requires Divine grace to make us sober, humble, and frank to say, 'I do not know'. The very fact there was so much in fulfilled prophecy that was not rightly understood until after it was accomplished, should check us from wild theorizings and dogmatic assertions in connection with unfulfilled prophecy. Scripture affirms, 'The coming of the Lord draweth nigh' (*James* 5:8), i.e., is ever getting nearer; and with

[31] *Studies*, 1935, p. 94.
[32] *Studies*, 1938, p. 381.

> *that* we should be content – no one is justified in saying, 'The coming of the Lord *is* nigh.' Will friends kindly note that we are not prepared to enter into any correspondence on the subject. If you think we err at this point, pray for us; as it is possible you may be wrong, pray for yourself.

The same attitude holds good for his views on baptism. 'Though the editor has strong convictions on the subject,' he wrote in 1936, 'for fourteen years he has refrained from pressing (or even presenting) them in this magazine.'[33]

While these enlarged views should have made it easier for Pink to identify himself with an organized church, they also served to hinder him. For he repeatedly found, as happened in Glasgow in 1935, that things which he could not regard as necessities were made conditions of fellowship. He wrote in 1936:

> What sectarian walls and barriers exclude some of Christ's sheep from other members of his flock! 'Wherefore receive ye one another, as Christ also received us, to the glory of God' (*Rom.* 15:7) is the Divine injunction. That does not mean 'receive' into church-fellowship (the Roman saints were already in *that* relationship: *Rom.* 12:4–8) but 'receive' each Christian brother and sister *into your hearts*, so that you interest yourself in their welfare, and do all in your power to promote their temporal and eternal interests. But today, Baptists, for the most part, will 'receive' none but a 'Baptist', the Presbyterians none but a 'Presbyterian', those known as the 'Brethren' none but one who is 'identified' with them. That is

[33] *Studies*, 1936, p. 14. See also his sentiments expressed to a young paedo-Baptist in *Letters*, p. 56. Pink wrote forty-six letters to Lowell Green before he even referred to the subject of baptism.

> one reason why – as a protest against sectarianism – the writer remains unattached.
>
> O what a lack of brotherly kindness, tender sympathy, and Christian affection now obtains! Instead of bearing each other's burdens, some seem most pleased when they can add to them. O for grace to sink our petty differences, and seek a practical union and communion with the whole family of God; loving those whom the Lord loves, and walking in affection with those whom he has redeemed with his precious blood. But this too often calls for self-denial and self-sacrifice, not sacrificing God's truth, not sacrificing any Christian principle, but mortifying our carnal pride which loves to have the pre-eminence.[34]

This is not the voice of a recluse but of an exercised Christian. His trials were indeed unusual, but out of them he became a man better fitted to help others. As he wrote to Lowell Green on August 15, 1937:

> Trying circumstances (as with Israel in the wilderness) are an essential part of God's disciplinary training of His children, and dull scholars we all are. We have to live and learn. It is an old saying that 'Experience is the best teacher', and I may add, her fees are high!

[34] *Studies*, 1936. p. 119. Pink was perhaps not allowing that denominations need to speak on issues they believe to be scriptural, yet are not essential to salvation. Too often, however, denominational differences among Christians become terms of fellowship.

11

'We Believe, and Therefore Speak'

From what we have so far considered of Pink's life it may seem easy to conclude that he ought to have recognized his restriction to a written ministry long before he reached his fiftieth year. But what may be clear to us now was by no means so clear at the time. As Pink would remind us, 'God's ways in providence, as well as in grace, are often "past finding out" (*Rom.* 11:33) not only by ourselves, but by those looking on – as God's ways with Job were misinterpreted by his "friends".'

There were, in fact, a number of circumstances which combined to make it appear improbable that much usefulness could be achieved by means of his pen. In the first instance, throughout the Christian world there was a marked absence of demand for 'a spiritual and helpful exposition of Scripture'. Neither the pulpit nor the religious press commonly catered for such a taste. Speaking of contemporary Christian literature, Pink wrote in *Studies in the Scriptures* in July 1929:

> There is much to interest the curious, much that appeals to the intellect, but little that searches the conscience or that feeds the soul. The best of the magazines, though giving much of the religious news

> of the day, are, for the most part, sadly lacking in that which promotes a closer walk with God. 'Signs of the Times' may make exciting reading, but they do not lead to more intimate communion with Christ . . . It was because of the lack of expository ministry, both oral and written, that seven and a half years ago we were asked and consented to publish a magazine devoted solely to studies in the Scriptures. This trust we have sought to fulfil. But we have learned that there are not so many who welcome a ministry of this type as we had thought.

Pink's early books had not been a publishing success. 'Our Hope', the publishing name of the Gaebelein organization in New York, had published his first commentary, *Gleanings in Genesis*, in 1922; thereafter Pink's increasing deviations from Fundamentalism had closed the door on any further items from his pen. Herendeen, at the Bible Truth Depot, Swengel, had started to publish his *Exposition of John's Gospel* in the mid-twenties but by the time that the third of the four-volume set was announced in 1929, Pink had to explain to readers of *Studies* that the high price (two dollars each!) was due to the small circulation.[1] Worse was to come. 'I am not at all surprised to hear that Mr Herendeen is experiencing a dearth of orders,' he wrote to Lowell Green on February 27, 1938. There was no possibility that the Bible Truth Depot could consider taking on any new Pink titles. To Lowell Green's plea that his articles on 'Divine Chastisement' in the *Studies* should be published together, he replies: 'No, I am sorry to say it is hardly feasible to re-issue my articles upon "Divine

[1] *Studies*, 1929, p. 169. Pink spoke of this material as 'the product of ten years' prayer and hard work'. Like his other earlier works it is marred by Dispensationalism and, in places, by over-dependence upon Brethren authors.

Chastisement" in separate form. They would make a large booklet even if condensed a little. It would cost $100 to print one thousand, and today the demand for such literature is so pitiably small that a publisher could not sell enough copies to "come out even".'[2]

Interest in Pink as a writer had thus decreased by the 1930s and, humanly speaking, the closer his own writings approximated to the 'Puritan school', the stronger the likelihood that they would share the almost universal neglect with which those authors were then treated. It was almost as though the works of old-school theological authors had passed into oblivion! Replying to a query from Lowell Green on second-hand books he writes: 'The last time I "scoured" the 2nd-hand book-shops of London, twenty-two out of twenty-four [shops] told me they had long since ceased carrying any theological literature – no demand for it!' And after recommending Manton, Owen and Goodwin to Green, he adds, 'if procurable!'[3]

In the second place, it has to be said that, not only was there a general lack of interest in serious Christian literature, but the circumstances in which Pink's magazine in particular had to operate were not, in 1936, conducive to the hope that it had a viable future.

Ten years earlier, towards the close of 1926, Pink had removed the subscription price from the magazine and replaced it with the words, 'Free to all who will read it'. He appears to have been motivated by a concern to act literally on the principle, 'Freely ye have received, freely give' (*Matt.* 10:8), and in part by the hope of obtaining a wider circulation by helping some who could not afford a subscription.

[2] Oct. 4, 1936.
[3] Jan. 3, 1937.

The first results were promising. 'Our circulation during 1927 has exceeded that of any previous year.'[4] It was soon clear, however, that there would be considerable difficulty in judging who were the real *readers* of a free magazine. Anyone whose address was sent to Pink received a copy without charge. Of course Pink indicated that the help of those who could pay for their copies was expected and donations came in; none the less he was faced with a financial problem as a brief note indicated in the issue of March 1929: 'The printing and mailing out of this magazine costs over £5 (25 dollars) every week. What is your *responsibility*? *Studies* was sent throughout 1928 to over 1,000 people who sent in no gift!'

Pink never took any financial remuneration from the magazine; on the contrary, at this date, he almost certainly supported it from his own slender resources. The last salary he ever received was in Sydney in 1928. From that date to the end of 1930 he was to receive less than 200 dollars (forty pounds) for preaching. At the end of 1929 he told his readers in a 'Personal Word' that, in connection with the magazine finances, 'we have been severely tested'. By this date, it will be remembered, Pink was back in the United States and sharing in 'one of the greatest financial collapses that ever struck that country, being followed by an acute and protracted industrial depression'. His 'Personal Word' at the end of 1930 carried no news of further difficulty; only in 1946 did he reveal that 1930 was 'our most trying year': 'We were firmly resolved to cease publishing rather than contract any debt, and so were kept on our faces before Jehovah-jireh (*Gen.* 22: 14), looking to him for the needed funds . . . On the morning of November 30 (the day our financial year closed) we lacked 1 dollar 75 c (seven shillings) and there

[4] *Studies*, 1927, p. 265.

was nothing in the post! There was an afternoon delivery, though it scarcely ever brought us anything. That afternoon there was one letter and it had 3 dollars in it, so we closed with a credit balance of five shillings. Of course we did: God never confounds those who confidently rely upon him!'[5]

Throughout the 1930s the struggle continued to find enough readers to keep the magazine going. Every year copies were sent out to new names of persons who might be interested, but in many cases Pink had to conclude, from the absence of any reply, that they were not proving to be new *readers*. 'We try out several hundreds each year, only to drop the great majority of them the following year,' he wrote to John Blackburn on December 22, 1933. That year three hundred and fifty who had received the magazine were thus removed: 'An unpleasant task, we assure you,' he wrote in the columns of *Studies*, 'Yet we dare not waste copies on uninterested ones, or on those who would take an unfair advantage of the generosity of others.' In 1934, at the very time that he was bereft of preaching opportunities, he reported, 'For several years past the number of names on our mailing-list has been slightly but steadily decreasing.' An increase followed this announcement but again it was not maintained.

At one point in 1935 he had to sustain the magazine funds by a temporary transfer from his personal account. To his friends Stanley and Elsie Pressel, who had acted as agents in the United States, he says in the course of a letter dated July 14, 1935:

> Stanley's conclusion that 'no doubt most of the readers are sending their letters and funds direct to

[5] *Studies*, 1946, p. 284.

> you' – seeing you are receiving so few – was a very natural one, but alas it is not the case. Nearly all the U.S.A., Canadian and Australian readers are as silent as the grave; in fact, had it not been for what has come in from English and Scottish readers, we could not have printed the last four issues of *Studies*. Outside of the small amount you received, totals of magazine gifts from U.S.A. were April $31; May $13; June $27; July, to date $6!

A short note in the issue of September 1935 read: 'We are much exercised over a decreasing circulation. Many who once relished this magazine, do so no longer. Death has removed quite a number of old readers, and their places are not being filled by new ones. Cannot you introduce us to some of the Lord's people who would value this monthly messenger?' The danger that publication might have to cease was real. 'Very few co-operate with us in seeking to make this magazine known to fellow-Christians,' he wrote in December 1935. 'How many would *really* be sorry if we are obliged to cease publication for lack of support? How many are endeavouring to *prevent* this by their efforts?' In the first month of 1936 – the year of his move to Hove – he wrote again, 'We are finding it extremely hard to obtain enough interested readers to justify our continuing to publish.'

Precisely how small the number of readers was which kept *Studies* going is hard to determine. In a letter to John C. Blackburn in March 1936 he comments: 'Funds have come in more freely for the magazine of late (our own needs are provided for, thank God), but we still have less than 900 on our list!' By 1938 the list was smaller than it had ever been and he says in *Studies*: 'The falling off in the number of readers often disheartens us, but we are thankful for those we do have. It is for the sake of the few really interested ones we continue plodding along.' The following year the position was worse with a further decrease of nearly seventy names on his list: 'During 1939 our circulation has shown a further marked decline, but for the sake of the handful who do appreciate this monthly messenger we hope to have sufficient readers to warrant our continuing for one more year . . .'

Somehow they did manage to continue. In the early 1940s the list to which the magazine was sent probably included about 700 names. One hundred still went to Australia, and the highest number, 'over two hundred', to the United States. Not until after the Second World War did demand in the United Kingdom exceed that figure. Moreover, the number of those who received copies was always higher than the actual number of eager supporters. It may be that the real backbone of his readership for many years was not much above one hundred! 'Had it not been that more than one hundred sent an annual donation which permits us to mail them an extra copy, we had been obliged to cease publishing years ago,' he was to write in 1948.

It is by no means easy to glean these figures from *Studies*, or from his letters, for references to numbers are very rare and in the extraction of the above quotations out of their contexts there is a danger that they may put Pink in the guise of a complaining editor. That was far from being the case. It was only sometimes in extremities – and then, chiefly, to appeal for prayer – that Pink spoke of his difficulties. Anything like direct or indirect appeals for money he detested. These quotations, however, are necessary to show that while he did come to believe that his whole public calling was now to be through the written word, it was a conclusion not easily drawn from the appearance of things! Circumstances alone could never have brought him to that decision. Rather he remembered that the same chapter of Scripture which commands that bread be 'cast upon the waters' also warns: 'He that observeth the wind shall not sow; and he that regardeth the clouds shall not reap' (*Eccles.* 11:4). Supremely, throughout its history, the ministry of *Studies in the Scriptures* was a work of faith. As he wrote in 1937:

> The fact is that it has been and now is literally a 'hand to mouth' experience in this matter of having enough readers to warrant our continuing to publish . . . And is not this experience of ours in connection with the magazine duplicated in some form or other in the life of each Christian reader? God has so ordered it that 'we walk by faith, not by sight'.[6]

Vera Pink was given the same faith with respect to the work in which she so much shared. To Evelyn Green she writes:

> The declension of readers has been a great trial to us both, but we are thankful that by his grace, we have been enabled to leave it with him to order as best he pleases himself – to cease worrying over it or letting it discourage us as once it did. I am sorry we were so weak as to let it worry us, but when all avenues seemed to be closing it was hard to think *Studies* would cease too.[7]

Again, on the ministry of the magazine she writes to Evelyn Green two years later:

> The Lord has been good these years – almost 20 now – to us in supplying everything needful to carry on such a work unattached and unheralded by any sect,

[6] *Studies*, 1937, p. 221.

[7] June 25, 1939.

> denomination, or 'big' person. It would take volumes to tell a part of his ways with us. 'The things which are impossible with men, are possible with God' seems to express in a few words what I could not state in a book. All the praise is his alone![8]

There is one particular practical matter in which the Pinks were clearly guided. In addition to the loose issues of *Studies* which went out every month, Pink had a very limited number bound up in one volume at the end of each year. In 1936 he told his readers that to send one monthly copy for twelve months cost him three shillings and sixpence or one dollar and to supply one bound volume four shillings. It was the bound copies supremely which were to give the ministry of *Studies* permanence in the years to come, as the life of many of the loose issues, all without covers, must have been short. Even the bound volumes were to become exceedingly rare, for Pink was able to keep no reserve supplies as each year passed.

* * * * *

There are a few things which should be said at this point about the ministry of *Studies in the Scriptures* as it took on, in the 1930s, the form in which it was to remain for the rest of its existence.

The sermons which had been a prominent part of the contents during the Australian years disappeared, and so did the long extracts from other writers. Pink settled to the practice of providing a balanced and varied diet from his own pen. After a short editorial on a spiritual theme such as Prayer, Self-Denial or Faith, first place was often given to articles in an expository series. 'Hebrews' ran

[8] July 21, 1941.

from January 1928 to July 1938 when it was followed by 'The Sermon on the Mount'. Other material given in expository form included 'The Life of David' (January 1932 to December 1939) and then 'Elijah' (January 1940 to November 1942). Along with this there were always articles of a more immediately experimental, spiritual character, as well as doctrinal series on such themes as Depravity, Perseverance, Justification and Sanctification.

Without question, the standard of the contents in the 1930s was higher than during the magazine's first eight years and it would have been impossible for Pink, or indeed for anyone else, to maintain this standard had it not been a whole-time ministry. Pink never queried whether the decrease of interest in the 1930s was due to any lowered standard on his part. He was right in believing that it was because he was being more discriminating and scriptural that the interest of some was falling away. The articles against Dispensationalism undoubtedly cost him readers. So did his sustained emphasis on scriptural godliness and on serious Christian living. He was to write in 1945:

> During the last twenty years we have probably lost many hundreds of readers because our endeavour to present the *standard* of holiness was so unpopular and unpalatable. The great majority of professing Christians in this evil day wish to hear only 'smooth things', and resent that which searches the conscience, rebukes worldliness, and condemns carnality.[9]

At the same time, it was no small part of Pink's usefulness that in an era when many were proclaiming 'victorious Christian living' as their every-day experience,

[9] *Studies*, 1945, p. 285.

he did not overstate the spirituality which distinguishes the Christian. He rejected both 'perfectionism' and any kind of 'defeatism', while presenting the high view of Christian living that one finds, for example, in the Puritans. He writes:

> The best of God's children (if there be any best!) are frequently affected with fits of unbelief and chillings of love. Today they find themselves earnestly proposing and resolving to do those things which are good, but tomorrow discover their zeal has somewhat abated, so uncertain and inconstant are their affections. Now hopeful, anon despondent, now singing God's praises, anon their harps upon the willows; now walking obediently in the path of the Divine precepts, anon straying off into bypath meadow. None differ so much from them as they often differ from themselves! Some will glorify God in one condition, but dishonour him in another. They may conduct themselves becomingly while God keeps them low, and then become fretful against him when they are exalted. On the contrary, others who tread softly in a time of prosperity are filled with murmuring when the cold winds of adversity smite them.[10]

Or again, writing in 1939 on David's last words in 2 Samuel 23:5, he says:

> As the believer nears the end of his course, he not only meditates upon the lowliness of his original estate and then the elevated position to which sovereign grace has lifted him, but he also reviews

[10] *Studies*, 1948, p. 275. 'No Christian enjoys a course of uninterrupted victory. No Christian perfectly realizes his own aspirations. The "perfect day" has not yet dawned.' *Studies*, 1935, p. 31.

his follies, bemoans his failures, and sorrows over the wretched returns he has made upon God's goodness. This is the common experience of the pious: as they journey through this wilderness they are sorely tried and exercised, pass through deep waters, experience many sharp conflicts, and are often at a loss to maintain their faith.

> Favour'd saints of God,
> His messengers and seers,
> The narrow path have trod,
> 'Mid sins, and doubts, and fears.

And at the end they generally have to mourn over the graceless conditions of some that are nearest and dearest to them, and exclaim, 'Although my house be not so with God'.[11]

A remarkable thing about Pink's ministry in the *Studies*, as already noticed, is the very small extent to which the articles are adversely coloured by his own experience. At the very times when one might expect that the severity of his trials and disappointments would cast a gloom over his writing in the magazine, as it occasionally did upon a few of his personal letters, he rises quite above his personal circumstances. For instance, in 1930 we find him writing:

> The Lord has been good in connection with the work which he has condescended to commit unto us. Were we given the opportunity, we would not exchange places with the President of the U.S.A. or with the Prime Minister of England. No, for by sovereign grace we are far better occupied than in winning laurels of earthly fame. We are an ambassador of the King of

[11] *Studies*, 1939, p. 10.

> kings. It is our blessed privilege to minister unto those who are joint-heirs with Christ. We are sowing seed which will yield an eternal harvest, and month by month the Holy Spirit replenishes our basket. Though we endeavour to apply ourselves, closely, constantly, to this written ministry, it never palls on us. There is a marvellous vitalizing power in God's eternal Word. Its pastures are ever 'green' (*Psa.* 23:2) and fresh. Its refreshing wells are exhaustless.

Even in his worst 'fainting fit' of the 1930s, in December 1934 at Cheltenham, we have noticed how he not only maintained the magazine at a level which leaves his readers oblivious of his inner conflict, but launched the next year into two of his most elevated series. He knew his duty was not to write his own experience but to teach the Word of God. Two months after that dark December day when he penned the despairing letter to Wallace Nicolson, printed above, he wrote to the Colemans:

> There are times when it seems little more than a mockery that I should be writing on 'Sanctification'. But enough: I have never been one to say much about myself and that much slipped out before I was hardly aware of it. I passed through a very trying season in December which shook me to my foundations. The Lord seemed to give Satan the full length of his rope towards me. I have not yet quite recovered. I do hope there may yet be some fruit from it to God's praise.[12]

Pink knew recoveries as well as failures. He could say with the psalmist, 'I was brought low and he helped me' (*Psa.* 116:6). When he wrote on prayer and the refreshing

[12] Quoted in *Reformation Today*, July/Aug. 1977, p. 32.

that comes from Christ, it is the reality of his own experience that gives force to his words. His articles were no mechanical output; behind them there was his enjoyment of new supplies of light and grace. Without so much as hinting at it, Pink's own pathway clearly lies behind the kind of paragraphs which we read in 'Union and Communion'. For example:

> None but Christ will be sufficient for us when we are called upon to pass through the valley of the shadow of death, and none but Christ can do us any real good now: what we need is to really believe that truth. And does not God take abundant pains to prove the truth of it to us? He removes this and withholds that, because he sees that our hearts are too much set upon them. We imagine that a certain thing would be very pleasant and profitable, and fancy that we cannot do without it; if we could but obtain it, we promise ourselves much satisfaction from it. If God grants it to us, do we not find that it is not what we expected? We dream dreams, build air castles, live in many a fancied paradise, only to be bitterly disappointed. God's purpose in those disappointments is to wean us from the world, to make us sick of it, to teach us that all down here is but 'vanity and vexation of spirit'.
>
> O my reader, it would make much for our peace and blessedness if we committed the management of the whole of our affairs into the hands of Christ. We need to continually pray him to save us from having any will of our own, to work in us complete subjection to and satisfaction with his holy will. By nature we are full of restlessness, covetousness, discontent – never satisfied with what we do have, ever lusting

> after what we do not have. But by grace we may live more happily than a prince, even though we possess nothing more down here than bare food and raiment: yea, shall do so if we seek and find all our satisfaction in Christ alone. Here is the key to the extraordinary history of Paul and Silas, Bunyan and Rutherford, Madame Guyon and many others. Why were they so contented and joyful while lying – some of them for many years – in prison? No doubt God favoured them with a double portion of his grace and comfort, yet the real explanation is their hearts were completely absorbed with Christ.[13]

Pink's own experience both in sorrow and in joy was Christ-centred and his portrayal of the Christian life is not one of gloom and drudgery. Writing on the words, 'My yoke is easy, and my burden is light' (*Matt.* 11:30), he says:

> While we cannot affirm that the Christian's life in this world is one of unclouded sunshine and unalloyed bliss, yet we must be careful lest we convey the impression that the believer's lot is far from being an enviable one and that, for the present, he is worse off than the unbeliever. Far, very far from it! If the Christian be using diligently the means of God's appointing, if he draws upon the fulness which there is in Christ for him, if he cultivates daily communion with him, if he walks in the path of his commandments, he will possess a peace which passeth all understanding and experience such joys as the worldling knows nothing about. The world may frown upon and the Devil rage against him, but a conscience approving instead of condemning, the felt

[13] *Studies*, 1936, pp. 213–14.

> smiles of God upon him, the sweet communion enjoyed with fellow believers, and the assurance of an eternity of bliss in the presence of his Beloved, are ample compensations, so that he would not, if he could, change places with a millionaire in his mansion or a king in his palace who was a stranger to Christ.[14]

To his closer personal friends Pink did occasionally speak of how the articles were 'hammered out on the anvil of our own heart'.[15] An example of this occurs in a letter to the Colemans, dated August 10, 1941. Turning from an article which he had just prepared on Elijah under the juniper tree (*1 Kings* 19:4), he starts his letter:

> For the first time in my Christian life I have today spent several happy hours under the 'juniper tree'. I confess I have, at different periods, spent some most unhappy seasons there, but today it has been quite otherwise, for in attempting to prepare an article thereon, I have been occupied with the Lord's love and grace and not with the prophet's dejection. What a truly wondrous Book the Word is! No matter what our circumstances there is something exactly suited to our need: no matter what may be our case – whether one of jubilation on the mountain top or one of consternation in the Slough of Despond – we find it accurately depicted therein in one or another of God's servants.

* * * * *

Pink was by temperament an ambitious man and, while that temperament was redirected in him as a Christian,

[14] *Studies*,1941, p. 140. [15] To the Colemans, July 21, 1932.

the apparent smallness of his circle of influence, at an age when many men are at their peak, must have entered into the discouragement he sometimes knew. The devil knows how to work on the pride from which no Christian is free. A temptation to self-importance is not extinct in the best of men. Pink's long-continued prayer that God would be pleased to enlarge the circulation and the usefulness of the magazine did not seem to be answered. He met this temptation with the shield of faith and with a growing humility.[16] He came to see more clearly that it was not for him to measure the significance of his seemingly little ministry. In this regard a verse he often quoted to others reveals what had meant much to him:

> Deeds of greatness as we deemed them
>   He will show us were but sin;
> Cups of water we'd forgotten
>   He will tell us were for Him.

Yet at the heart of Pink's desire for a wider ministry was his burden that so few cared for a deeper understanding of the Word of God. It distressed him that so many struggling Christians remained unfed. He spoke the sober truth when, on one occasion, he compared his feelings with those of Paul: 'While Paul was at Athens and saw the city wholly given up to idolatry "his spirit was stirred in him", and as we behold the reckless and irreverent handling of the Word of God by many, and witness the pernicious effects it has produced in the minds and lives of many, we are moved by what is, we trust, a

[16] Accustomed to speak plainly to others, Pink did not take offence when others took the same liberty. An incident was remembered in Kentucky, for instance, of how a man in 1929, disliking what he perceived as his critical spirit, told him one day on the street, 'Mr Pink, you are just a Pharisee.' Instead of being ruffled, the accused simply replied, 'Perhaps you are right.'

holy indignation.'[17] It was from this same spirit that he prayed for more readers. The prayer, as we have seen, was not granted or, at least, so it seemed at first. The answer, in fact, had begun to take place before Pink realized it. He writes in August 1947:

> God moves in a mysterious way his wonders to perform, yet is it not infinitely superior to any which our short-sighted policy would devise? For many years past we have prayed that God would 'enlarge our coast' (*1 Chron.* 4:10), that a greater number of hungry souls might share with us some of the wondrous riches of his grace. Yet instead of our circulation increasing, it has decreased considerably from what it was twenty years ago. This has puzzled and exercised us, for all other requests concerning the magazine have been so manifestly granted. Only of late have we clearly perceived that the above has been no exception.

The explanation, as he goes on to state it, was that it had come to his knowledge that the material in *Studies* was increasingly being of help to preachers. One reader, after giving him information to this effect, continued: 'It is a case of God's overruling for his own glory, and we rejoice to know that he has given you a sort of vicarious oral ministry when we least expect it. Your articles on — are forcibly preached, and attended with great blessing.' 'Thus,' writes Pink, 'in supplying seed to other sowers our labours are being multiplied, and through the mouths of many ministers the substance of our articles is reaching thousands of people who do not read them. Our prayer helpers will rejoice to know that this magazine is now being taken by over one hundred preachers!'

[17] *Studies*, 1933, pp. 14–15. This was part of his Introduction to 18 articles on Dispensationalism.

The fact is that the extended ministry of Pink through the preachers who read *Studies* was a good deal more significant than he could know. Paul Tucker, for example, who was later to exercise an influential ministry at the East London Tabernacle, and elsewhere, has recorded how Dr Martyn Lloyd-Jones advised him in the year 1945:

> He spoke to me about the ministry and said that if I was called to be a minister he would advise me as follows: 'Don't waste your time reading Barth and Brunner. You will get nothing from them to aid you with preaching. Read Pink.' At that date, when Pink's writings had a limited circulation, I was thus introduced to *Studies in the Scriptures* long before Pink became the almost cult figure that he is today. I was grateful for the Doctor's advice.[18]

This recommendation was the result of Lloyd-Jones' own regular reading of *Studies.* Paul Tucker was not alone in receiving this advice from Lloyd-Jones. In a letter of Pink's to a correspondent in October 2, 1946, he writes of 'Mr Douglas Johnson of Epsom Downs, and then Mr D. M. Lloyd-Jones of Ealing', as 'those who were the instruments of introducing *Studies* to you'. Pink clearly did not know who these men were. Dr Johnson (1904–1991) was the influential founder and leader of Inter-Varsity,[19] and Dr Lloyd-Jones was at the centre of the recovery of doctrinal Christianity then beginning in England. Four years later, when the minister of Westminster Chapel suffered from a temporary depression

[18] *Lloyd-Jones, The Fight of Faith*, p. 137.

[19] An obituary by John Taylor, Bishop of St Albans, in the *Independent* for 11 Dec. 1991, said of Johnson: 'Relatively unknown in Christian circles and virtually unknown outside, he did much to shape the church of the late twentieth century.'

in 1949, it was as his eye fell on words from a sermon of Pink's that help came to him 'like a blaze of light'.[20]

Lloyd-Jones and Pink never had any personal contact.[21] It was by faith that Pink began to see the wider purpose of God. While he could not anticipate that the preachers who read him were to become many thousands across the world within twenty years of his death, he did start to believe that the church would pass through and out of the shallows of unbelief and worldliness of which he had seen so much. Gone was his old outlook that there was nothing worth expecting save 'the end of the dispensation'; instead we find him declaring:

> In God's appointed time, when his judgments have accomplished their designed work, the Spirit will return again to a purged Christendom and the testimony of God be established again in its midst.[22]

What a contrast there is in attitude between Pink's dark view of the future of the church upon earth as seen in *The Redeemer's Return* and the attitude of his later writings! Commenting on Elijah's dejection, for example, he exhorts preachers to remember that God's purpose 'includes *tomorrow* as well as today! The Most High is not confined to any one agent. Elijah thought the whole

[20] *Lloyd-Jones, The Fight of Faith*, p. 209.

[21] It may be that it was A. V. Gilbey, one of Lloyd-Jones's deacons at Westminster Chapel, who arranged for him to receive *Studies*. In a letter to Gilbey, Pink once asked him if the 'Mr Jones', who welcomed the *Studies*, was Martyn Lloyd-Jones, the preacher. He learned that he was.

[22] *Studies*, 1943, p. 215. At an earlier date Pink was very doubtful about anyone labouring in the wider church scene but now he had a new hopefulness in his desire to help such men. He wrote to Lowell Green in August 1948: 'Please make it a matter of definite prayer, thought and inquiry, to see if you can locate up to a dozen selected young men now preparing for the ministry, and young pastors in rural districts with small salaries, who are likely to welcome the *Studies*.'

work was to be accomplished through *his* instrumentality . . . Do your duty where God has stationed you: plough up the fallow ground and sow the seed, and though there be no fruit in your day, who knows but what an Elisha may follow you and do the reaping?'[23]

Above all else, the ministry of *Studies in the Scriptures* surely demonstrates the life-principle of all true witness-bearing: 'We having the same spirit of faith, according as it is written, I believed, and therefore have I spoken; we also believe, and therefore speak' (*2 Cor.* 4: 13).

[23] *Studies*, 1942, p. 84, or *Elijah* (London: Banner of Truth, 1963), p. 242.

12

'Twenty Thousand Letters'

Arthur Pink was a letter-writer extraordinary. Not given to exaggeration, he could say in 1946 that he had written 'by hand well over 20,000 letters'. Sometimes, as already noted, he wrote as many as ten in one day and these were not mere hurried notes but pages full of thought and consideration depending upon the situation of his correspondent. He also thrived on the letters which came back. To his old friends the Colemans in Australia, referring to 'the many letters which the Lord is graciously and continually sending in', he says, 'Eighteen arrived by a single mail a couple of weeks since.' To another correspondent, as a New Year approached, he wrote, 'Soon I hope to be nearly "swamped" with letters from those who write me but once a year!'

While he prized correspondence as a source of Christian fellowship there is no doubt that he saw its chief importance as a ministry to be exercised alongside *Studies*. Because he recognized the limitations of a printed ministry read by very varied classes of readers, he coveted every opportunity of giving more personal help to any individual who wrote to him. While he never advertised his willingness to reply to letters, it is obvious that many of the circle who were regular readers of *Studies* felt that the author had a pastor's heart and that they could write to him freely. Indeed for not a few who were unable to find any 'church home' where they could belong, A. W. Pink truly was their minister and to those friends whom he knew to be in such circumstances he would generally close his letters with the words, 'Yours by Divine Mercy, Arthur W. Pink – your Pastor'.

Some of his correspondents had once sat under his ministry in various places. Their numbers naturally decreased as the years went by, and by far the greater part of those who wrote to him he had never met face to face. Their bond was a common love for the Word of Christ. Occasionally Pink makes reference to the kind of people who provided the mainstay of his readership and we may assume that they were also prominent among his correspondents. To John B. Culver he wrote in 1943:

> We greatly appreciate your kindly efforts to secure new readers for us, but I wonder if they are being directed along the *most likely* channels. Long experience has shown that nineteen times out of twenty the *Studies* are unacceptable to theological professors, preachers and missionaries, unless someone makes them a present of the same, and then it is doubtful if they do more than glance over them. You are likely to have more success in locating those who are hungering for spiritual food among the laity – simple souls, in the background.[1]

As he later came to realize, more ministers were reading *Studies* than he knew in 1943, but, whatever the reason, comparatively few of their number seemed to write to him. To another helper of *Studies* he wrote in 1949, 'I appreciate the efforts you have made to secure new

[1] *Letters of A. W. Pink*, p. 118.

readers: young converts and shut-ins are the most likely ones!'

Many seem to have written to him for the first time because of some personal problem. Pink rarely mentions the case of others in his letters but the following to Lowell Green gives us a glimpse both of his correspondence and of the spirit in which he undertook it:

> Of late I have had some exceedingly difficult letters to answer: among them one from a Sister who allowed her heart to run away with her head . . . She thought she was doing God's will, is now satisfied she was deceived by Satan, and wanting to know *how* the promptings of the Holy Spirit may be distinguished from those of the Evil One. Another from a preacher of many years' experience: had a nervous breakdown; eventually went to a 'Prayer Healer' (a servant of the Devil), since which the spirit of prayer has been stifled in his own soul, all assurance of salvation gone, so that he no longer dares to preach to others. What saddens me so much is that there seem to be so very few today unto whom these poor souls can turn for helpful counsel. Many who can preach gospel, doctrinal and prophetic sermons appear to be quite incapable of entering into the experiences of the perplexed and distressed and giving them 'a word in season'. Unless pastors are Divinely qualified to be doctors of souls they are 'physicians of no value', as Job had to say unto those who failed to diagnose his case and minister to him in his trouble. Such 'qualification' cannot be acquired in any Seminary or Bible School![2]

[2] July 10, 1939.

Pink's letters, that is to say, those which have survived, reveal a great deal of spiritual wisdom. He has no set formulas for responding to the needs of various correspondents. Nor does he assume that the writer can be depended upon to give a right account of what his needs may be. A downcast correspondent, for example, giving a sad account of himself and perhaps expecting commiseration from Pink, might well be exhorted to stir himself. 'Thank God', he tells one correspondent, 'the way is always open for us to confess to God our failures and start anew. It is at that point there is ever encouragement for the most discouraged soul: at the mediatorial throne "mercy" may be found to remit the past and "grace" to help in the present (*Heb.* 4:16). Never allow the sense of failure to keep you from that throne: it is sprinkled with blood, the Friend of sinners is seated thereon, mercy and grace is what he dispenses therefrom . . . O my dear, I do want you to bear this in mind: that whatever the future may hold for you, whatever tight corner you may get into, Christ is your *Friend*, and desires you to make use of him, to be free and unreserved with him, never to doubt his love, sympathy and care for you, no matter how his providences may seem to frown.'

In his letters there are often passages rich in sympathy, yet with sympathy he always gives direction and a reminder of appropriate spiritual duties. Such sentences as the following, taken from various letters to the Colemans in Sydney, are characteristic:

> Greetings in the blessed Name of him who informs us, 'Thy God hath commanded thy strength' (*Psa.* 68:28). Each of his living children has received personal proof of that statement . . . While I doubt not that the primary reference is a spiritual one, yet

> inasmuch as the greater includes the less, we should not exclude the physical. God has also 'commanded' our physical strength and beyond what he has wisely ordained we cannot go. I believe one reason why he causes so many of his people to remain on earth till they are aged and feeble is to make them increasingly dependent upon himself. Do not be unduly depressed by your growing infirmities and evidences of old age: they are but the appointed order of nature and to be expected. If you cannot concentrate on reading as formerly, do more quiet musing and praying . . .
>
> Much of what Brother C. says about his own personal failure is duplicated in my own experience. God will not suffer us to love and admire ourselves, but has written death on all our members . . .
>
> Many of God's dear children are passing through deep waters at the present time: some exceedingly distressing cases came to my immediate notice during the past few months. It is only as *faith* is really in exercise that we can have comfort from Romans 8:28! To merely 'bow to God's sovereign will' is not sufficient when the Mohammedan does that! – there needs to be a *trusting* in his *goodness* and a confiding in his wisdom also, if the heart is to be kept in peace and if we are to be 'giving thanks *always* for *all* things' (*Eph.* 5:20). In recent years I have thanked God fervently for several withholdings of his which were sore disappointments in the past!

To a correspondent who sought advice on a headstrong son he wrote: 'You will need both wisdom and patience. While seeking to set before him the holy standard of God, yet do not expect too much from him in the way of measuring up to it. He is but a *babe* in Christ and you know the old saying that we "cannot put old heads on young shoulders"! Each of us had to learn from painful experience the folly of leaning unto our own understanding and following the desires and devices of our own hearts, and must not think that those who follow us will provide any exception. While not condoning his faults, seek to bear with his infirmities. This may be a part of God's wise discipline for you.'

Little space is given in Pink's letters to his view of authors but what he does say, in answer to requests for advice on reading, is of interest. Of the Puritans his favourites appear to have been Matthew Henry, John Owen, Thomas Manton, John Flavel and Thomas Goodwin. '*Pilgrim's Progress*', he tells one correspondent, 'is a very fine, helpful, spiritual book, which I would earnestly advise you to read and re-read.' 'The four volumes by Gurnall', he writes to another, 'are very spiritual and helpful, but need reading slowly, and meditate on each section.' At one time he considers Flavel's *Mystery of Providence* to be that author's best book, but later it has given way to another, and he replies to a friend: 'Glad to see you are acquainted with Flavel's *Fountain of Life*: it is my favourite of his works and I recently read the whole of it to my wife – one chapter each evening.'

The names of a number of other Puritan authors occur in his writings; he studied them enthusiastically and widely but not blindly. He is ready to designate John Howe 'the driest of the Puritans'. In another letter he says to a correspondent, 'Personally, I think you were guided by God in passing by Trapp's commentaries – he has many 'quaint' sayings, but is a poor expositor.' It was his conviction that God has not given all the light to any one school of writers. Despite his change on prophecy he never gave up Brethren writers entirely and, in starting his series on 'The Doctrine of Sanctification' in *Studies* in 1936, he wrote, 'On some aspects of *this* subject he has found the Plymouth Brethren much more helpful than the Reformers and the Puritans.' Of the German authors whom he knew, the Lutheran E. W. Hengstenberg was chief; of the Scots he quotes most from Thomas Boston, but he came to know the nineteenth-century Free Church of Scotland theologians such as Patrick Fairbairn, George Smeaton and William Cunningham. From his correspondence with John Blackburn it is evident that he had some of the works of the Southern Presbyterian leaders and notably J. H. Thornwell who did not impress him as a writer. C. H. Spurgeon, he regarded as 'always good' and ever spoke of him in the highest terms.

To all his correspondents who sought advice on books he would say, 'A few really helpful books thoroughly assimilated count for far more than skimming through many ordinary books.' John Culver, for instance, received this exhortation: 'The works you have procured by Jonathan Edwards and John Owen are most excellent and should last you a couple of years.[3] Don't hunt around for others until you have thoroughly absorbed these. One book read slowly, meditated upon and assimilated, is worth twenty skimmed through hurriedly.' The books in his own library were carefully marked and indexed. 'I have devoted ten or probably twenty times more hours on one or two authors than I have on fifty others put together', he tells one friend.

[3] It should, however, be noted that he did not advise young Christians, going to the Puritans for the first time, to start with Owen!

Nonetheless, his reading was remarkably broad and he strongly disliked the practice (especially in ministers) of reading none but those with whom one is in agreement. While accepting John Blackburn's conviction that wide reading is 'dangerous unless one is first well grounded in the teaching of Holy Writ', he nevertheless exhorts Blackburn to enlarge the circle of his authors. Similarly when another correspondent quotes Alexander Maclaren and, half-apologetically, adds, 'though apparently he was an Arminian', Pink responds: 'He was, though not nearly so extreme an one as some. He is always worth reading on any subject, yet with caution. I have often received helpful suggestions from his writings and believe he was much used of God. I would have been greatly the loser had I confined myself to Calvinistic works!'

When it comes to the 'high' or hyper-Calvinistic authors Pink is prepared, with caution, to suggest some of them to *some* of his correspondents. Speaking of Samuel Eyles Pierce, he tells one correspondent: 'Though I would hardly recommend them to anybody, his two volumes, *Letters on Spiritual Subjects*, would be worth your reading, especially when you felt you needed, or could enjoy, spiritually speaking, a glass of champagne! There is much in them that is sweet and precious.' On the other hand, when a younger Christian, only beginning to find his way, asks his opinion of William Huntington, the late-eighteenth-century 'hyper', Pink speaks very plainly:

'You ask if I have read any of Huntington's Works? Yes, I have gone carefully through the 3,000 pages of the same. 1st, my suspicions were aroused when I discovered that in his middle and late life, such large crowds attended his preaching – bad sign, Galatians 1:10. 2nd, it soon became apparent why such large numbers attended his ministry, viz. because of the novelties he set before them

(*Acts* 17:21); he was all the time *straining* at presenting "original" interpretations of Scripture, which is what most appeals to that (large) class who have "itching ears"! 3rd, mixed up with considerable truth (or none had so readily swallowed his poison) were errors of a serious nature, such as his repudiation of the free gospel offer to all who hear it, his denial of "duty repentance" and "duty faith", and his insisting that the Moral Law is *not* the Christian's "Rule of Life", in all of which he departed from the uniform teaching of the godly Puritans – i.e. from the Word of God. Alas, his errors were embraced by William Gadsby and J. C. Philpot and are perpetuated to this day by *The Gospel Standard*. Each of my three observations above applies equally to James Wells.'[4]

A Christian's reading, Pink would say, needs to be balanced. Orthodox authors of different eras have different strengths. Some excel in setting forth the Faith objectively, others are pre-eminent in dealing with the subjective. 'Both of us', he tells Lowell and Evelyn Green, 'have greatly enjoyed Romaine's Works for his magnifying Christ and seeking to get the believer occupied with him. Yet one also needs to read Owen so as to preserve the balance: Romaine is almost entirely the honey of the gospel – Owen brings in more salt. Romaine's ministry was a special one – needed particularly in his day to deliver the saints from legality and too much introspection.'

Remarks like these, as I have said, occupy small place in Pink's letters. His patent concern is to deal with questions arising directly out of Scripture. The enquiries he especially welcomed were those from readers who wanted help on biblical truths, provided they were major

[4] Letter to John T. McNee, May 1947. Pink was widely read in Philpot and, on occasions, quoted him with approval. He had read carefully some twenty volumes of Philpot's magazine *The Gospel Standard*!

truths and that the enquirer was concerned with their *practical* value. To one correspondent who wrote to him in 1933 with a problem on verses in Revelation, chapter 7, he offers no solution, only the advice, 'I have long since turned my attention to more vital and practical concerns than puzzling my brains over the symbols of Daniel and Revelation, and only wish I had done so much earlier.' To another, asking for light on the Jews' place in Palestine, he answers succinctly in 1946, 'God will work out his own eternal purpose, though personally I do not now profess to know what that involves regarding the Jews.' With these exceptions he positively encouraged the raising of difficulties. Thus to Lowell Green, in the early days of their correspondence, he writes in August 1935:

> It is indeed much to be thankful for that the Most High has been pleased to reveal to you the blessed truth of his Sovereignty, and I trust he will now make just as clear to you the equally important (and equally hated!) truth of our relationship to his Law. I wish you would carefully re-read my articles thereon in last year's *Studies* (p. 18, etc.). As you read, and meditate thereon, jot down on a slip of paper any particular difficulties which occur to you and any objections, or any passages which appear 'on the other side'. Thus, D.V. arrange them in definite form and send them to me, and I will endeavour with God's guidance to help you thereon.

To the same correspondent, on another occasion, he adds this postscript:

> When replying, please have this letter before you and make some comment on my remarks upon Psalm 25:9: I want to see if you have really grasped them.

Many of Pink's letters were more like an elevated correspondence course, with personal tuition in the Scriptures, than anything else. There is never the slightest hint of any grudge that a correspondent is taking up his time; on the contrary he spares no effort in giving of his best to every enquirer. His willingness to help is transparent. To John T. McNee, to whom he lends a booklet on 'the Law' and urges to read the 'Sermon on the Mount' articles in the February-April issues of *Studies*, 1939, he says, 'Take a week or two in thoroughly digesting them and within a month write me frankly and definitely thereon – you need *not* fear "hurting my feelings" but I long to *help* you. May the Lord teach each of us his way more perfectly!' To another he writes: 'Instead of just writing me annually, I wish you would do so every two or three months, concerning any personal problems, subjects or passages of Scripture on which you desire fuller light.' To a certain class of correspondent he gave priority, as he told an old friend in 1945: 'For the past two or three years I have devoted most of the time available for correspondence to writing to *young* Christians, for long experience has taught me that people are most impressionable and influenced while between fifteen and thirty.'

William Naismith was one of Pink's younger correspondents in later years. To a first letter from Naismith (who was then a student) Pink replies, 'Yes, I welcome questions, for I long to be of help unto souls; yet a child can ask me many I cannot answer.' But after a few letters in which Pink has taken the measure of his young correspondent, he begins to make Naismith himself deal with questions. The following well illustrates Pink's teaching method with individuals:

While it is nice to have our problems solved and difficulties removed by others, it is not always best for us. Instead of continuing to answer your questions, I feel I might be of more service if I put you in the way of answering them for yourself. That man is the greatest help to me who most casts me back upon God and stimulates me to the study of his Word. 'Study', I say, for while there are many who *read* it daily, and use the concordance, scarcely any *study* it. The first requirement is, of course, a spirit of dependence upon the Lord (distrusting our own competency), yet prayer is not meant to encourage slothfulness, and is no substitute for the diligent use of whatever talents God has bestowed upon us . . . I could easily give you three or four reasons which conclusively determine whether 'the gift of God' (*Eph.* 2:8) refers to 'salvation' or 'faith', but had rather you obtained them for yourself. Let me assure you, first, that there is nothing whatever in the Greek which requires the slightest alteration, or even modification, of the Authorized Version rendition of Ephesians 2:8–10. I want you, during the next week or so, to concentrate on those three verses, analysing, and pondering each word in them. Particularly seek answers to these questions: 1. What is the precise force of the opening 'For' of v. 8? It must be given due weight and its meaning ascertained *before* you are ready to apprehend what follows! 2. Why is the 'through faith' *added* in v. 8: are not vv. 8–9 grammatically and contextually complete without those two words? 3. What is the antecedent of 'And *that* not of yourselves'? 4. How does the determining of that antecedent serve to settle whether the 'gift of God' refers to salvation or faith? 5. With *which* of

> these two (salvation or faith) is v. 9 the more accordant and pertinent? 6. What is the precise force of the opening 'For' of v. 10 in *relation* to vv. 8–9? 7. What light does the first half of v. 10 shed on the 'that' and 'gift' of v. 8? Later, D.V., send me your 'findings'.

The most remarkable set of manuscript letters to survive are those exchanged between Pink and Harold J. Bradshaw of Norwich, England. Written between February and November 1943, the letters of the two men run to forty-eight closely typed foolscap pages when copied from the originals. The correspondence is an example of Pink's dealing not with a young Christian but, this time, with a mature believer who is troubled by his lack of full assurance.

Bradshaw opened the exchange with a query concerning two pages written in the January 1943 *Studies* where Pink denied any faith to be 'saving' unless it works by love, purifies the heart, and overcomes the world. 'Saving faith', Pink wrote, 'is not an isolated act which suffices for the remainder of a person's life, rather it is a living principle which continues in activity, ever seeking the only object which can satisfy it.'[5] Does this not make faith in Jesus insufficient for assurance? Bradshaw asks. Pink, in reply, explained that his point was not to unsettle weak believers but to expose 'empty professors' whose 'faith' bears no fruit; at the same time, he tells Bradshaw that it is faulty teaching which accounts for the weak assurance of many true believers. When Bradshaw asks him to explain the latter remark, Pink points to the passivity advised by 'hyper-Calvinists, Plymouth Brethren, or rank Arminians' when it comes to assurance – the

[5] *Studies*, 1943, p. 5.

absence of instruction for God's people in the teaching of these groups on taking 'the whole armour of God', and the failure to explain the several parts of that armour and *how* to use them. For reading, he directs Bradshaw to current articles on 'An Honest Heart' in *Studies* (March and April 1943). The same letter contains a rare personal reference in answer to a direct question from Bradshaw:

> No, alas; I am doing no preaching these days, nor have I had the holy privilege for ten years past. For years I was in the Baptist pastorate in the U.S.A., but withdrew because I could not fellowship with what was going on. Then I became a 'free lance', speaking at Bible Conferences and special Conventions, addressing from 500 to 2,000 people, but as time went on I found less and less with which I felt free to associate, and in many places my messages were not acceptable. We had several years in Sydney, Australia, and then back to America. I gave up in despair in 1934 and returned to England.

On the main theme of the correspondence Bradshaw remains unsure, and Pink therefore takes up the subject at much more length, stating at the outset, 'I dare not take it for granted you are a regenerated soul.' In Pink's view Bradshaw was suffering from difficulties characteristic of those brought up among the 'Gospel Standard' section of the Strict Baptists:

> To state it rather baldly, the impressions obtained by those who sat or sit under their preaching are something like this. *Negatively*: a mere intellectual belief of the truth is a non-saving one. *Positively*: I must have a feeling sense of my lost condition, a feeling sense of Christ's suitability and sufficiency for

my desperate case, a feeling sense that I have trusted in him and that I am clothed with his righteousness; ratified by a peace which passeth all understanding possessing my heart. Under some powerful sermon, or alone in my room, that feeling sense is granted me, perhaps accompanied by a voice which says, 'Thy sins are forgiven thee,' and I go on my way rejoicing. But soon the joy is dampened. I am conscious of sin raging within, and perhaps breaking out into open act, and now I have serious cause to fear that sin still has 'dominion' over me. I am staggered. Yet I still find some satisfaction in prayer, and in meeting with God's people; and I ask myself, could this be the case if I were unregenerate? I am sorely perplexed. I read and hear sermons which have not a little to say about the perplexities of God's people, about their ups and downs, about their walking in darkness, etc.; and I am somewhat comforted, hoping this may, partly at least, *explain* my contradictory experience. Much of my thought and time is now devoted to seeking diligently for 'marks of grace' in myself. At certain seasons (particularly on Sabbaths) I am encouraged to hope I can really perceive some of those 'marks' in me; at other seasons (especially during the week) I am greatly cast down because 'iniquities prevail against me', and I am at a loss to reconcile this with those 'marks of grace'. Thus my 'assurance' is like a seesaw. That, I think, is a fair, if crude and general, description of the inner workings of the average Strict Baptist.

Now let me try and show *why* his 'experience' is (inevitably) such, and wherein the preaching he sat or sits under is defective:

1. Because only a one-sided view of the gospel and way of salvation has been presented to him. Nothing, or next to nothing, was told him of the *claims* and *requirements* of Christ: that there must be a forsaking of sin (*Isa.* 55:7), a complete surrender of ourselves to him, a receiving of him as LORD (*Col.* 2:6), a taking of his 'yoke' upon us, a willingness and resolution that he should 'reign over' us (*Luke* 19:14) in order to be saved!

2. Because only a one-sided view of the Christian life has been presented to him, nothing, or next to nothing, having been told him of Christ's *demands* upon his people. Those 'demands' are made known in his commandments and exhortations, but instead of dwelling upon the *precepts*, they are largely side-tracked for the promises. Strict Baptist pastors do not instruct their members that the chief concern and business of the Christian should be – not seeking for 'marks of grace', nor making a god of inward peace and happy feelings, but the practice of obedience. Moreover, the general tenor of Strict Baptist preaching has sadly failed to preserve the *balance* between either the gloomier and brighter sides of the Christian life, or between the experimental and practical aspects of it. Few of their people know much about 'the joy of the Lord' being their 'strength' (*Neh.* 8:10), or that John wrote his epistle to the saints that their joy 'may be full' (*1 John* 1:4); rather are they encouraged to entertain the idea that doubts and fears are the normal and common experience of Christians. As to the *practical* side of the truth bearing on the Christian life, how many Strict Baptist members have received any explicit teaching on *how*

> to 'mortify' their members, *how* to take unto themselves 'the whole armour of God', *how* successfully to resist the devil, *how* to obtain answers to *prayer*, *how* to be fruitful branches of the Vine?
>
> 3. Because an erroneous presentation of the *ground of* assurance has been made unto them. My persuasion that I have been regenerated and accepted in the Beloved is *not* to rest upon a discovery of 'marks of grace', or upon peace within, but the testimony of a good conscience that I have the approbation of God, because I am genuinely and sincerely endeavouring with all that is within me to abstain from everything he hates and practise everything he enjoins (see *2 Cor.* 1:12).

In all this Bradshaw agrees that Pink is partly right: 'Your knowledge of Strict Baptists is far wider than mine, but I am sure that practical godliness is earnestly contended for amongst the present-day 'Gospel Standard' section, though there is a great lack in emphasising Christ's demands upon his people and of exhorting to obedience . . . I am convinced that I am suffering from defects.' Nevertheless, he argues, is Pink not putting the 'practice of obedience' too high and thus in danger of basing assurance upon sanctification which would lead to the very emphasis which Pink wants to avoid, namely, the constant pursuit of 'marks of grace' on the part of believers? To support his fear he quotes John Owen's warning against Christians putting obedience before 'frequent actings of faith upon Christ' and he quotes John Gill's interpretation of 2 Corinthians 1:12 as contrary to Pink's.

Pink's answers to this objection run (in their typed form) to four foolscap pages in which he patiently defines the issues with more exactness, points to certain confusions which he believes exist in Bradshaw's thinking, and gives him some questions to ponder and to answer! He has dropped the possibility that Bradshaw may not even be a Christian, yet he urges him not to be offended at his plain speaking. 'A postman may be gruff, even surly, but that is (relatively) a trifling matter if he hands you a valuable letter! I am an 'earthen' and not a golden vessel. I may not be as suave as you might wish, I may even appear harsh, but I hope you will not suffer such defects in your would-be physician to prejudice you against his *treatment* of your case. This is a day which calls for *plain dealing*, not Judas-like kisses.'

With respect to Owen, Pink replies:

> You say J. Owen gives a solemn warning against my emphasis upon the practice of obedience 'coming before "actings of faith upon Christ"'. Here again I think you show confusion of thought. The actings of faith upon Christ and the practice of obedience must not be pitted against each other, as though there was a danger of one displacing or taking precedence over the other. Are you not familiar with the words, 'the obedience of faith' (*Rom.* 16:26)? Have you not been taking much too circumscribed a view of what is *included within* 'acting faith on Christ'? – i.e., restricting it to acts of faith on his *promises*, or at least going no further in your mind than acting faith on his Person, for grace and comfort? Are we not also to 'act faith' on his *authority*, on his *precepts*? Did not David say, 'I have *believed* (i.e. appropriated to myself) thy commandments' (*Psa.* 119:66)?

Bradshaw's response, at equal length, acknowledges the

help he is receiving from Pink (and especially from his *Studies*), and yet he wants to pursue further the note which he finds in Owen and Gill, whom he quotes further, as well as a passage from John Newton 'such as, I feel, dear Mr Pink, would not come from your pen'. Pink's approach, he suggests, is out of balance 'with an *over*-emphasis of the human responsibility side of things, and a corresponding *under*-emphasis of the fact that it is the Lord who must work all our works in us – even to *will* as well as to do of his good pleasure'.

Far from being offended, Pink replies:

> I like your last letter better than the previous ones. I knew when I wrote mine of May 23rd that it would *test* you: nine out of ten professing Christians would have been so 'disappointed' and 'hurt' with it as to decline any reply. I much appreciate your frankness and kindness in writing so fully.
>
> Much of your criticism is to the point. I freely grant that quite a number of my recent articles have been very unbalanced, stressing the human responsibility side more than the operations of God's grace; and the same applies to most of my letters written to high and hyper-Calvinists. It is just because they have (many of them, most of their lives) sat under a ministry *the very reverse*, that I felt such disproportionate emphasis necessary on my part – to counteract, and help them obtain a due balance. And if you could read the letters I have received during the past two years from 'Gospel Standard' Baptists in England and 'Primitive' Baptists in the U.S.A., you would own that God has been pleased to bless my poor efforts – and 'poor' I well *know* them to be. In like manner, when, 25 years ago, I published my

book on *The Sovereignty of God* (now out of print) in the U.S.A., and devoted most of my time to preaching on *that* subject, many criticized my *lopsidedness*: so in the Foreword to the 2nd Edition I said: 'Probably 95% of the religious literature of the day is devoted to a setting forth of the duties and obligations of men. The fact is that those who undertake to expound the responsibility of men are the very ones who have *lost* the "balance of truth" by ignoring very largely the Sovereignty of God. It is perfectly right to insist on the responsibility of man, but what of God? – has *he* no claims, no rights? A hundred such works as this are needed, and ten thousand sermons would have to be preached throughout the land on this subject, if the "balance of truth" is to be *regained* . . . Surely there is far more danger of making too much of man and too little of God, than there is of making too much of God and too little of man.' Yet the very opposite of this would apply to 'Gospel Standard' circles.

I freely grant that, not only 'at times' *but frequently* of late years, there has been a 'legalistic ring' in my writings, and that is because I was so much engaged (in this day of abounding *lawlessness*) in holding up the standard of obedience and our duty of conforming thereto. I take no offence whatever at your saying that you feel the blessed paragraph you quote from John Newton 'would not come from *my* pen': it all depends upon *which* class I was writing to or for!

At this point the discussion was only reaching its halfway mark! There can scarcely have been a like correspondence going on anywhere in the world in 1943. The grounds of assurance continue to be the main theme. Bradshaw remains persuaded that a special experience of God's love (which he identifies with Romans 8: 16, 'The Spirit himself beareth witness with our spirit') is a higher ground of assurance than any assurance derived from a good conscience. If the conscience is sufficient, he asks, what special need is there of the witness of the Spirit? Pink will not accept this antithesis and there is further debate on the meaning of both 2 Corinthians 1: 12 and Romans 8:16. Pink brings in testimony from Thomas Goodwin and Jonathan Edwards, while Bradshaw employs John Gill and J. C. Philpot. Finally Bradshaw appeals to the experience of 'most of the Lord's people', only to receive this riposte:

> I wonder what *percentage* of 'the Lord's people' you have even so much as met! That such is the 'experience' of many, perhaps most, of those who have deeply imbibed the teachings of Mr Philpot and men of his party, I can well believe, but *that* is a vastly different thing from what obtains among the Lord's people in general. I have personally met scores of German, Swiss, Dutch, Danish, Swedish, Norwegian, Syrian Christians, was for several years pastor of some of them, lived in the homes of others of them, and was intimately acquainted with still others, in addition to many hundreds of British Christians, all of whom lived holy lives, and possessed a humble but unshakable assurance of their acceptance in the Beloved. I have preached, not merely once or twice, but dozens of times, in Methodist, Friends', Presbyterian, Dunkards, United Brethren, Campbellite, as well as General and Particular Baptist churches in literally scores of towns and cities from

> one end of the U.S.A. to another, as well as in Canada, Australia, England, Wales and Scotland. So I have something more than a theoretical or hearsay knowledge of what characterizes the Lord's people at large – *not* that I regarded anything like all the members of those churches as regenerate souls. And this I can say, and must say, that so far from the doubting and doleful spirit which marks so many of the Strict Baptists being duplicated in the Christians I have been privileged to know, on the contrary, nine-tenths of them were those who rejoiced in the Lord and enjoyed daily communion with him as they trod the path of obedience, though still groaning over inward corruptions and longing for complete deliverance from indwelling sin.

Our quotations give but little idea of the thoroughness of the discussion between these two equally exercised Christians. In so far as the debate had a resolution it lay in their agreement that there is more than one strand of scriptural truth necessary to a right doctrine of assurance. Bradshaw pointed out that in the correspondence Pink appeared to be insisting on one element only, namely, the believer's responsibility to walk in obedience; to which Pink answered that it was *this* truth, he considered, which needed 'a much larger place' in Bradshaw's own thinking and acting, but in *Studies* his correspondent should recognize he did teach other aspects of assurance including the place of direct faith in Christ.

* * * * *

Readers will have noticed the number of letters we have quoted in these pages from Pink to Lowell Green. The preservation of these letters has added much to this biography. As a young man in Georgia, Green first wrote to Pink in July 1932, after reading his *Sovereignty of God*. Thereafter letters were frequent and they show how interested he was in all the affairs of those whom he sought to help. As well as spiritual counsel, there is very practical advice on matters related to such things as business, saving for the future, the need to have a will written, and the pros and cons of a location for a home after he married. In that marriage the Pinks had a special interest for Lowell married Evelyn Sorrells, a young lady in another part of Georgia, who was also in correspondence with Pink, as we have seen in previous pages. When a letter in March 1935 brought the news that these two warm supporters of *Studies* in Georgia were engaged to be married, Pink was delighted. 'I have cherished a secret hope that the Lord would graciously fit you for each other,' he wrote in response to Lowell's news.[6]

After the Green-Sorrells wedding in the summer of 1935, it was normally Vera Pink who wrote to Evelyn, and one letter of advice on setting up home gives us a glimpse of Mrs Pink's own routine at this period:

> I am pleased to learn that you are finding house duties take up a goodly portion of time, and your days do not drag, as so many young wives fear while the husband is away all day. I have found it very helpful to take a portion of each morning for reading a chapter or two from God's Word, spend a season in prayer, and then meditate on what I have read. My plan has been as follows: after we have worship I

[6] Lowell Hanson Green lived 1909–1981. We were privileged to know him as a bright witness for Christ. That witness Mrs Evelyn Green (b. 1910), in advanced years, continues to this day (May 2004), while their son, David Green, is an esteemed leader among pastors in New England.

> get my morning duties done and before taking up some work like sewing or going out, or writing, I have a whole hour quietly to myself. In the afternoon I seek to read some good book or the *Studies*. Then in the evening I read another chapter and pray. So with the duties of the day my time is filled and I find no time for idling.[7]

Vera Pink's correspondence with Evelyn Green, which survives in a large bundle, reveals much of her charm and spirituality. Her thinking is no mere echo of her husband's. She rejoiced in her own personal study of the Scriptures and can speak of weighty truths in simple sentences, as the following quotations indicate:

> I like those words, 'Our life is like the weaver's web' for it is so true to life. We only see the wrong side of the fabric now, for the Weaver has not finished his work. But in the Day to come, where we shall see it from his side, then we shall behold the beauty of his work and not the knots and ends which our sins and failures have caused.

> Election is a truth more widely and hotly persecuted than any other in Scripture. Perhaps it is because God is given his rightful place and man put in the dust that enmity is so stirred up.

> I cannot live by your faith, nor you by mine – we must each act faith on our own account and are each responsible for the way we use it. We cannot please the Lord if we wrap it in a napkin to keep, but we must *use* it, exercise it and the more we do so the more we will find we have.

[7] Oct. 13, 1935.

> It is wonderful to view the Divine Hand in everything. The flakes of snow, the scales of fish, the wings of the despised moth, all show the wonder of the Divine Mind in creation, wonders too tiny for the eye to see with a powerful lens. Each has its part to perform, each has its place in the universe.
>
> There are times in the lives of all women when the changes which the years bring on are trying, but it is a wonderful opportunity for us to prove and prove again, and yet again, his sufficiency. Ah, how patient he is – how longsuffering! The more we lean upon him the more we please him.
>
> Yes, indeed, his coming is a glorious prospect, but it is a blessed privilege to be witnesses for him in this Christ-rejecting age while we are left down here.

Like her husband Vera Pink writes little of herself. Occasionally there is a quote from her grandfather or from an 'old saint' she knew in her youth. Sometimes she speaks of household things and gives advice on cooking or on health. Although she had become British, her affection for the United States was enduring: 'I remember the kindness there used to be back home in old Kentucky – I expect it is much the same as then.'

In many letters spanning more than twenty years there are only two which ever suggest that she could be cast down: the prevailing tone is bright, contented, thankful and prayerful.

In their correspondence, as in all else, God blessed Arthur and Vera Pink with a union of spirit which adorned the gospel.

13

The Hidden Ministry of Greatest Usefulness

From 1936 until his death at the age of sixty-six in 1952, Pink's life was so wholly given to the ministry of the magazine that virtually no biography can be written for these years.

When the Pinks went to Hove, on the south coast of England, in late March 1936, they booked accommodation, which they had seen advertised in *The Gospel Standard* magazine, for one week. In the event the rooms on the upper floor of 31 Colbourne Road so suited them that they decided to settle permanently. Before moving from Glasgow to this coastal resort, adjoining Brighton, Pink wrote as follows of their anticipations to Lowell Green, 'We shall have the advantage of being away from the rush and roar, grime and smoke of the city, and be close to the sea – which we both so much enjoy.' These hopes were fulfilled. 'It is wonderful to us,' Vera Pink wrote to Evelyn Green, 'how this place was provided for us. A more restful and quiet place one could not find if one searched for days.' At the end of 1936 he told the readers of his Annual Letter: 'In our outward circumstances things are now more pleasant for us than for years past . . . For another twelve months each of us has been favoured with excellent health.

Since the home-going of our parents our temporal needs are fully provided for, and all that is sent in to us we apply to the expenses of *Studies*.'

Pink's parents had both died during his last years in the States – his mother, past eighty, in the spring of 1930, and his father at Surbiton on August 14, 1933. Speaking of the latter event Pink had written to a friend at the time: 'Less than a month ago we received the news of the home-going of my beloved father: he had turned 85, all his faculties preserved to the end: only a day or two of sickness (exhaustion from the great heat) and he passed away peacefully in his sleep.'

Although the portion of Thomas Pink's estate which came to them was to relieve them of personal financial concerns for the remainder of their days, Arthur and Vera Pink continued to live in the simplest possible manner. From the time of their return from the States and for the rest of their lives they never rented more than two rooms! For three-and-a-half years their large living-room in Colbourne Road was the scene of all the daily work needful for the continuation of *Studies*. In the winter they heated it by a gas fire, augmented by an oil stove if the cold was severe. Vera Pink rarely mentioned her own part in maintaining the written ministry, but sometimes in her letters she speaks of her concern at the extent of her husband's labours:

> No one realizes the hours and hours of hard brain work entailed in composing and going over and over the ground to make sure no error is printed to lead some sheep astray from the green pastures. Then the proof reading — one man's job — apart from the composing. Last but not least, the correspondence to care for. So you see Mr Pink does really three

> men's work. For that reason I do all I can in the way of book-keeping, typing, and addressing the envelopes to help him.[1]

There was little for them to do beyond the walls of that room. As already noted, no invitations to take meetings in London or anywhere else were forthcoming. Sometimes they walked on the promenade, or elsewhere if it was crowded on fine summer days; and sometimes he would stop and talk with boys in the neighbourhood. On their arrival in Hove in 1936 they had gone on occasions to the nearest Calvinistic congregation, Galeed Strict Baptist Chapel, Brighton, where the aged J. K. Popham ministered, and to which the two ladies from whom they rented their accommodation belonged. But as that church held to the same 'Gospel Standard' articles which had led to Pink's removal from the Belvoir Street Church in Sydney, membership was not an open option. Nor was he 'at home' in the Galeed services.[2] Aspects of Mr Popham's ministry appealed to him, but he felt a certain air of fatalism which chilled him. In a letter to Evelyn Green, full of spiritual things, Vera Pink allows herself to say: 'Sometimes I wish we were near enough to talk of these precious things in person and not have to limit ourselves to letters. We know no one here – I am sure it is for our good – with whom we can have heart to heart talks on the things of God.'[3]

On Sundays, the observance of which he regarded as a high privilege, Pink would give time to spiritual correspondence. 'It suggests an extraordinary picture of a

[1] Letter to Evelyn Green, June 25, 1939.
[2] Pink would have found the ministry of Benjamin A. Warburton at the Tabernacle, West Street, Brighton, much more congenial, but it was not until 1938 that Warburton began to serve that church.
[3] Oct. 30, 1939.

Sunday in those rooms in Hove,' writes Sinclair Ferguson, 'with the ladies of the house preparing for their services, and bells ringing from the towers of local churches, while this man, with his unusual ability to apply the Word of God, sits silently at a table writing to one or other of his many correspondents throughout the world, opening and explaining the mysteries of Christ.'[4]

Despite everything, Vera Pink did not doubt that they were guided of God. 'Though it has been trying for one who has been called to preach, and is gifted to preach, to have his mouth closed, yet we can see it is best,' she writes to Evelyn Green, 'so far more time is needed to write.'[5] She was, however, aware that her husband's almost unremitting work was unwise and saw it was responsible for the sleeplessness and the inability to relax at the end of the day from which he suffered.

In their travels around the world Vera had made a habit of collecting stamps for children and for friends, and now a comment she had heard concerning the late King George V gave her an idea: the king when over-tired would ask for his stamps! 'So I suggested Mr Pink start collecting some on his own,' she tells Mrs Green. 'At first he refused, but I finally got him to make a start. When he is over-tired and has a headache through constant brain work, an hour before he retires looking at the colours, seeing what the date and so on is on each stamp helps him in a remarkable way. He only has a few, for he has only been collecting a short time, but to see the effect it produces – without having to resort to drugs, etc. – I am sure it is good for him.' Thereafter Lowell and Evelyn Green were to send supplies to help the new hobby!

[4] The words are from a draft of Pink's life which Dr Ferguson prepared while editing *Letters of A. W. Pink*, 1978.
[5] Feb. 6, 1938.

In 1938 and 1939, when the world at large was debating Hitler and Mussolini, Munich and the fall of Czechoslovakia, Pink was absorbed with such themes as The Kingdom of Christ, A Tender Heart and The Doctrine of Election. It was not that he had no political awareness; his letters to Lowell Green reveal that he was abreast of contemporary news; but he saw it as the business of ministers to give 'the nourishing milk of God's Word' and not the 'water of current happenings in the world'. Nothing distressed him more than the prophecy purveyors who saw history as material for their latest ideas: 'Instead of being exercised as to how they may please God, young converts are now having their minds diverted to how soon the battle of Armageddon is likely to be waged . . . Instead of giving themselves to earnest prayer for the revival of vital holiness, they are doting upon a "revived Roman empire".'

After the commencement of the Second World War, writing on the verse, 'Meditate upon these things; give thyself wholly to them' (*1 Tim.* 4:15), he says:

> A few of our readers (very few, we trust!) may have been disappointed at finding in these pages no articles devoted to the making of comments on current events, no reference to the progress of the war, and no attempts to show the position of present national convulsions in the scheme of Divine prophecy. We have not done so because we have sought to profit from the folly of those who pursued such a course in the last great war, because we felt it was altogether outside of our province, because we could perceive no spiritual benefit for the soul, and especially because this word 'Give thyself wholly to them' (Divine things) positively precludes our doing so.[6]

[6] *Studies*, 1940, p. 285.

The War, however, was soon to come to Pink. After the 'phoney' alerts and needless preparations against gas attacks in 1939, air raids began in earnest in the summer of 1940 and Hove, being immediately opposite the French coast now occupied by German forces, was in the direct flight path of many enemy planes. At first, as a quiet coastal resort, the town had received thousands of children evacuated from the major cities, but when the whole of northern France had fallen it was evident that the south coast of England would be in the front line of any invasion and the children were hastily removed by the government. By August 1940 many of Hove's permanent residents had also fled to safer parts. Writing to Lowell Green during that month, Pink says:

> Our warning signal consists of a loud wailing siren for two minutes, when everybody forsakes the streets and takes cover – either in a public shelter (below ground), private one (steel, covered with earth, in one's garden), or just in the house. We have no private shelter. We reside in a small, frail modern building – brick and stucco – of two storeys; our part being upstairs – so there is only a thin roof between us and the enemy's bombs, *if* we left out of consideration the protecting hand of our God.[7]

After the beginning of July, when their neighbourhood had been machine-gunned from the air, the danger from night air-attacks was so real that the Pinks had slept on top of their bed with their clothes on. When an 'alarm' sounded at night they shared the draughty hall downstairs with their landladies, Vera Pink using a small camp-bed and Arthur a straw mattress. On the night of July 2 machine-gun bullets had missed their bedroom by about

[7] August 18, 1940.

four feet before burying themselves in the chimney stack of a house across the street. From their home in Atlanta, Georgia, the Greens urged the Pinks to come to live with them, an offer which, though much appreciated, they declined. 'For the present, at any rate, I feel definitely that we should remain here,' Pink replied. 'First, to maintain a testimony to the Lord, who is able to preserve us in the midst of great perils (*Psa.* 91:1–11). Second, it was clearly the Lord who brought us to our present abode . . . Third, even if we desired, Uncle Sam would not allow us to enter the U.S.A. I was born and educated in England and never took out my "naturalization papers" in the U.S.A., and though my dear wife was born and bred in Kentucky, when she married an "alien" she lost her American citizenship. We greatly value your prayers, but please do not be unduly concerned about us. We are in Good Hands. I am thankful to say we have been able to "Rest in the Lord", knowing that "Not a single shaft can hit, till the God of love sees fit".'

When Pink writes to the Greens again on September 15, matters were worsening. Since September 4 Hove had experienced twenty-eight air-raid warnings and bombs had fallen in the vicinity of their home. In one raid some fifty people were killed. It was certain that the lightly-built house in which they lived could resist neither a blast nor incendiary bombs. The next week, when a friend in the north-west of Scotland renewed a call that they should move there, they believed it was God's time for them to leave the place which they had enjoyed for four-and-a-half years.

After considerable difficulties involved in the need for hurried packing, including the slimming down of Pink's library (some of which went to the Greens for safe-keeping for the duration of the war), they left Hove on

September 24, 1940. This was to prove the last of their many journeys. The first stage was by train to London, but their ultimate destination was a great deal further. They had not yet reached it when Vera Pink wrote of their experiences to Evelyn Green from Wallace B. Nicolson's manse at Lochmaddy, North Uist, in the Outer Hebrides of Scotland, on October 14, 1940:

> Though we passed through some difficult and nerve-racking times, yet as I look back – as I did yesterday while spending the day in bed resting – I cannot help but be thankful for the experience, because I have learned, in a practical way, valuable lessons on God's keeping power, his quietening and calming mercy, causing the flesh to be still and the heart to wait as I realized we were in his hands. Lying on mattresses on the hall floor downstairs, we have more than once thanked our heavenly Father for the kind and loving friends he has given us. We knew you and many others were bearing us up in constant prayer. The contrast of our being able to lie calmly and wait, and the nervous racing back and forth of the poor people we lived with, was so marked that Mr Pink and I often said we would be the same but for the prayers of God's people.

Pink reports their long journey in the Annual Letter for 1940:

> It meant travelling across the city of London, and a bomb fell near the station where we were waiting for our train, but we were unharmed. It meant a five-hundred-miles journey to Glasgow, but we reached it safely, and had a week's rest with dear ones who devotedly ministered to our every need, so that we

> were much refreshed both spiritually and physically. Then another railway journey of a hundred-and-seventy-miles, and then a twelve-hours' sea trip, which was accomplished without any untoward event. A few days' fellowship in the home of another kind friend and his wife, and then a short sea trip and our 'haven' was safely reached. We are now situated on an island far removed from the scene of conflict, where we can quietly study and conduct the work of the magazine in peace, and what is still better, we are once more in a place where we can have fellowship with some of the choicest of God's people.

Their new home was in the small town and port of Stornoway, on the island of Lewis, in the north-west extremity of the British Isles, where, in comparative isolation, a Gaelic-speaking community was maintaining a Christian form of life and culture. On the upper floor of 27 Lewis Street they resided with Mr and Mrs MacIver who were also the owners of number 29. Their only further move before Pink's death, twelve years later, was to move to 29 Lewis Street!

Speaking of the last stage of their journey from North Uist to Stornoway and their four hours by boat, Pink wrote to the Colemans on November 4, 1940:

> The sea was very rough and I was quite sick and being so run-down was like a flat tyre for the next day or two, but Mrs Pink is a splendid sailor and did not suffer at all. I have lost a stone in weight and am the lightest I have been since a boy – 9 st. 6, which, strange to say, is exactly Vera's too – she has not lost a lb – in fact she is 10 lbs heavier than when she left Sydney. We have been in Stornoway almost two weeks and feel well repaid for all the strain in getting

> here. Everything is quiet and peaceful. Our landlady is a very godly woman, with whom Vera has happy fellowship.[8]

The situation in Stornoway was entirely new to Pink, for the culture, while imbued with Christian influence, differed from anything he had known before. Surprise has been expressed that he did not settle happily in either of the two Calvinistic congregations that existed in the town – Free Presbyterian and Free Church. But neither congregation held Sunday morning services in English, Gaelic being the predominant language. He reported to Blackburn: 'Many cannot speak English and those who do consider it almost a barbarous language in comparison with Gaelic.' It is true, these congregations provided afternoon services in English, and during their first three months the Pinks attended them. Unused to strangers in the midst these churches had no provision for the welcoming of visitors, and, worse than that, Pink thought the temperature of the services themselves decidedly chilly. How far that again was due to Highland culture, where congregations might be deeply moved and yet outwardly appear utterly unresponsive, we cannot say. A hundred years earlier C. H. Spurgeon had also noted how the first impression of a Highland service 'was hardly encouraging'.[9]

We do not know who was the preacher in the Free Presbyterian Church at this date, but in the Free Church was the Rev. Kenneth MacRae. Possibly Mr MacRae was not the preacher when Pink visited the Free Church. If he were, Pink was not put off sufficiently to desist from

[8] Despite Pink's care in reporting anything relating to the War the censor's scissors cut six gaps into the letter which eventually arrived in Sydney.
[9] C. H. Spurgeon, *Autobiography, Vol. 2, The Full Harvest* (Edinburgh: Banner of Truth, 1973), p. 253.

writing to him, asking if they could meet. A meeting never took place for MacRae was not available at the time Pink proposed, and in later years, as he told the present writer, he greatly regretted that he had not appreciated the kind of man that had been in their midst. The Stornoway minister was involved in immense labour in a large congregation, visiting for three hours daily, five days a week. With most others in Lewis, he had read nothing by Pink,[10] yet it is a startling fact that he never met the man who lived only a few hundred yards from his manse door. It was not without justification that Pink wrote on February 14, 1945, 'The Scots are ultra-clannish and the great majority look upon me as a foreigner.' The Pinks did not continue their afternoon church attendance.

From the side of the Stornoway people, who are eminently sociable, the whole lifestyle of the newcomer looked odd. While Pink guarded his time with military precision, they knew no such 'bondage' to the clock, and enjoyed nothing better than a long talk. They could not understand what the Englishman could possibly be doing, week after week, and with only brief appearances in public. Even their ministers, with, presumably, far more work to do than 'Mr Pink', followed no such habits.

More serious, for almost the entire population of Lewis, at this date, church attendance was a high duty. The Puritan literature which some of them read told them that 'God gives a curse to private means, when they are used

[10] Probably the first Pink title read by MacRae was *The Sovereignty of God* (London: Banner of Truth, 1961). This was ten years after the author's death. In a personal letter to me in 1963 MacRae said this about that title: 'There is no mincing of matters here, yet the author cannot for a moment be accused of any tendency to Hyper-Calvinism. Both in doctrine and practice the book is soundly scriptural and makes edifying and should be helpful reading. The chapter on prayer is especially good.' The present writer was responsible for the *Diary of Kenneth A. MacRae: A Record of Fifty Years in the Christian Ministry* (Edinburgh: Banner of Truth, 1980).

with neglect of the public'.[11] It is certainly true that if Pink, instead of only visiting the orthodox congregations, had joined fully with one of them, he would have found a better welcome. He knew human nature well enough to understand that fact, but at the age of fifty-three it was more than he could do to adjust himself to some of the traditional church customs that were required of all members. The exclusive psalmody, followed in both Free and Free Presbyterian churches, did not repel him, nor did the practice of infant baptism, although, for him, neither of these things was biblical.[12] But the ethos of the churches, established over many years, had elements that he could never embrace. To his friend John Blackburn (who was a Southern Presbyterian minister) he wrote on February 24,1941: 'Denominationalism has its value, but sectarianism is a curse. Very few want to have much to do with us now they have discovered we are not prepared to join *their* church. O for a broad heart as we tread the narrow way!'

It is no doubt true that by this time in his life Pink did not make new friends in the manner which had been true in his earlier years. He was still capable of warm relationships, but his experiences in the 1920s and 30s may have accustomed him to a measure of withdrawal from social contacts. While he was still at Hove, he had put the following note in *Studies*: 'We regret that it is not convenient for us to receive any visitors, and respectfully ask readers who may visit these parts to kindly refrain from calling upon us, but please note that we are always glad to hear from Christian friends.'[13] Some read this as an

[11] Richard Sibbes, *Works, Vol. 3* (reprint ed., Edinburgh: Banner of Truth, 1981), p. 511.
[12] 'Personally, I enjoy the singing of Psalms, but do not agree with those who decry "man-made hymns".' *Letters to a Young Pastor*, pp. 28–9.
[13] *Studies*, 1938, p. 383.

indication that he had no need of Christian fellowship. Pink saw it differently. He was tired of the repeated advice of well-wishing callers who urged him to be 'up and doing'! They simply did not understand the way he had been led. Further, because he had no telephone, such callers always came unannounced and generally failed to understand that although he resided in such a quiet way in his home he was as *busy* as any man in the country! As he wrote in 1951:

> Very few realize the vast amount of time and labour which is involved in composing a monthly magazine of this size and character. Every article has hours of hard work in it, for we do not just scribble down the first things that enter our mind. Moreover, writing sixty articles each year for several hundreds who have had at least half, and probably fifty who possess the whole, of the previous volumes, and to prepare fresh articles for them, would be impossible unless the Word of God were inexhaustible. Yet to do so requires increasing thought and study in order to bring out of the Divine treasury things new and old. To maintain the standard we have set before us keeps us busy the year round, night as well as day. We trust that friends will understand our position and realize that the hour we might spend in entertaining, or in writing them an extra letter, is used in preparing a message for over a thousand readers.
>
> We desire neither to be unsociable nor to live the life of a hermit, but we are 'not our own', and are resolved by grace to devote the whole of our energy in an endeavour to feed Christ's lambs and sheep. We highly value such a privilege and honour, and are jealous of anything which tends to encroach upon

> the same. We are deeply thankful that the Lord has brought us apart from 'the strife of tongues' and has so graciously provided us with a 'peaceable habitation' (*Isa*. 32: 18). Not that we urge anyone else to follow our example! Others must take their place in the firing-line and each soul should seek to perform his or her duty in whatever position providence has assigned them.[14]

Nonetheless, it is hard not to believe that Pink's detachment from social life had some relationship to the rejection he had encountered in earlier years. He did not brood over past hurt, but occasionally there are brief allusions to it. To Lowell Green he says in a letter of June 20, 1943:

> Numbers of those who loved to attend every meeting I held in their vicinity, even though it meant a hard journey of several miles, and who could not say and do enough to express their appreciation and gratitude, within a few years cooled off, and would not hear me today if I spoke in the house next door to them.

* * * * *

Once removed to Lewis, the Pinks saw no more of enemy action, but the conflict which had engulfed Europe and other parts of the world – although rarely mentioned in *Studies* – was very much upon their hearts. They were earnest in intercession for cities suffering from air-attack, particularly Glasgow – 'There are many of God's dear servants there, some of the choicest', Vera wrote to the Greens. A number of young men in the armed services slowly entered their correspondence. The war also

[14] *Studies*, 1951, pp. 285–6.

affected the magazine. The number of overseas countries which could receive copies was reduced to fifteen, and magazines to some of these destinations did not always arrive. All the copies of *Studies* for March and April 1941 sent to the United States were sunk in the Atlantic. 'If we are permitted to have the 1941 vol. bound,' the editor wrote to the Greens (who had missed their copies), 'it will contain all twelve issues, and perhaps by then Uncle Sam may see more plainly his duty to be willing to do his share in convoying stuff across the Atlantic!' As Vera Pink says in a next letter, their confidence was that 'a war can have no effect on his supplies'. Yet throughout these years the survival of the magazine remained a test of faith. In 1942 the printers (in Bath) were bombed, and paper became increasingly difficult to obtain. At length it became a problem to find any printer willing to bother with a monthly magazine having such a short run. In 1945 inflation had doubled the pre-war cost of the magazine.

Perhaps it was a side-effect of the War which induced George MacIver, their landlord (who ran a store in the town), to turn the good-sized plot of ground at the back of the house to productive use, giving the Pinks a part to plant for themselves. Pink helped MacIver with the initial digging and then the ladies took over, as Vera Pink reports to Evelyn Green: 'Mrs MacIver and I have planted out quite a large vegetable garden and the things look good. Mr Pink and I are indoors so much that we really enjoy going out two or three times a day weeding and cultivating, for it gets us out in the air and is a diversion from close concentration and writing.'

When the Second World War came to its end in 1945 Arthur and Vera Pink had no thoughts of moving. Despite its isolation they spoke of Stornoway as 'a delightful place'. On February 14 of that year, in response to a letter from Blackburn asking for news of his 'personal affairs', he replied:

> Really, there is practically nothing to write about. My whole time is devoted to study, preparing articles and writing letters – many to young Christians and preachers, offering suggestions. I go out from noon till one, six days a week, to 'shop' and get a little exercise, otherwise I never leave my study . . . We have no radio and spend only ten or fifteen minutes a day on secular literature. We have no visitors. Yet we are quite contented, rejoicing in the Lord, and I would not change places (if we could) with anyone on earth. The Lord is very gracious to us and has favoured us above many. He continues to give us just sufficient readers (but no more) to warrant our continuing to publish *Studies*. We have no financial worries: our tastes are almost spartan and living here is relatively cheap: abundance of fish but no fruit.

Within a few months of the above letter to Blackburn, a visitor was to arrive unexpectedly on their doorstep in Lewis Street. He was Harold J. Bradshaw whose extended correspondence with Pink we have referred to in the previous chapter. The two men lived at opposite ends of the British Isles and would never have met had Bradshaw not planned a holiday in the north of Scotland in 1945. What followed we give in Bradshaw's own words:

> I felt I would try to fulfil a great desire I had had to set eyes on and speak with this remarkable man of God. But after prolonged correspondence two years earlier with him, in which there was some disagreement, I felt he might say 'No' to a request to

see him personally. So I started off from Inverness by train, hoping I would at least have the pleasure of just seeing him and shaking hands with him. Arriving at Kyle of Lochalsh in the evening I stayed at a nearby guest-house for the night where they promised to call me very early and give me breakfast next morning in time to catch the boat for Portree in the Isle of Skye. On boarding the boat I was accosted by a gentleman who asked me if I would 'keep an eye' on his three children who were going to relatives for a holiday in Skye. I saw my charges safely off the boat at Portree where a relative was waiting for them, but remained aboard myself to go to the next port of call, Tarbert in the Isle of Harris. It was raining heavily when we reached Tarbert, and the coach for Stornoway was not due to leave for two hours. The journey which then began was through beautiful scenery across Harris and Lewis but with dismal conditions of drizzle and poor visibility which had cleared by the time we reached Stornoway – at about 7.20 p.m. I had no trouble in finding the Pinks' house, and wondered what sort of reception I would get as I knocked on the front door. It was Mrs Pink who answered. She was astonished to see me when I disclosed my identity, coming from so far away, and said she really did not know if Mr Pink would see me as he did not like visitors! Would I wait while she went upstairs to see? I hurriedly said that if Mr Pink did not feel he could talk with me just then, I would be satisfied if I could just shake hands with him and go at once. However, she immediately returned and asked me to come upstairs, and led me into their bed-sitting-room, crowded with furniture, with books and papers lying about. And there, in the middle of the smallish room, at a table sat the man I had come so far to see – in shirt sleeves, no parting in his greying hair which was brushed straight back over his head.

I was pleasantly welcomed, and sitting down in front of him, we at once fell to talking, Mrs Pink sitting by, listening mostly. He was obviously pleased to see me, and made me feel at ease. We kept off controversial subjects, specially those he had written to me about; but he told me something of his life: of his ministry in the U.S.A. and Australia, and of his coming to England and eventually, finding nowhere for the exercise of his ministry in the south of England, and greatly bothered by the bombings in the early 1940s, how he came to Stornoway in the far north so that he could continue working on his *Studies in the Scriptures.* He told me he went out for about one-and-a-half-hours each morning for exercise, and for his daily visit to the Library to have a look at the papers.

Mr and Mrs Pink were interested in my relation of my own family affairs and in my business affairs and how the Lord had appeared so wonderfully in providential matters; and then (this would be after about two-and-a-half hours talking) he suddenly said in a not-very-friendly voice, 'Now you have stayed your welcome!' I was asked if I would like a cup of cocoa before I left, and Mrs Pink left the room and brought in some sections of jam sponge with a hot drink for the three of us. I have never forgotten the way Mr Pink asked God's blessing on the food. He seemed, as he clasped his hands and bowed his head, to have a tremendous sense of the glory and majesty of the God he was approaching. The tone and

> deepest reverence of his voice made such an impression on me at the time that I have many times recalled it. I left and caught the midnight boat to the Kyle of Lochalsh.

Bradshaw was right in believing that Pink had enjoyed the evening, which concluded towards 10 p.m. He mentioned the visit soon after in a letter to the Colemans, and the same letter shows that there had been more than one visitor:

> One, raised a 'Gospel Standard' and whose family for several generations were such, but who latterly became dissatisfied with their deadness, and who, under God, has been helped by the *Studies* and many letters I have written him, called on us in July – having come all the way from Norwich, a very difficult and trying journey. He wrote us later to say, 'While memory lasts I shall never forget that evening.'
>
> Another, a lieutenant in the U.S. army, used his first leave to come all the way from Germany on purpose to spend five hours with us. I do not encourage these visits for I believe I can help them just as much by writing. Undisturbed quietness is essential for the best fruits of unremitting study, meditation, writing, though some friends in Scotland fail to see that and are inclined to consider us as being 'unsociable' etc. However, the Lord knows our hearts and motives.

* * * * *

By 1946 the ministry of *Studies* had been going on for a quarter of a century, with Pink himself writing almost seven thousand pages, and he lists the articles that had appeared to that date as series as follows:

> John's Gospel 72 articles, on Exodus 72, Hebrews 127, Sermon on the Mount 65; the Life of David 96, of Elijah 36, of Elisha 30. Doctrinal articles have been: on the Atonement 24, Justification 10, Sanctification 34, Election 24, Impotency of man 24, Perseverance of Saints, 26, Reconciliation 36. The Divine Covenants 50, the Antichrist 22, Union and Communion 25, Dispensationalism 18, the Law 21, the Sabbath 19, Faith 18, Assurance 14, Profiting from the Word 10.
>
> On the Attributes of God we wrote 24 articles, on the Glories of Christ 41, on the Person and work of the Spirit 65. On the Heart 10, Spiritual Growth 30, Prayer 20, and the Prayers of the Apostles (to date) 36.[15]

Before we conclude this chapter, a glimpse of correspondence sent to Pink at this period will give some conception of what the ministry of *Studies* meant to those who read it regularly. Once a year it was Pink's habit to include in the magazine about two pages of short extracts from letters he had received, under the heading 'Welcome Tidings'. Correspondents were normally designated only by their country of origin or sometimes by the branch of the armed services to which they belonged: their age, employments and denominations were clearly very varied. Due either to War-time duties or to the absence of sound preaching, many of those who wrote clearly looked upon the magazine as their chief source of spiritual help. A member of the Australian Forces writes: 'My work in the army is such that I am very much on my own, and consequently your magazines have been what one might call a little sanctuary.' 'I receive much spiritual help from

[15] *Studies*, 1946, p. 285.

your writings,' says a Canadian soldier, and another of the same nationality writes, 'Those of us who are isolated look forward to *Studies* as they contain food for our souls: we get not only doctrine, but reproof – something we are surely in need of, but I know of no other religious magazine which gives it.'

For a number of readers the ministry of *Studies* was a staple part of their lives and there was much concern and prayer when, early in the war, Pink expressed the fear that the magazine might not be able to continue. From North Dakota a reader writes in 1940: 'I cannot refrain from expressing my deep regret that there is any thought of your discontinuing the *Studies*. Where, oh where, are we to receive spiritual ministry? We do not get it from the pulpit any more. Good, sound, expository books are fast going out of print. I can only plead with you to continue on for the sake of the few . . .' From Australia, New Jersey and Scotland come the following respectively: 'I have been reading the *Studies* now for ten years, and I thank the Lord for them'; 'I am still enjoying *Studies* and do not know how I would get along without them'; 'Long may you both be spared to carry on with the publication of the *Studies*: they bring comfort to many a starved heart.'

The reading matter provided by the magazine fitted into the lives of readers in many different ways. One subscriber in Wales throughout the war years used to read them for a devotional hour in the morning before going out to work, from 4.30 to 5.30 a.m.! Some preferred the other end of the day. A munitions worker wrote: 'At the moment I am so busy on war work, fourteen and a half hours per day (Sunday excluded), that I find my brain and mind very tired at the end of the day. So a helpful spiritual ministry like yours is a tonic to my soul.' An American husband and wife wrote: 'Our evening worship is not complete unless we read an article, or at least part of one, with our Bible reading and prayer. We never forget to remember you both in our devotions.' Another couple say: 'I cannot but express how much your work has meant to my wife and me. I feel as though we were one in fellowship. We have grown to know and respect you highly, not only as an able expositor of God's Word, but as a friend. By that word "friend" we mean all it connotes. When the mail arrives bringing your *Studies* we feel as though you too had stepped through our door to pay us a visit.' To which sentiment Pink added, 'Many of our readers feel the same way.'

There was unanimity about the qualities which gave the magazine its chief appeal, as the following extracts indicate: 'Your *Studies* stir me up to make more diligent use of the means of grace and to seek more earnestly those things that belong to my peace.' 'Your articles make my own Scripture reading more serious and deeper.' 'I am writing to tell you what a tremendous blessing they have been to me both in their acute analysis of spiritual truth and their warm expression of devotion to our Lord Jesus.' 'There is a wholesome refreshment in reading them, and they are new when re-read.' 'I enjoy your *Studies* next to my Bible. As one gets older he wants something different from information for the mind: he wants something that touches the heart.' 'To me *Studies* is worth more than all the religious magazines I know of put together.' 'You give the entire glory to Him to whom it wholly belongs. You stimulate investigation, and "give the sense" (*Neh.* 8:8).'

That younger preachers were being helped in various ways is very clear. In a number of cases Pink not only helped them but redirected their studies. One 'young preacher' wrote, 'Your numerous quotations from the writings of the Puritans are making many conscious of the real value of their works.' And another said, 'Your written ministry has not only helped me in my preaching, but especially so in my personal life. How thankful I am that you have been led to deal with the practical side of the Scriptures. In no one else's works that I have ever read, am I so exercised and probed by the Word as by yours.'

Perhaps the extract most worthy of quotation here comes from the letter of a New Zealander in 1942: 'I have no doubt that these *Studies* will be helpful to people in many lands long after you have gone to your rest, though valued in these days by comparatively few.'

Pink did not receive such letters every week, but we can well understand why he says that these 'unsolicited testimonies' were cause for fervent thanksgiving and 'encourage us to plod along in the face of much which is disheartening'. The character of his readers is certainly part of the explanation for the long-term fruitfulness of his writing. God gave him the support of men and women of faith and of prayer.

14

'All Things Well'

By the time that the post-war years arrived it was as though the Pinks were prematurely old. In 1946, the year in which they completed twenty-five years of editing and publishing the magazine, Vera Pink, writing to Evelyn Green on November 15, notes, 'We were able to do without a small fire only one week this whole year', but adds: 'The sea air keeps our winters from being severe, so we feel it is an ideal place for an old couple.' Two years later, when he had reached the age of sixty-two, Pink wrote in 'Our Annual Letter':

> We have now entered upon what must be at least the beginning of 'the evening' of our life, for forty years have passed since the editor preached his first sermon . . . Since then, without any break, it has been our holy privilege, yet solemn responsibility, to sow the good seed, either orally or by the pen – the latter exclusively the last twelve years.

Such comments, far from being made as a reason for reducing their endeavours, occur in contexts which confirm their increasing commitment to the call which God has given them. 'It is not the revealed will of God that his people should spend their old age in idleness. He does not preserve them through all the dangers of youth and the trials of maturity that they should be mere cumberers of the ground.'

Most Christian leaders in their sixties have passed beyond years of trial and seen their work established. But it was not so with Pink. After a quarter-century of publishing the magazine, Vera Pink noted in 1946, 'As far as getting the magazines printed is concerned, this has been our most trying year.' A severe shortage of paper and an unenthusiastic printer were the main difficulties. Further, instead of any recovery from the low circulation to which the magazine had fallen by the beginning of the War, he feared that its ministry – 'which seeks to expose a worthless profession on the one hand, and to promote a closer walking with God on the other' – would 'meet with less and less acceptance. Nevertheless God's order to his servant remains unchanged: "Thou shalt speak *my words* unto them, whether they will hear, or whether they will forbear" (*Ezek.* 2:7). May the Lord enable us to do so unto the end!'[1]

The next year (1947), while there was no actual increase in the circulation of *Studies*, as we have already noted, Pink had become sure from evidence of its usefulness to preachers that God was enlarging its ministry 'mediately rather than directly'. 'Our prayer-helpers will rejoice to know that this magazine is now being taken by over one hundred preachers!'[2] As the work of *Studies* approached its conclusion it is clear that God blessed his servant with an increase of faith and he speaks more confidently of the future. Thus, commenting on the monument which Joshua erected in Gilgal as a memorial, he writes that it 'teaches us that we should take thought of and seek to

[1] *Studies*, 1946, pp. 1–8.
[2] *Studies*, 1947, p. 190. See above, p. 210.

make provision for the rising generation. That cairn of stones was erected with the express desire of evoking enquiry from those who should later behold it. God would have the wonders of his power and mercy preserved for posterity. There was to be a permanent witness of what God had wrought for his people. It was meant as a sure pledge that God would continue to show himself strong in Israel's behalf . . . Thus, we rejoice when readers of this magazine purchase the bound volumes with this design before them. At least one is now thankfully reading those volumes which his mother (now in heaven) purchased from us twenty years ago, when he was unconverted. We cherish the hope that the bound volumes will be read by many long after we are called home.'[3]

In 'Our Annual Letter' for 1948, while he notes that the smallness of the magazine's circulation 'is still our acutest problem', there is the same note of expectation in respect to the future. Writing on a favourite verse, 'In the morning sow thy seed, and in the evening withhold not thine hand . . .' (*Eccles.* 11: 6), he says: 'The figure of "sowing seed" is a very suggestive one, among other things implying the exercise of *faith*, for to outward sight, so far as immediate results are concerned, it seems to be love's labour lost. For the same reason, it is an act of *hope*, performed with the expectation of a future yield. So it should ever be with the servant of God.'

As far as its circulation was concerned it was in 1948 that the magazine quietly turned a corner. After taking into account necessary removals from the mailing list of the previous year Pink noted that the number of readers had increased by fifty. While 1949 was to record 'another slight increase', in 1950 he can speak of 'quite a marked

[3] *Studies*, 1947, p. 228.

improvement in our wee circulation.' In his 'Our Annual Letter' for 1951, which was to be the last full year of his editorship, he wrote, 'Our circulation, though still a very small one when compared with that of more popular religious magazines, *has increased fifty per cent*! Considering the nature of the articles that appear in these pages, that is surely the Lord's doing, and it is marvellous in our eyes.'[4]

In the course of a letter to Evelyn Green, written on July 17, 1951,Vera Pink says:

> We have been much encouraged over the way names have come in this year. There seems to be an unusually nice tone to many of the letters we receive from time to time. We feel it is most gracious of the Lord to give us to see the effect of his blessing upon the work we are seeking to do for him and his dear people scattered abroad.

But the Pinks' deepest cause for thankfulness, in the mature grace of their later years, lay in God himself. The agitation and occasional near-despair of some earlier years were gone. They were fully assured of the goodness of divine providence and could set their seal to the words,

> This will set my heart at rest,
> What my God appoints is best.

More clearly than ever, they saw that the life of faith is the only truly joyful life. 'The writer can testify', he writes at the age of sixty-two, 'that after forty years of Christian experience, in his travels around this earth, he has never

[4] *Studies*, 1951, p. 286. There was now also a financial surplus and Pink, never retaining gifts for the magazine for himself, distributed it to the Trinitarian Bible Society, the Scripture Gift Mission and the *Gospel Magazine*.

met with a single person who trusted God and found that his promises mocked him. At the close of his long life Joshua said unto Israel, "Ye know in all your hearts and in all your souls that not one thing hath failed of all the good things which the LORD your God spake concerning you: all are come to pass unto you" (*Josh.* 23:14).'[5]

The note of praise is now increasingly prominent in *Studies* as it was in Pink's own heart. 'Praising and adoring God is the noblest part of the saint's work on earth, as it will be his chief employ in heaven.' This spirit now also affected his hopes for the churches. God can replace 'the spirit of heaviness' with 'the garment of praise,' and he does this, he wrote in 1950, 'when the churches are granted a time of reviving after a season of deadness, such as obtained in the days of Whitefield and may yet in ours'.[6]

* * * * *

It is to be wished that we knew more of the human side of Pink's life in Stornoway. He did try to maintain the stamp collection which he had started at Hove and, while work in MacIver's garden had to be given up, his interest in nature endured and one of his pleasures was to send packets of flower seeds to his old friends the Pressels in Pennsylvania. He never owned or drove a car, and there is no record of their ever exploring the scenery of their island home. But he did enjoy walking, although it seems that, on account of frailty, Vera was no longer able to go with him as she had done at Hove. The speed of the wind was a subject of regular interest to him. 'I love a real strong breeze,' he tells Lowell Green in one letter, 'and regard the ocean at such times as a grand if awesome sight.' In the same letter he confesses that, when the wind

[5] *Studies*, 1948, p. 184.

[6] *Studies*, 1950, p. 239.

had recently registered 90 miles per hour, he had to 'buck' his usual outing!

The Pinks had been seven years in Stornoway before Vera, writing to Evelyn Green on February 6, 1948, gives the following description:

> You were asking me to tell you something of our little Isle. Well, it is one of the little places, but it is important in many ways. It is a great place for fishing and sometimes the harbour is quite full of fishing boats from Iceland, Shetland, Norway and lots of places. They put in here for shelter and bring with them loads of lovely fish. The climate is a very even one – not as cold as you would think, being so far north. The Gulf Stream lies near our West Coast and that is what keeps it so mild and protected. We get a little snow and ice, but it does not last long. Plenty of rain falls and lots of wind — sometimes so strong you feel like it is stripping your clothes off and yet scarcely any damage done. It is a very healthy place as you can expect from it being a rain-swept and wind-swept Isle.
>
> The people are religious. Stornoway has nine church buildings and it is little more than a large U.S.A. village. Mainly Presbyterian, only one Episcopal and one Brethren Hall. Of the seven they are divided into four, shall we say, branches and each one having no more to do with the other than Baptists and Methodists in the U.S. They preach and speak Gaelic, the native language: so we are foreigners, as we do not know a word of Gaelic. But we stay on, for we like the quiet and peace, and on our own we can carry on our work undisturbed.

In another letter Vera writes,

> As we do not visit the people here there is very little contact except through letters. The magazine keeps us both busy from day to day. I do get a good bit of reading done, for I feel I need it since I do not go to church. Just now am reading a book by Matthew Henry and it is very, very good.

The above should not be read as though they had no friends. We have already noted 'happy fellowship' with Mrs MacIver from whom they rented their accommodation. Among other friends who came to know Pink personally was James MacLean, who has provided the following memories:

> At first Pink worshipped in the Free Presbyterian Church in Stornoway, but after a time he felt that he could no longer associate with that denomination. However, he did have some intimate friends in the congregation, including the lady in whose house they resided.
>
> In the town of Stornoway he had a few close friends whom he met during his daily hour-long walk around the town and piers. Most of them he spoke with either at their places of business or on the streets, but hardly ever in a social setting. The conversation was always centred on the Scriptures and he often opened the discussion with a question such as, 'Have old things passed away? I'll come back to hear your answer tomorrow.' One friend of those days says: 'I can recall that he used to question me so closely on his *Studies* that I made a point of doing my homework before I met him!'
>
> Every morning – Monday to Saturday – he could be seen striding along the main street towards home, sometimes having bought groceries on the way, and

invariably carrying a parcel containing two herrings. Mrs Pink, during her husband's lifetime, shopped in a small store near their home, and rarely visited the shops in the town centre. Theirs was a home with no luxuries, where everything was used from turnip tops to apple peelings.

While Mr Pink was alive, Mrs Pink visited us only once, Mr Pink having made arrangements beforehand as to the time of her arrival and departure, and no afternoon tea was to be offered.

The practice of handshaking, so prevalent in Lewis, he did not appreciate.[7] On one occasion, on being greeted by a friend with the words, 'How are you keeping, Mr Pink?', the reply came, 'I'm not keeping, I'm being kept!'

He was a strong character – hard, austere and flint-like; yet on one occasion, on entering my shop, he broke down and wept as he handed me a letter to read. This letter had come from a missionary who at that time was recovering from leprosy. Many years before, in the U.S.A., he had been converted through a sermon preached by Mr Pink on the text, 'I thirst.' At that time Mr Pink and the man's brother had spent a whole night praying for his conversion, but this letter was the first indication he had had that this person had come to the Lord and also of his subsequent work for the Master. 'You are the dearest friend I have in this world,' the letter stated.

* * * * *

'Our Annual Letter' published in the December issue of 1951, when *Studies* had completed the third decade of

[7] This 'practice' in Lewis was not exactly what was normal elsewhere. Even long-time friends in Lewis, who had said goodnight to one another at bedtime, commonly shook hands again the next morning.

its history, began with comment on the words, 'He that glorieth, let him glory in the Lord' (*1 Cor.* 1:31). 'Everything', he concluded, 'must be traced back to God's sovereign goodness: to his special favour, his all-sufficient grace, his unceasing faithfulness, his longsuffering to usward. Even when our duty has been performed, we are but "unprofitable servants" (*Luke* 17:10)!' Through the grace of God, he observed that he had been enabled to compose no less than two thousand different articles, averaging four pages each. 'Those bare figures can convey only a faint idea of the immense amount of toil involved in their preparation, or the strain on our devoted wife as she has typed out the same amid her domestic duties. Truly we serve a great God, and he is greatly to be praised, for during the whole of these thirty years the editor has not had to spend a single day in bed for over twenty years past. We have looked definitely to the Lord for the needed health and strength, and he has never failed us.'

But there were signs that his constitution, which was never robust, was failing. Vera noticed an increasing loss of weight – a fact which seemed to become more pronounced as soon as he reached his sixty-sixth birthday on April 1, 1952. The enlarged circle of his readers was now bringing more correspondence and for the first time its demands were becoming too much for him. A last letter to Lowell Green on May 8, 1952, began, 'Greetings in Christ, the believer's All in all for time and eternity', and concluded, 'I am feeling the infirmities of old age, which compels me to considerably curtail my correspondence.'

His thin figure was still to be seen about the streets of Stornoway but James MacLean noticed with apprehension that on coming into his shop he would now need to take a seat and rest before moving on. His illness, which was a form of anaemia, 'was a painful one', MacLean writes, 'but almost until the end he refused to take any drug which might dull his mind and hinder him from completing his work.' The editor pressed on with the various series which were currently occupying the pages of the magazine. Just as Calvin, in the last months of his life, was occupied with the exposition of Joshua, so was Pink. He had finished chapter 21 by the beginning of July. In his parallel series on 1 John the last article before he had to lay down his pen was on chapter 3:1, 'Behold, what manner of love the Father hath bestowed upon us,' and was entitled 'Amazing Grace'.

Many years earlier, at the end of his 'Life of David', he had written, 'David made all the preparations for his departure with unruffled composure because he knew that his death did not end all.' Pink now did the same. 'He had already settled all his affairs,' writes James MacLean, 'and had instructed Mrs Pink concerning the funeral and those who were to be present.' On his last walk outdoors (about June 15th) he bought an Air Mail letter, telling Vera that it was for her to use to send the news to Elsie and Stan Pressel 'when I go away'. On July 15, 1952, he entered into the full joy of the words which he had long delighted to quote:

> He and I in one bright glory
>   Endless bliss shall share;
> Mine, to be for ever with him;
>   His, that I am there.

The funeral of Arthur Pink appears to have taken place on July 17. 'It was to be a simple affair,' writes James MacLean, 'not an expensive coffin nor a cheap one. In accordance with Pink's request, based on Acts 8:2 ('and devout men carried Stephen to his burial'), eight of his friends laid his remains to rest in Sandwick Burial Ground, just outside the town. It was another illustration of the pervasiveness of Scripture teaching and example in his life. On our return to Lewis Street we sang Psalm 23 to the tune Coleshill, followed by a short reading and a prayer. The owner of the house, Mrs Pink, my wife and two or three other ladies were also present at this short worship, and afterwards we had tea prepared by Mrs MacIver their landlady.'

As he was many months ahead in his preparation of material for the magazine there was no question of its immediate termination, and thus, in the September issue, Vera broke the news of 'The Late Editor's Last Days':

> Several months before the end I saw he was failing and it worried me very much. Each time I made a reference to it he would always say, 'It's old age, my dear. Thank the Lord it is so. I am thankful I am so near the end, and not just beginning life. I am heartily sorry for the young men of today who are just starting out. It will be terribly hard for those who are conscientious. The times are so dark and will get much darker for them, but the Lord will keep his own.' Many times he appeared so weary and exhausted as he was losing his energy, that I would press him to rest so that he would be better able to do his work. To which he would ever reply, 'We must work while it is day. The night cometh when no man can work. I desire to be found at my post when the call comes.' He would not stop work except for the short intervals he was accustomed to go out each morning, which he continued until three weeks before his death.
>
> He never ceased to praise the Lord for bringing us to the Island of Lewis, and for placing us in the home

in which it has been our happy privilege to reside for twelve years. He felt it was a mark of distinguishing favour that we should be with those who love and honour the Sabbath as we, too, have always done. He loved the Sabbath. It was a sacred and holy day to him, and he loved those who had the same reverence for it. In the peace and quietness here in Lewis he pursued and enjoyed his studies away from the maddening crowds of the cities. More than once he told me that he had no desire whatever to be anywhere else, and never expected to leave till the Lord took him to glory.

One night in May he had a seizure which lasted several minutes. After it passed he said, 'I shall soon be home in glory, I cannot go soon enough. "Bless the Lord, O my soul and all that is within me, bless his holy name." I am so happy, I feel like singing through that psalm.' He observed I was weeping and asked, 'My dear, why do you weep? You should be rejoicing that I shall soon be home.' I told him I was weeping for myself at being left behind. I knew it was good for him, but I dreaded the separation. He gently said, 'The Lord has been so wondrously good to us all these years and brought us safely through until now. He will not desert you in your hour of greatest need. Only trust him with all your heart. He will not fail you.'

After that night he was making plans and getting all things in order for his departure as if he was going on a long journey, and he would be telling me what to do. Among other things, he wanted me to publish in *Studies in the Scriptures* all the material he was leaving with me before closing down the magazine. As he saw his time was short he applied himself more strenuously to composing articles so as to leave as much as he could and to complete as nearly as possible some series he was working on. 'The Lord is good and doeth good', was daily on his lips. He rested as few have done on the sovereignty of God and seemed to be completely resigned to his will for him to such an extent that he said many times, 'Let him do with me as seemeth him good.' Once when we were speaking of the past and present dealings of the Lord in our pilgrimage journey he said, '"He hath done all things well." *All* things, my dear, not *some* things!'

On the Wednesday morning before his death the following Tuesday morning, while still in bed and I about my duties in the room, he began to speak: 'The darkness is past and the true light now shineth. Yes, it shineth more and more unto the perfect day.' Lifting his hand toward the ceiling he said, 'All is glory before me. I cannot say with Mr Rutherford, "Dark, dark hath been the midnight," for my experience has been so different from his. But I can say, "Day-spring is at hand, and glory, glory dwelleth in Immanuel's land." I am leaving the darkness behind to you who have still to finish your pilgrimage.' I said to him, 'That is all very beautiful for you,' to which he quickly replied, 'And it can be for you too if you will cast aside your doubts and fears and put your whole trust in him.' He sat in his chair most of the day dictating an article with great effort, for he was so desirous to finish it, but he said he felt he had left it too late to get it done. We lacked only four sentences when he stopped, put down his paper and glasses, and said, 'Put me to bed.' I shall never know how I got him to bed, but by the Lord's mercy

I did, supporting him for over an hour till he got relief and I could lay him down. After a few minutes' rest he said, 'Get your glasses and paper and pencil and come to the bed, and I will give you the last four sentences and you can type them when I am gone.' I took them down and when I had completed writing he said, 'My work is finished. My race is run. I am ready to go. I cannot go soon enough.' He never rose after that, but still remained happy and praising the Lord.

The 23rd Psalm was almost constantly on his lips, spoken both to myself and the Christian nurse, and many wonderful things he said to us, among them being, 'Not one good thing hath failed of all the good things he hath promised.' Another time we heard him say, 'He hath not dealt with me after my sins, nor rewarded me according to my iniquities.' Again, 'Wearisome nights are appointed me, but I have nothing to say, for the Lord has so wondrously spared me bodily pain all my life through till now.' Once we heard him ask the nurse if she knew those lovely lines, 'The King of love my Shepherd is, whose goodness faileth never; I nothing lack if I am his, and he is mine for ever.'

Once in great agony he said, 'O taste and see that the Lord is good, blessed is the man that trusteth in him.' A dear friend came in to relieve the nurse and be with me and we beheld his face radiant many times, and we felt sure he was having visions of glory. Then we heard him say, which were his last words, 'The Scriptures explain themselves,' showing us what his mind was on. So having finished his course, and completed his work, he has gone to be with him whom he loved and served for so many years. 'O magnify the Lord with me, and let us exalt his name together.'[8]

* * * * *

Studies in the Scriptures are not only Arthur W. Pink's memorial; the very title suggests what grace had made the supreme characteristic of his life. He studied the Word of God and studied it for its own purpose – to promote the glory of God and holiness of life. In a man-centred age, when the wisdom of men was exalted and divine revelation cast down, Pink proclaimed the Word of God. As he read it, prayed over it, taught it, he found it to be only broader, deeper and fuller. 'What a laborious and thankless task would it be,' he says, 'to read through the ablest human productions twenty times!' But he found that the attractions of Scripture only increased with the years. In all the problems which he encountered with the magazine a fresh supply for its contents never troubled him: 'With the inexhaustible Word of God to turn to, with endless variety of spiritual riches available, with the Holy Spirit to instruct him, there is no need to explain why he should never "run out" of material.'

More than this, his life exemplified how far the Word of God can and ought to rule the life of a Christian. While conscious of how greatly he fell short, the standard at which he ever aimed as a servant of Christ was the rule of Scripture. In a brief comment upon her husband Vera Pink gave the chief characteristic of his life: 'Two verses of Scripture have always guided Mr Pink in his work, viz. – "Whatsoever thy hand findeth to do, do it with thy might" (*Eccles.* 9: 10); "Cursed be he that doeth the work of the LORD deceitfully" (negligently) (*Jer.* 48:10). It is a solemn thing to undertake to do the work of the Lord.'

[8] *Studies*, Sept. 1952.

The life of A. W. Pink reminds us that 'Mr Valiant-for-Truth' of *The Pilgrim's Progress* does not belong to the seventeenth century alone. Not that he resembled Bunyan's character in every respect, for of the latter it was said, 'When the day that he must go hence was come, many accompanied him to the river side.' Pink passed from his pilgrimage as unnoticed as much of his life had been. But in heart commitment to the Word of God he was indeed like the character of whom he had first heard his father read to them on those peaceful Sundays of childhood in Nottingham:

> Then said Great-heart to Mr Valiant-for-truth, Thou hast worthily behaved thyself. Let me see thy sword. So he shewed it him. When he had taken it in his hand, and looked thereon a while, he said, Ha! it is a right Jerusalem blade.
>
> *Valiant.* It is so. Let a man have one of these blades, with a hand to wield it and skill to use it, and he may venture upon an angel with it. He need not fear its holding, if he can but tell how to lay on. Its edges will never blunt. It will cut flesh and bones, and soul and spirit, and all.
>
> *Great-heart.* But you fought a great while; I wonder you was not weary.
>
> *Valiant.* I fought till my sword did cleave to my hand; and when they were joined together, as if a sword grew out of my arm, and when the blood ran through my fingers, then I fought with most courage.

The Pressels were the first in the States to hear news of Pink's death and they soon circulated word of it to others. Vera Pink was herself temporarily under the care of a doctor. In a first letter to Lowell and Evelyn Green on August 27, 1952, she wrote:

> Your kind Air Mail letter came safely to hand for which I thank you. I can only say 'He hath done all things well' . . . My dear one is now in glory where he so longed to be with Christ. Oh what bliss is his, and how empty and cold all is down here without him. I am feeling somewhat stronger in my body now, and able to get out some. The doctor urged me to and also the friends. Yes, the Lord has given me many kind hearts to help me and truly I have been overwhelmed with acts of love and kindness.

The difficult work before Mrs Pink was the termination of *Studies*. There was no question of an immediate end, for Pink had been so far ahead with his articles that there were enough ready in the Joshua and 1 John series to run in successive months to April 1953, but it was a question whether enough readers would renew their subscriptions to make a further year possible in view of the editor's death. She found it very hard, after thirty years, to think of the magazine's 'coming to an end and closing down'. Her hope was, as she wrote to Evelyn Green, 'that it may end triumphantly, as the late editor finished his course', and at length decided to go ahead for a final year, with reprints of articles from earlier years supplementing the unused manuscripts. In mid-December 1952, while working on the magazine, she suffered a stroke affecting her right side from head to foot:

> It came on insensibly while sitting in my chair after typing the last article – 'The Manna a Type of Christ'. Upon reading it through I put the sheets on the table and attempted to rise, but found I was helpless. Many things played their part in bringing this about, no doubt, but to me it was most wonderful that the Lord in his goodness put me to bed to rest, for rest I could

> not. He took everything from me – grief, worry and corruptions – into his loving hands, leaving me without care in peace and quietness to rest. I trust I can say to God's glory that before this trouble came upon me he had for some days, particularly that night while reading through the above-mentioned article, graciously filled me with his holy presence, which was a great strength and comfort during those critical days which followed. 'His way is in the deep, and his footsteps are not known' – to carnal sense, but faith perceives them as it hears his voice, 'Follow thou me.' Oh, the wonder that he never requires his people to go along a path that he has not first trodden!
>
> Oh, how He helped me! Alone in the world, a widow, broken-hearted, helpless and near death, he gave me the kindest of kind hearts and hands to minister unto me night and day and take over the care of *Studies in the Scriptures* during those weeks. Royalty could not have had more untiring and faithful attendance from physician, nurse and friends than I was privileged to receive.

To a friend in the United States Vera Pink wrote, January 10, 1953:

> The Lord has been wonderfully kind to me and has gone through the waters of bereavement with me upholding and supporting in a way which has caused me to marvel and in my illness he has raised up the kindest of friends to minister to myself and also to the magazine work.

Vera Pink recovered in good measure from this stroke, although she was unable to type again, and once more, as in the far-off autumn of 1923, Elsie Pressel came to her aid from the other side of the Atlantic, typing articles from former issues of the magazine which were needed to complete the numbers for 1953.

The last volume of *Studies*, as all those before it, was to be full of Scripture. Almost hidden amidst it were a page and a half in the February issue giving 'Extracts From Letters', from which we must briefly quote:

> It is the loss of a friend whom having not seen we loved . . . his work will live long in those whose appetites for the deep spiritual things of the Word were made keener and whose witness will continue to glorify our Lord whom he loved.

> We have lost a father in Israel. We have and will have great cause for thankfulness to the Head of the Church for his gift, and we bow to his sovereign will in taking back his gift . . . We cannot help but mourn with many who have been blessed of the Lord through his ministry.

> How many, many times I have marvelled at his amazing knowledge of the Bible, and how by comparing Scripture with Scripture he showed so clearly what was Truth.

> We feel there is not anyone with such spiritual insight into the Word as our brother Pink, and none which has laboured so untiringly to bring the message needed for the times as he did. This has left in our hearts an aching void which will be hard to fill after such a long period of sweet fellowship around God's Word.

> The death of your beloved husband is a great loss to the whole Christian Church – but the Lord knows

> best when His servant's work is done in this earthly sphere. We feel like orphans, with our spiritual father and best earthly friend taken from us.
>
> I cannot express to you what a help Mr Pink was to me. I have *Studies in the Scriptures* in bound volumes and read them now in preference to anything else I have or get.
>
> The privilege and talent and light given him through his studies of the Bible, which he lived only to pass on to others, were a great blessing. He found the true light. Being dead to his work, his writings will live on. Praise the Lord!

The sense of loss among the circle who looked to *Studies* for spiritual food was clearly profound. Elsie Pressel expressed the feelings of so many when she wrote to Lowell and Evelyn Green, 'Over the years we had had some twenty Christian periodicals but none can compare with Pink's expositions.'

On August 1, 1953, Vera wrote to the Greens:

> The work – my part of it – is done in connection with the magazine. So by his great mercy I can rest. The days have been lonely and sad but God has been with me and helped me and my dear kind friends have been so thoughtful of me these days – even the dear nurse has been several times and all were a help. I can never praise him as I desire for his great care for me. What wonders he has wrought for me! Not one word has failed of all he promised. When he wounds he has promised to heal, and enable to endure what he in his love sends for our good.

The end of the year brought the magazine to a conclusion with the last Annual Letter coming from Mrs Pink's pen:

> This is the final issue of *Studies in the Scriptures.* It began in 1922 as a 'labour of love' for the poor and needy seeking water and finding none. Well do we remember the beginning and progress as year after year the little messenger found its way to the ends of the earth, taking words of salvation and comfort in its pages. Being frail, I never thought it would fall to me to finish the work so dear to each of us; but the Most High has shown that his thoughts are not as ours, by causing to come to pass what I never expected. Many were the difficulties and trials through which *Studies in the Scriptures* came, but the rough places have been made plain, and the crooked straight, as each has been faced, so that it has been a pleasant task, as one would expect a 'labour of love' to be; all praise to him who doeth all things well! In looking back over the past, nothing stands out more wonderfully than to recall how, in all our journeys around the world, not an issue failed to be printed and posted. What can one say of such things, but, 'It is the LORD's doing, and it is marvellous in our eyes'? 'In all thy ways acknowledge him' has been in mind as I have attempted to write this piece. I am not qualified for such a task, but since it came upon me I have sought to carry out my dear late husband's wishes to the best of my ability, fully realizing that my best is far, far below the standard. Looking to Him alone for enablement to perform what I felt I could not do in bringing the magazine to a close, he has not failed me, but has done wonders greater than

could have been imagined. But then, is he not a great God, and doeth great things? Should I not expect him to do great things? I feel we should all be profoundly thankful to the Lord that *Studies in the Scriptures* continued so many years.

'In all thy ways acknowledge him' – in the hard equally as in the pleasant. To bow submissively to his most holy will, resting in the thought, 'Let him do what seemeth him good.' Unreservedly to resign all into his loving hand – 'The LORD gave, and the LORD hath taken away. Blessed be the name of the LORD.' So having cast his bread upon the waters and finished his course on earth in glory, my dear husband, the late editor, shall find it again. For me I seek to follow on in weakness in this vale of tears unto that better land where nothing that defileth or maketh a lie cometh. What a prospect! Done with sin for ever! I commend you, my dear friends, whom we sought to serve so long, unto the care of him who has promised, 'Lo, I am with you alway, even unto the end of the world.' Remember me at the throne of grace. By wondrous mercy, Vera E. Pink.

Vera Pink survived her husband by ten years. Of that period James MacLean has written:

As Mrs Pink now had more time to spare, she mixed more freely, visited a number of friends, and had lots of callers herself. One of her closest friends at this time was the Rev. K. A. MacRae. She was an elegant and gracious lady with a radiant expression and a loving and lively interest in people. During this period her income came from interest on money they had inherited somewhere in England.

The room in Lewis Street remained her home where

she was 'mothered' by Mrs MacIver, until it was necessary, after a second cerebral haemorrhage to remove her to hospital.

One could wish that the wide circle of true Christian friends had been found earlier in their time in Lewis. When the present writer visited Stornoway in 1958 the radiant testimony of Vera Pink was common knowledge among the Christians of different denominations. The Free Presbyterian minister, the Rev. James Tallach, who arrived in Stornoway just a few months after Pink's death,[9] was as much pleased to visit her as was Kenneth MacRae and it was at Mr Tallach's suggestion that we made our way to the hospital where it was a spiritual blessing to be in her bright presence. Four more quiet and peaceful years she was to spend in the Stornoway hospital until she also 'went home' on July 17, 1962, at the age of sixty-nine.

In the truest sense the ministry for which the Pinks had lived did not 'close down'. They had sought to serve their own generation by the will of God and it was also God's will that the work which had honoured him should remain fruitful for generations to come.

[9] See Fraser Tallach, *Fraser: Not a Private Matter* (Edinburgh: Banner of Truth, 2003).

15

Pink as a Teacher

A characteristic feature of A. W. Pink as a writer is that he almost invariably induces a response of one kind or another in his readers. Most of those who give any degree of attention to his writings are compelled to take sides; few are likely to put him aside with indifference and unconcern. The reasons for this are at least threefold.

Firstly, Arthur Pink did not write out of a theoretical interest in his subject, and never did he view literary work as a means of livelihood. Writing was a *ministry* and he believed he had to exercise it with the authority which belongs to the office of teaching the Word of God. Once assured that his case was scriptural, his business was to 'speak, and exhort, and rebuke with all authority' (*Titus* 2:15). He meant to speak plainly and directly, and deplored any presentation of the truth which might be construed as asking men 'to do Christ and his cause a favour'.

Secondly, the clarity of Pink's method of teaching was conducive to bringing people to definite conclusions. Believing as he did in the necessity of the Spirit's work in illumination he was, none the less, insistent that the presentation of the truth ought to conform to such rules as are necessary for effective instruction.

Thirdly, Pink's propensity to drive people either to commitment or rejection is related to his conviction that his work was not finished once he had communicated a right understanding of the meaning of Scripture. Equally important is 'the use' to which that understanding is put: principles have to be understood in order to 'the regulating of our daily walk', in order to convict and stimulate, to comfort and strengthen. Right teaching *must* include application:

> To spare no pains in endeavouring to arrive at the meaning of God's Word, that he may give a sound interpretation of the same, is only a part of the duty resting upon the minister of the gospel. Another part of his work, equally necessary and exacting, is for him to make practical application unto his hearers of each passage he takes up, to point out the various lessons it inculcates, to accommodate it unto the present condition and circumstances of those to whom he ministers. Only so will he emulate the example left him by the Divine Teacher of the church: only so will he pursue the same course that was followed by his apostles: only so will he be of greatest service unto his needy, tried and often sorely perplexed people.[1]

While these three things go some way to explain the very different reactions which occur among those who read A. W. Pink, they do not adequately explain the extent of the criticism to which his reputation as a teacher is sometimes subjected. It is not, after all, only non-Christians who respond adversely to his ministry. There are those, sympathetic to his commitment to Scripture, who may take up one of his books and put it down without wanting to read another. Some knowledgeable

[1] *Gleanings in Joshua*, 1964, p. 310.

Christians seem to have so many reservations about his value as a teacher that they would not care to recommend his books at all. How is this fact to be evaluated?

It must at once be said that there are grounds for criticism, the chief of which is the unequal value of his literary output. In assessing any Pink title it is essential to know *when* it was written. Perhaps not a great deal of what he wrote before the 1930s is of abiding importance and most of his earlier writings do not represent the outlook to which he came in his maturity. Pink himself frequently referred to this matter in writing to friends. Speaking of his book *The Redeemer's Return* (1918), he wrote in 1934, 'More light has been given me on some things, and on others I would be less dogmatic. It is the tendency of youth to be speculative.' In 1938 he put it more strongly, 'My book on *The Redeemer's Return* was written 20 years ago, and as I stated in the Foreword I merely echoed what others had said; in those days (as a 'child') I believed all my elders told me.'[2] Similarly, writing to R. Harbach, December 20, 1943, he said bluntly, 'I would not recommend my book on *The Antichrist* which was written twenty years ago.'[3] In *Studies in the Scriptures* he writes in 1947:

> 'If any man think that he knoweth any thing, he knoweth nothing yet as he ought to know' (*1 Cor.* 8:2). To the very end of his earthly pilgrimage the best instructed Christian has reason to pray, 'That which I see not teach thou me' (*Job* 34:32). Even the theologian and the Bible-teacher is but a learner and, like all his companions in the school of Christ, acquires his knowledge of the truth gradually – 'here

[2] To Lowell Green, Jan. 17, 1938.
[3] *Letters to a Young Pastor*, p. 6.

a little, there a little' (*Isa.* 28:10). He too advances slowly, as one great theme after another is studied by him and opened up to him, requiring him to revise or correct his earlier apprehensions and adjust his views on other portions of the truth, as fuller light is granted him on any one branch thereof . . . Like the rising of the sun, spiritual light breaks forth upon both preacher and hearer by degrees. The men who have been the most used of God in the feeding and building up of his people were not thoroughly furnished for their work at the outset of their careers, but only by dint of prolonged study did they make progress in their own apprehension of the truth. Each preacher who experiences any real spiritual growth views most of his first sermons as those of a novice, and he will have cause for shame as he perceives their crudity and the relative ignorance which marked the production of them; for even if he was mercifully preserved from serious error, yet he will probably find many mistakes in his expositions of Scripture, various inconsistences and contradictions in the views he then held, and which a fuller knowledge and maturer experience now enables him to rectify.

What has just been pointed out explains why the later writings of a servant of God are preferable to his earlier ones, and why in a second or third edition of his works he finds it necessary to correct or at least modify some of his original statements. Certainly this writer is no exception. Were he to re-write today some of his earlier articles and pieces, he would make a number of changes in them. Though it may be humiliating unto pride to have to make corrections, yet it is also ground for thanksgiving unto God for the fuller light vouchsafed which enables him to do so.[4]

In his lifetime Pink was not faced with any demand for the reprinting of his earlier writings. Had that demand occurred it is certain he would not have allowed republishing without revision and, in the case of some titles, he would not have authorized reprints at all. Thus he made it clear to Vera before his death that *Studies in the Scriptures* were not to be reprinted in their entirety. His wishes have not, however, been honoured, owing to the fact that no executors have exercised a copyright control over his literary work. Pink never dreamed of the possibility that within twenty years after his death publishers would want practically *anything* he had written. The unhappy result was that a great deal of Pink came into print, taken from all parts of *Studies* and, almost invariably, with no indication to the reader of the period of the author's ministry to which a particular title belongs.

This irresponsibility on the part of some publishers has certainly contributed to the conflicting assessments which are currently made of Pink's value as a teacher. Those who would judge him should be sure that they are judging the best. His *Life and Times of Joshua*, for example, written for *Studies* between 1946 and 1952, is in a different class from his *Gleanings in Genesis* and *Gleanings in Exodus*, volumes first published in the 1920s. His articles on 'Dispensationalism', published in *Studies* in 1933–34, contain views directly contrary to earlier published material. The same is true of his book *The Sovereignty of God* which will be discussed in the next chapter.

[4] *Studies*, 1947. p. 19.

To aid readers in making a classification of Pink's writings we are supplying an Appendix giving the dates of all his major writings.

* * * * *

The reason for the uneven value of Pink's writings will be apparent to the reader. Leaders in the churches have often been men who entered the Christian ministry after a sound theological training, and by this means they were established in lifelong convictions at an early stage of life. The advantages of such training, where it is reliable, are great. Pink, on the other hand, had to struggle to find his own way. At no point did he sit under able men who might have led him to the beliefs that became his own. Instead, he had to learn and unlearn, being self-taught both from Scripture and from authors that he was slowly to discover and to evaluate. Such self-training, as Dr Belcher has wisely pointed out in his biography of Pink, has real dangers, and these are apparent in most of Pink's early writings.[5] But if Pink were conscious of the deficiency, he was also convinced that theological education, in the early twentieth century, was commonly a very poor preparation for faithful ministry. He was not wrong. There were few seminaries anywhere in the world at that time that pointed their students to the value of Reformed and Puritan authors, and who were outspoken on the contemporary spiritual needs of the churches. Had Pink gone through the mould of formal training it is probable that he would never have become a 'trail blazer' for the recovery of historic Christianity. As Belcher concludes, 'This writer is satisfied to recognize that God has a variety of works for his servants to fulfil, and that

[5] Belcher, *Arthur W. Pink*, chapter 4, 'Early Ministry and Study'.

He best knows the preparation that is needed, whether it be the disciplined self-study of a Pink, or whether it be the training under gifted and well qualified Bible-believing men.'[6]

Pink's early mistakes were not without their benefit. It led to a general change in his writings, and a concern to guide younger men away from the pitfalls he had known. His abiding concern became to direct attention to primary truths, not secondary or more theoretical ones. Thus, he did not exchange dispensational and premillennial teaching for an exposition of other opinions; he rather put such issues to one side. There were greater priorities. Some ideas merely prompt talk and theorizing; it is the fundamental truths which are fruitful in spiritual power, prayer and communion with God. 'The faith of God's elect' has to be bound together with 'the acknowledging of the truth which is after godliness' (*Titus* 1:1). He writes in 1947:

> How little is now heard, even in the centres of orthodoxy, of 'walking worthily of the Lord unto all pleasing'! Will not the Lord yet say unto many an unfaithful occupant of the modern pulpit (and editors of religious magazines), 'You have not spoken of me the thing that is right'? You did not make known the high requirements of my holiness, nor teach my people those things which would most 'adorn the doctrine' they profess. You have been tithing mint and anise and cummin, but omitting 'the weightier matters'; concerned with politics, wrangling over forms of church government, speculating about prophecy, but failing to insist on practical godliness.

[6] Ibid., p. 33.

> No wonder the 'churches' – Calvinistic, equally with others – are in such a low state of spirituality.[7]

Through the last twenty years or so of the thirty years in which he published *Studies*, he kept the big things before his readers. His endeavour was not to align his readers with any denominational emphasis or any theological system, but to teach what it means to be a Christian and how to live upon the great things of the Word of God.

With this change went a deepening concern that the magazine should not only expound truth but do so in scriptural balance and in due proportions. There is ever-recurring emphasis on the need to avoid partiality and lopsidedness in understanding the Scriptures. He insists upon divine sovereignty *and* human responsibility; the law *and* the gospel; free justification by Christ's righteousness *and* personal, subjective holiness; God's infallible preservation of his people *and* the necessity of their keeping themselves; the direct dealings of God with Christians *and* the necessity of the means of grace. To anyone who questions whether these things can be harmonized he is content to respond: 'God's Word is to be received with childlike simplicity, and not quibbled over: received as a whole, and not merely those parts which appeal to us or accord with our own views.'[8] His Calvinistic friends are not spared:

> We may think it vastly more honouring to God to write or say ten times as much about His sovereignty

[7] *Studies*, 1947, pp. 53–4. Practically the whole of this quotation is omitted from the Moody Press reprint of the series of articles from which the words come: cf. *Gleanings from Paul, Studies in the Prayers of the Apostle*, 1967, p. 237. Yet this volume gives no warning that editorial revision had taken place.

[8] *Studies*, 1947, p. 267. 'Error', he says elsewhere, 'is truth perverted, truth distorted, truth out of proportion' (*Studies*, 1932, p. 54).

as we do upon man's responsibility but the business of God's servant is not only to contend earnestly for the Faith but to set forth the truth in its scriptural proportions. Far more error consists in misrepresenting and distorting the truth than in expressly repudiating it.

Pink exercises the same care to avoid lopsidedness in dealing with living the Christian life. Thus in opposing the theory of 'victorious Christian living', he is ready to show that the Scriptures are equally against any 'spiritual defeatism'. 'It is a favourite device of Satan's', he warns, 'to drive us from one extreme to another. One element of truth must not be pressed to such an extreme that another be denied, but each given its due and distinctive place.'

This question of balance brings us to another feature of *Studies* which is of importance in any assessment of Pink as a teacher. The twenty-four pages of *Studies* were mostly taken up with four major articles which each ran on through many issues of the magazine. His treatment of 'The Divine Covenants', for instance, ran from July 1934 to December 1938. It could have been completed much earlier had he been prepared to give it more space but it was his wisdom that prevented him from doing so. He wanted *each* issue to provide a varied spiritual diet. So along with material which was more heavily theological he would place expository articles which were virtually extended commentaries on books or passages of Scripture (Old and New Testaments often appearing concurrently in the same issue). Nor was this all. In each issue there would always be one series of articles which were pre-eminently practical and experimental, dealing with the Christian life in a more subjective manner than in those articles in which the explanation of objective, doctrinal truth was the main purpose. The annual numbers of *Studies* reveal that Pink gave close attention to maintaining this balance. 'It is desirable', he wrote in beginning a series on 'The Doctrine of Reconciliation', 'that there should be an alternation between and a proportionate emphasis upon both the objective and the subjective sides of the truth.'[9]

The books which publishers have compiled out of *Studies* are made up of the consecutive articles on a given subject. Apart from a few early works, none of them was actually selected by Pink for publication in book form, and these books necessarily separate the strands that Pink was concerned to keep together. He knew that certain articles would be more suitable and helpful to some of his readers than they would be to others. But with the many themes of his various series of articles now divided into individual books there is at least the likelihood of a purchaser taking up Pink on a subject which may prove less beneficial in his present stage of spiritual understanding than another title by the same author. The point to be recognized is that there is considerable variety in Pink, not simply between early and later writings but also between the varied types of material which he handled.

* * * * *

Pink's literary output, broadly speaking, can be classified under three headings, theological, expository and experimental or devotional. Of course there is an overlap. His experimental writings proceed upon the basis of doctrine, and his more strictly theological or expository articles do not lack spiritual application, yet the difference

[9] *Studies*, 1944, p. 61.

is there and it has to be recognized in an evaluation of Pink's work.

Pink is not equally strong in all these areas. Certainly he does not rank with the eminent theologians or doctrinal instructors of the church. His doctrinal articles are at their best when he accurately popularizes – as he often does – Pauline divinity recovered in the Reformation and the Puritan eras. In the occasional instances when the Reformed thought of those periods had to be brought into closer conformity with Scripture (as it was in the work of later theologians of the Princeton school) Pink generally follows the earlier understanding and loses thereby. His treatment of the word 'covenant' may be cited as an example. Similarly, where he has to face a theological question scarcely considered three hundred years ago – whether, for instance, man is bipartite or tripartite – he may come down on the wrong side. In general, however, his theology is reliable and while the student will go to other authors for more exactness, Pink has been immensely important in reviving and stimulating doctrinal reading at the popular level. The same can be said of few other twentieth-century authors.

As with theology, Pink does not belong to the front rank of commentators. He lacked some of the gifts necessary to make a careful exegete. It would not have been a loss if his early expositions of Genesis and Exodus had not been reprinted. The same applies, though not so markedly, to his work on *The Gospel of John*. All these volumes contain good material, but better is to be found elsewhere. His expositions of Hebrews, the Sermon on the Mount, Joshua and 1 John have higher value. But few of the older authors, to whom he often looked, were available when he wrote these works. That is no longer the case. Many books for which Pink had to search hard to obtain second-hand copies are now in print again, and some will prefer to read the sources from which Pink himself gained much. It would be both a compliment and a criticism to say that Pink's expositions read somewhat like a modern 'Matthew Henry', yet, whatever their deficiencies, the truth is that their simplicity and spirituality will long give them an appeal to those who love the Bible. It is no small indication of what Christians have felt about his helpfulness as a commentator that his exposition of *The Gospel of John*, despite its size, reached a fourteenth printing in 1979!

It is in the practical and devotional field that Pink really comes into his own, and that he is almost uniformly uplifting, stimulating and often inspiring. Here he needs to lean on none. He speaks what he has 'seen and heard' when he takes up such subjects as prayer and self-denial, communion with Christ and growth in grace. His grasp of the ways of God in conversion and in spiritual experience is masterly and reveals a gift which has been exceedingly rare among preachers and writers of our times. He has sound counsel for the spiritual infant and for the mature Christian. As a spiritual physician who knows the heart in all its multiplicity of need he talks like one of the Puritans. He is able to walk, and to assist others to walk, through that Valley, which says Bunyan, 'is as dark as pitch', where there is 'on the right hand a very deep ditch' and on the left 'a very dangerous quag, into which, if ever a good man falls, he finds no bottom for his foot to stand on'.[10]

This pastoral ability and discernment is surely Pink's foremost strength as a teacher. His longing is to help people. The words of Paul to the elders at Ephesus to take heed 'to all the flock' and 'to feed the church of God'

[10] *The Pilgrim's Progress* (Edinburgh: Banner of Truth,1977), pp. 66–7.

were at the centre of his living. And yet it is just at this point, as we have noticed, that there is a seeming contradiction in his ministry. How could a man rightly fulfil the pastoral function throughout a quarter of a century in which he not only had no pastoral charge but was not even connected, for the most part, with the life of any congregation of Christian people?

We have already commented above on this subject yet something more may be said. It is arguable that, although Pink shed his Dispensationalism, he was never *wholly* free from the way in which that system had influenced his thinking upon the subject of the church. As we have seen, in the 1920s he believed that the church in its organized form was in the final stages of apostasy and shortly to be smitten with judicial blindness.[11] The rapture of true believers was imminent. 'The House of God on earth is a ruin.'[12] Even when he had given up his earlier views of unfulfilled prophecy he could write in 1941 to his friend, John C. Blackburn, who was still a minister in the Southern Presbyterian Church:

> Things are much worse in Christendom than you yet realize. As you know, I reached the conclusion upwards of a decade since that all corporate testimony *owned of God* is a thing of the past. Since then, so far from meeting with anything which has caused me to modify such an extreme and gloomy view, *everything* which has come beneath my notice has sadly confirmed it.[13]

As we have noted above, Pink's view of future history did not remain so consistently pessimistic,[14] yet his

[11] *The Sovereignty of God*, 1929, p. 154.
[12] *Studies*, 1931, p. 143.
[13] Feb. 24, 1941. These words were written at the darkest point in World War II.
[14] See above, p. 212–3.

experience in the 1930s – particularly the reaction of so many to his teaching, as it became more thoroughly biblical, seemed to confirm him in the view of the churches that he had grown up with among Dispen–sationalists. 'Even now', he once commented, 'I have to exert myself in order to refuse to look at things through their spectacles.'[15] Nor was it only his own experience that influenced him. He knew that a number who took *Studies*, and loved the magazine's teaching, were equally at a loss to find a true 'church home'. One reader spoke for many when he wrote to Pink from Australia: 'Your expositions of the Scriptures are now appreciated more than ever. A testimony on these lines, of course, involves a cutting off from most, as they will not accept it.'[16] Douglas Craig reports the following concerning his father who lived in Swansea, South Wales:

> I recollect my father telling me when I was a young Christian, reading Mr Pink's *The Sovereignty of God*, of the time in the early 1920s when it first came into his hands and his initial reaction to it; bearing in mind that my father was among the 'Brethren' and was thus steeped in Arminianism and Free-will teaching. He was not taking the *Studies* at that time and he wrote Mr Pink telling him what he thought of his book and that the contents needed to be taken with a generous 'pinch of salt'. Mr Pink replied in very forceful terms but asking for humility in comparing its contents with Scripture and asking the Lord for light. I cannot trace this letter but one thing is certain, my father became, through the over-ruling and mercy of God, one of his strongest supporters, and,

[15] *Divine Covenants* (Grand Rapids: Baker, 1973), p. 79. Quoted by Richard Belcher.
[16] *Studies*, 1948, p. 190.

as far as this part of the country was concerned, for many years, from 1925 to 1950, he stood alone among evangelical Christendom spreading the truth of sovereign grace. This so incensed the 'Brethren' among whom he had spent all his spiritual life, that they excommunicated him from their fellowship; called him a 'heretic' and he found himself in exactly the position experienced by Mr Pink – a fast closed door and in complete isolation.

Yet if such experiences were not uncommon among Pink's correspondents, his position on church attendance was not just as clear-cut or extreme as some quotations would suggest. On the one hand, he spoke strongly at times in favour of separation – the believer should be outside 'the corrupt systems' where his Master is absent. He once advised no church membership at all in preference to sitting under an Arminian ministry. On the other hand he disavowed withdrawal from 'imperfect churches'. 'There has never been a perfect church on this earth, and never will be.'[17] He warns that there is no warrant 'for Christians forsaking "churches" or companies of God's professing people where Christ is owned, honoured, worshipped.' But occasionally in *Studies* he advocated non-attendance at orthodox churches which may be judged lifeless and powerless. To support that conviction he quoted Paul's words, 'Having a form of godliness, but denying the power thereof: from such turn away' (*2 Tim.* 3:5), and defended his argument with such words as these:

> One may sit under what is termed a 'sound ministry', and through no fault of his own, derive no benefit from the same. There is a 'dead orthodoxy' now

[17] *Studies*, 1932, p. 70.

widely prevalent, where the truth is preached, yet in an unctionless manner, and if there be no life in the pulpit there is not likely to be much in the pew. Unless the message comes fresh from God, issues warmly and earnestly from the preacher's heart, and is delivered in the power of the Holy Spirit, it will neither reach the heart of the hearer nor minister that which will cause him to grow in grace. There is many a place in Christendom where a living, refreshing, soul-edifying ministry once obtained, but the Spirit of God was grieved and quenched, and a visit there is like entering a morgue: everything is cold, cheerless, lifeless. The officers and members seem petrified, and to attend such services is to be chilled and become partaker of that deadening influence. A ministry which does not lift the soul Godwards, produce joy in the Lord, and stimulate to grateful obedience, casts the soul down and soon brings it into the Slough of Despond.

Only the Day to come will reveal how many a babe in Christ had his growth arrested through sitting under a ministry which supplied him not with the sincere milk of the Word. Only that Day will show how many a young believer, in the warmth and glow of his first love, was discouraged and dismayed by the coldness and deadness of the place where he went to worship. No wonder that God so rarely regenerates any under such a ministry: those places would not prove at all suitable as nurseries for his little ones. Many a spiritual decline is to be attributed to this very cause. Then take heed, young Christian, where you attend. If you cannot find a place where Christ is magnified, where his presence is felt, where the Word is ministered in the power of the Spirit, where

> your soul is actually fed, where you do not come away as empty as when you went, – then far better to remain at home and spend the time on your knees, feeding directly from God's Word, and reading that which you *do* find helpful unto your spiritual life.[18]

While there is an element of truth in these statements, they also contain a real danger. They encourage separation from what may often be true churches, and they provide an excuse for the Christian who fails to see that he ought to meet with fellow-believers (even if they are weak and the occupant of the pulpit dull) rather than remain in isolation. Surely there needs to be serious heresy in a church to justify the counsel, 'Better to remain at home'? The apostolic injunction to 'turn away' in 2 Timothy 3:5 is *not* a reference to congregations of believers deficient in their degree of life, and it is exceedingly hazardous for any visitor to an orthodox congregation to make his own subjective judgment on whether or not 'the power' of godliness is there denied.

There are, then, aspects of Pink's views on the church which must be regarded as indefensible. Yet his very inconsistencies in this area sometimes serve to show that, whatever his mistakes, they were not those of a narrow partisan with a closed mind. He did not hesitate to go back on his earlier view that the end of Christendom was emphatically 'at hand'. In 1947 he is ready to remind his readers that the same 'proofs' that 'the Lord is at the very door' had been urged a century before. And despite all he had said about being 'outside' the denominations he was prepared to recognize that more interest in the truths contained in *Studies* might be found there than among those (the Brethren notably) who believed in 'separation'.

[18] *Studies*, 1945, pp. 259–60.

While there were, as already said, a number of his readers and correspondents 'cut off' from church fellowship, others to whom he wrote with regularity maintained connections which he personally had not found it possible to sustain. He did not, in his later correspondence, seek to discourage church attendance and at times encouraged Christians to look around.

Although he had taken many 'knocks' from Brethren sources (and sometimes allowed himself too much liberty in denouncing Brethren distinctives) he maintained friendships among them. To William Naismith, a student at Cambridge, he writes of the Brethren:

> I suppose they have an 'assembly' in Cambridge and that you are attending it. If not, I wish you would ascertain if there is a 'Strict and Particular Baptist Church' within handy reach and 'sample' a few of their services. I 'hold no brief' for them, though they are staunch 'Calvinists', but the experience would widen your horizon. I trust it may please the Lord to bring you into contact with a few of 'his own' in Cambridge.[19]

A quotation such as this confirms that Pink did not want to make his own experience normative for others. The same feature is evident in another letter to Naismith who had sought Pink's counsel on how far he should feel himself free to help various churches by preaching for them when invited to do so. Pink's answer is semi-personal in nature but it is without the dogmatism which some might expect from him:

> Your query re preaching the gospel in a 'church' of doubtful orthodoxy requires pondering from *several*

[19] Jan. 29, 1951.

> *angles.* There was a time when I would have given an unqualified 'Yes' but today I hesitate, and am inclined to think it is a question on which, after prayer, each one should be free to form his own judgment and be 'fully persuaded in his own mind'. I have personally refused many such invitations, because I felt that my (even temporary) presence in their pulpit sanctioned what was done in that 'church'. Some might say, 'There can't be much wrong there or Mr Pink would not have entered its pulpit.' Suppose you went, would you not be merely 'beating the air' unless the Spirit clothed your message with power? Would he do so in a place where he was 'quenched'? Ponder Acts 16:6–7. On the other hand, don't 'grieve the Spirit' by being a party to sectarianism or submit to any tyranny which denies that you are 'the Lord's free man'.[20]

The question then remains, How far did Pink's withdrawal from the corporate life of the churches affect his teaching? In reply two things may be said.

It tended to promote the negative, critical element which is sometimes too much to the fore in his writings. When allowance is made for his blunt, plain speaking and, more important, for his conviction that rebuke and warning are a part of the pastor's duty, we are still left wondering at times whether he is not unnecessarily harsh and sweeping. In his relative isolation, and in his removal from the encouragements to be witnessed in normal church life, the temptation to feel, 'I only am left' was powerful. If even the apostle Paul *needed* like-minded brethren and could write, 'God, that comforteth those that are cast down, comforted us by the coming of Titus'

[20] Feb. 19, 1950.

(*2 Cor.* 7:6), Pink could not be immune from the loss occasioned by the absence of such fellowship. He felt the loneliness keenly. He sought to counteract it by correspondence, sometimes urging an individual to write more frequently, yet at the same time he knew, as he admits in one letter, that correspondence is a more or less unsatisfactory medium of communion, lacking as it does 'the life and warmth of personal contact and speech'.[21]

There were days when, as Pink took his solitary morning walks around Stornoway, the skies were too dark, and the sharp expressions which might then fall from his pen about 'apostate Christendom' originated, at least in part, in the effects of his restricted fellowship. Perhaps there is another feature, too, occasionally present in his writings, which has to be related to his isolation. He lacked the healthy discipline which comes from working with fellow ministers of Christ. He did not have the benefit of cut-and-thrust discussions with equals. There was no one of stature at hand whose disagreement with some of his views could have been salutary. His wife Vera was an outstanding Christian, deeply exercised in the Scriptures, and without her companionship, as he freely said, he would have been overwhelmed, but, of necessity, she could not provide the 'iron which sharpens iron' at the level of deeper biblical issues affecting the work of the ministry.

In the total absence of personal fellowship with other pastors and teachers through such a long period, Pink was at times prone to express his individual views with a dogmatism which does not always enhance his writings. 'Most of us, if we are honest,' he writes, 'must acknowledge that there is quite a bit of the pontiff in us,

[21] Letter to H. J. Bradshaw, July 17, 1943.

and therefore we should not be surprised . . . that a spirit of intolerance and uncharitableness has often marred the characters of real Christians.'[22] He was aware of the evil, and such was his spirituality that there is little of it in his writings, and yet we suggest that, where it is present at all, the fault is connected with the fact that as a teacher he stood too far apart and alone.

But there is a second thing to be said about Pink's removal from any congregational or denominational connection. While it does not justify his failure, it is worthy of observation, for it was overruled to strengthen an aspect of his teaching which has vital significance. As we have already seen, Pink's problem with respect to church relationship after he left Sydney was connected with his certainty that God had called him to teach. Teaching, however, was what he could not do in all the groups and congregations which he attended, at least *not without taking up their denominational positions.* Brethren, Strict Baptists, Scottish Presbyterians, would indeed all have welcomed him to their pulpits if he had conformed to their distinctives, but so long as he came among them only as a visitor, uncommitted to their denominational standpoint, his help was not invited.

As a result of his own spiritual development, Pink in the 1930s found himself to be a representative of no contemporary denomination. The men to whom he stood closest in thought and spirit were dead. Their denominational commitments had been varied. It was the *great* things which those men had in common – whether they were Presbyterians as Thomas Manton and Matthew Henry, or Independents as John Owen and Jonathan Edwards, or Baptists as Andrew Fuller and C. H. Spurgeon – that Pink had come to regard as essential to

[22] *Studies*, 1950. p. 117.

powerful, experimental, vital Christianity. *These* were the things which he laboured to see revived, and the more he saw the various church groupings giving undue stress to secondary issues, and circumscribing their fellowship so largely by agreement on those issues, the more he determined to maintain his freedom.

The solution which some offered to the problem of denominations, namely, that they are all 'man-made' and that a re-gathering 'unto the Lord' is demanded, did not commend itself to Pink. He considered that those who spoke in this way were often 'more sectarian than any of the denominations'. 'They have separated themselves not only from false systems, but from the great majority of God's own people.'[23] His belief was that secondary differences on church issues would remain, and that 'members of the one Flock are found in many different ecclesiastical folds'.[24] What was needed was not the end of the secondary differences but the restoration of the big things upon which the health of the whole kingdom of Christ depends. Therein true believers would find their unity and be welcomed as helpers in one another's churches. The following is a good summary of his outlook:

> Instead of dwelling so much upon minor things – concerning which God's children, most probably, never will all see eye to eye down here – we should be occupied with the major things which we all enjoy in common . . .
> Whatever blame may or may not rest upon men for the existence of the various evangelical denominations in Christendom, let not the superintending

[23] *Studies*, 1929. p. 59.
[24] *Studies*, 1945. p. 287.

hand of God therein be lost sight of. In our readiness to criticize former leaders – which charity requires us to believe were at least equally devoted to the Lord and as anxious to conform to his Word as we are – we need to be much on our guard lest we be found quarrelling with Divine providence. While it is true that a measure of failure marks whatever God entrusted to men, yet let it not be forgotten that 'Of *him*, and through him, and to him, *are all things:* to whom be glory for ever. Amen' (*Rom.* 11:36). We are either very ignorant of history or superficial readers thereof, if we fail to perceive the guiding hand of God and his 'manifold wisdom' in the appointing and blessing of the leading evangelical denominations . . . The present writer is not prepared to hold a brief in defence of every peccadillo in any denomination, system, or company of professing Christians; on the other hand, he desires to freely recognize and gladly own whatever is of God in all of them. Though himself unattached ecclesiastically, and a partisan of no single group, he wishes to have Christian fellowship with any and all who love the Lord and whose daily walk evidences a sincere desire to please him. We have lived long enough and travelled sufficiently, to discover that no one 'church', company, or man, has all the truth, and as we grow older we have less patience with those who demand that others must adopt their interpretation of Scripture on all points.

There should be a happy medium between sectarian narrowness – and the world's 'broadmindedness', between deliberately compromising the truth and turning away from some of the Lord's people because they differ from us on non-essentials. Shall I refuse

> to partake of a meal because some of the dishes are not cooked as I like them? Then why decline fellowship with a brother in the Lord because he is unable to pronounce correctly my favourite shibboleth? It is not without reason that 'endeavouring to keep the unity of the Spirit in the bond of peace' is immediately preceded by 'forbearing one another in love' (*Eph.* 4:2, 3). Probably there is as much if not more in me that my brother has to 'bear' with, as there is in him which grates upon me. As good old Matthew Henry said, 'The consideration of being agreed in greater things should extinguish all feuds over lesser ones.'[25]

There is much to the same effect in the pages of *Studies*. Under the heading 'Love to all the Saints', he several times quotes these words from E. Adams:

> How should I regard Christians who 'follow not with us'? a young believer may ask. Well, how would that Great-Heart, the apostle Paul, have regarded them? Are they not children of God? Hearts may agree, although heads differ, and God sees grace where we see none. If you think that these people have less light than you, their need is a claim upon your help; and, believe it or not, they can teach you something! Be on your guard against viewing them with suspicion or contempt. You are made of exactly the same flesh and blood as they are, and the same grace is at work in them as in you. God loves persons rather than places.
>
> Each group or school of thought has its own emphasis, and sometimes its own phraseology. Don't attach too much importance to pious phrases; the

[25] *Studies*, 1935, pp. 94–5.

> same truth can be expressed in different ways. We should learn to welcome all the truth, through whatever channel it may come to us. And the gifts of Christ are for *all* his people.[26]

To this quote Pink adds:

> The above emphasises one aspect of the truth which some extremists need to take to heart. There is a happy medium between refusing to walk with 'those in error', and declining to have fellowship with any who fail to pronounce all our shibboleths.

Elsewhere, on the same theme he quotes the words of C. H. Spurgeon: 'If churches are to agree one with another, they must not make rules that ministers who are not of their denominations should not occupy their pulpits. I should be ashamed of you, if you passed a resolution that no one dissenting from us should stand in my pulpit.' 'That honoured servant of Christ', Pink continues, 'had too much of the love of God in his heart to close his pulpit against fellow-labourers in the vineyard, who were sound in faith and orderly in their walk. Something much higher than sectarian considerations regulated that noble and greatly-used man of God. Alas, how few resemble him in this, or in any other respect! It needs pointing out that one may keep strictly to the Narrow Way without being of a narrow and contracted spirit. Fidelity to God does not require any to act uncharitably to his servants. Those churches which shut their pulpits to all who wear not their particular livery are grieving the Spirit, and oftentimes depriving themselves of the very help they much need. None can act in defiance of the unity of the Spirit without themselves being the losers.'[27]

[26] *Studies*, 1937, p. 255. [27] *Studies*, 1941, pp. 118–19.

The point was so important in Pink's teaching that it warrants two more quotations:

> Even where there was oneness of mind respecting the fundamentals of the faith, godly men have differed considerably in their ecclesiastical views . . . While on the one hand we must admire the wisdom of him who has *providentially ordered* as great a variety of types in the ecclesiastical sphere as he has in the physical and social, which though not a rule for us to walk by, is a subject for our admiration – yet on the other hand we cannot but deplore that they who are united on the same foundations and agreed in all the cardinal truths of Holy Writ, should lay such emphasis upon their circumstantial differences in sentiment as to prevent the exercise of mutual love and forbearance, and instead of labouring in concert within their respective departments to promote the common cause of Christ, should so often vex each other with needless disputes and uncharitable censures. Far better be silent altogether than contend for any portion of the truth in a bitter, angry, censorious spirit.[28]

> A spirit of bigotry, partisanship and intolerance is a mark of narrow mindedness and of spiritual immaturity. On first entering the school of Christ most of us expected to find little difference between members of the same family, but more extensive acquaintance with them taught us better, for we found their minds varied as much as their countenances, their temperaments more than their local accents of speech and that amid general agreement there were wide divergences of opinions and

[28] *Studies*, 1937, p. 323, or *Exposition of Hebrews*, vol. 3, pp. 325–6.

> sentiments in many things. While all God's people are taught of him, yet they know but 'in part' and the 'part' one knows may not be the part which another knows. All the saints are indwelt by the Holy Spirit, yet he does not operate uniformly in them nor bestow identical gifts (*1 Cor.* 12:8–11). Thus opportunity is afforded us to 'forbear one another in love' (*Eph.* 4:2) and not make a man an offender for a word or despise those who differ from me. Growth in grace is evidenced by a spirit of clemency and toleration, granting to others the same right of private judgment and liberty as I claim for myself. The mature Christian, generally, will subscribe to that axiom, 'In essentials unity, in non-essentials liberty, in all things charity.'[29]

As already indicated, this is not to say that Pink dismissed secondary differences. Such an attitude would have been impossible for him, for such differences have to do with scriptural issues, and the master principle in all his thinking was the absolute necessity of submission in all things to the supremacy of the Word of God. 'Beware of allowing any influence to come between your soul and God's Word . . . The origin of all sectarianism is subjection to men, human authority supplanting the authority of God.'[30] On secondary things, also, the Christian is to be 'regulated by what appears to be the revealed will of God', but the duty of mutual forbearance means that he is to leave others to do the same, according to their own light and conscience. 'Let every man be fully persuaded in his own mind' (*Rom.* 14:5). 'Perform what you are assured to be your duty and leave others to do

[29] *Spiritual Growth or Christian Progress*, p. 193.
[30] *Studies*, 1950, p. 164.

likewise: thereby the rights of the individual are preserved and the peace of the community promoted.'[31] As examples of such areas where forbearance is needed Pink instances the observation of such days as 'Christmas' or 'Easter' which are kept by some Christians and set aside by others. 'Much grace is needed if fellowship is to be maintained.'[32]

We believe that God guided Pink in this stress upon a biblical catholicity and upon distinguishing the truths that most urgently needed recovering among Christians. In a strange way, as we have said, his chequered, lonely path contributed to this emphasis. He might have been faithful to Scripture and served a church or denomination as others did in the same period; instead he was guided to a wider ministry with a little magazine in which he resolved to take up nothing of a sectarian nature, 'endeavouring to steer clear of whatever would give unnecessary offence, confining ourselves (with rare exceptions) to "those things which are most surely believed among" God's people at large'.[33]

When he died unnoticed in the remoteness of the Scottish Hebrides the full meaning of this policy had not been seen. It was only as a new era dawned, as a deeper hunger for the Word of God reappeared in the English-speaking world, and as the Puritans and other older writers were rediscovered and reopened, that Arthur Pink became one of the leading teachers of a new generation. He served to inspire a vision which was wider, grander and more fundamental than what so many found in their own church situations. Readers turned to him, not because he was a Baptist or a Presbyterian, but rather because they

[31] Ibid., p. 140. These two quotations are from articles on 'Private Judgment'.
[32] *Gleanings from Paul*, pp. 23–31.
[33] *Studies*, 1941, p. 285.

found an unction in his words which moved their hearts with new zeal and love for Scripture. By the gracious providence of God, Pink's books are now vastly more influential than was his ministry in the days when the cold shoulder of an unsympathetic generation reduced him to silence in conventions and in churches.

'Your own history is very staggering', a friend once wrote to him. 'It is most mysterious that your mouth should be closed as to a public oral ministry.' Now, half a century later, we may see a little more of its meaning and give thanks to God. The present writer can do no better than concur with the opinion that Dr Belcher gave at the conclusion of his biography of our subject:

> He feels he is not worthy to tie the shoe strings of a man such as Arthur W. Pink. That was not the conviction of this writer when he began his long study of Pink, though even then he had a respect for him. That is the conviction of the writer now as he has got to know the man and his heartbeat through his many writings.[34]

[34] Belcher, *Arthur W. Pink*, p. 118.

16

Pink on *The Sovereignty of God*

As we have seen, it was in the area of his opposition to Arminian belief that Pink found himself especially isolated in the years when he sought public ministry. His book *The Sovereignty of God* (1918) did much to shut doors on him. Yet after his death, when a major renewal of belief in Calvinistic theology occurred – in no small part aided by his writings – it was the rediscovery of the sovereignty of divine grace, and the certainty that Christ's redeeming work cannot fail, that gave his writings so much appeal to many. An extraordinary reversal occurred: the truth once so widely rejected had become a magnet and while Christian authors popular in Pink's lifetime faded from view, he became widely read.

It is said that in 1982 Zondervan Publishing House was steadily selling between 1,500 and 2,000 copies of his *Exposition of the Gospel of John* every year. Baker Book House at that date had published twenty-two titles by Pink, with combined sales of almost 350,000 copies.[1] There was the same success with his *Life of Elijah* and *Profiting from the Word*, published by the Banner of

[1] For these figures I am indebted to Richard Belcher's *Arthur W. Pink*.

Truth. Of all his titles, however, it is *The Sovereignty of God* that has done more than any other in redirecting the thinking of a younger generation. The Banner of Truth republished it in 1961, and to date it has sold more than 177,000 copies, plus others in foreign translations.

Pink did not adopt the title of Calvinist, nor did he require a person to be a Calvinist in order to be a Christian, but he did believe that the truths usually identified with that name are vital ones and, more than any other, it is his book *The Sovereignty of God* that explains why. But the edition of *Sovereignty* revised by the Banner of Truth in 1961 was not identical with the first edition of 1918, and this is a subject that needs explanation. We have already noted that the 1918 edition was revised by Pink in 1921.[2] Then another revision was done by him when he was at Morton's Gap, Kentucky, in 1929. In the Foreword to that edition he wrote: 'During the last ten years it has pleased God to grant us further light on certain parts of his Word, and this we have sought to use in improving our expositions of different passages. But it is with unfeigned thanksgiving that we find it unnecessary to either change or modify any doctrine.'[3] The reader needs to keep these dates in mind in what follows.

How far Pink changed the book in 1929 we cannot tell, for while the text of this third edition has been reprinted many times since, no copies of the editions of 1918 or 1921 have been available to us to make a comparison. But what is certain is that, had he revised it again *after* 1929, more changes would have been made as his understanding of Calvinistic belief matured. From

[2] See above, p. 61.

[3] Foreword to third edition, reprinted in *The Sovereignty of God* (Swengel, PA: Bible Truth Depot, 1959).

the 1930s onwards his references to hyper-Calvinism become very noticeable and strongly critical.[4] The characteristic of that system of thought is the teaching that it is not the *responsibility* of gospel hearers to believe savingly on Christ. But Pink came to see that his own teaching on human responsibility was defective in the 1929 edition of *The Sovereignty of God.*

In part his deficiency at that date concerned a confusion in terminology, a confusion which endangered his whole argument. It has been near universally believed in Christian theology that human responsibility means that men are free moral agents – they are not machines, deprived of voluntary choice. But in 1929 Pink denied 'free moral agency' (pp. 171, 175, 177, 282 etc.),[5] apparently on the grounds that he believed it had been destroyed by the Fall of man. He wrote, 'Strictly speaking, there are only two men who have ever walked this earth who were endowed with full and unimpaired responsibility, and they were the first and last Adams' (p. 303). Such a statement inevitably suggests that sin has diminished if not removed the responsibility of everyone else for 'the natural man is not a "free moral agent"' (p. 177). Pink said this because he wanted to safeguard the biblical truth that man's fallen nature renders him spiritually dead and thus unable, without divine grace, to obey God. No Reformed Confession, however, has ever sought to present inability in terms of the cessation of

[4] 'The unbalanced teaching of hyper-Calvinism has produced a most dangerous lethargy – unperceived by them, but apparent to "lookers on". Those who dwell unduly upon the Divine decrees are in peril of lapsing into the paralysis of fatalism.' *Studies*, 1948, p. 134.

[5] My quotations here, and following, are all from the 1959 printing of *The Sovereignty of God* which retains the text of the 1929 edition. This same edition has been subsequently re-issued, but with different pagination after 1984, by Baker, Grand Rapids. This publisher's 'fourteenth edition' of the book was published in 1995.

free agency and voluntary choice. It is over what determines choice that Reformed doctrine differs from that of others.[6]

This is not to say that in 1929 Pink was unconscious of the need to show that men are accountable to God. On the contrary, his purpose in his chapter on 'God's Sovereignty and Human Responsibility', retained in the 1929 edition of his book, was to meet the question 'how the sinner can be held responsible for not doing what he could not do'. But in addressing this question he advanced a theory which he believed could cut what he called 'the Gordian knot of theology', namely, 'The Scriptures distinguish sharply between natural inability and moral inability' (p. 188). Using this distinction, then, it could be said that Blind Bartimaeus had 'natural inability' – he lacked the ability to see – thus differing from men in general whose 'inability' is a moral one; it lies, not in the lack of natural faculties, but in their depraved hearts. 'The sinner', Pink argued, 'possesses natural ability, and this it is which renders him accountable to God' (p. 191).

So the unconverted person will be held accountable for not doing what he has 'the natural ability' to do, that is to say, read the Bible, use the means of grace, cry to God about his inability and so on. 'The fact of man's responsibility rests upon his natural ability' (p. 200). This argument is supposed to show that God does not, after all, call on men to do what they cannot do, namely, believe on Christ, and so the problem of responsibility is supposedly solved. Yet Pink himself, in a passing sentence, contradicts his case in the following words: 'Each sinner

[6] See John Murray on 'Free Agency' in *Collected Writings of John Murray* (Edinburgh: Banner of Truth, 1977), vol. 2, pp. 60–6. As Murray says, free agency does not mean that the will of man is capable of volition good or bad, apart from any previous conditioning of our moral and religious character.

who hears the gospel is "commanded" to believe (*1 John* 3:23). Therefore every sinner is *responsible* to repent and believe' (p.195).

It may be that Pink inserted the last quotation in his 1929 revision without considering how it ran counter to an earlier statement that responsibility depended on 'natural ability'. Certainly the 'Gordian knot' was not cut after all. It is the more strange that he allowed his earlier explanation of ability to stand in the 1929 edition in that, only two years earlier, when he was in the midst of his first encounter with hyper-Calvinism, he had written an article in *Studies in the Scriptures* entitled 'Gospel Responsibility'. In this article his theory that God requires of men only what it is within their 'natural ability' to perform is entirely, and rightly, abandoned.[7] He wrote:

> There are some who say, The unregenerate are dead, and that ends the matter – they cannot have any responsibility. But this is manifestly erroneous . . . The hyper-Calvinist is fond of asking, 'Would any sensible man go to the cemetery and bid those in their graves come forth! Why, then, ask anyone who is dead in sins to come to Christ, when he is equally incapable of responding?' Such a question only betrays the ignorance of the one who puts it. A corpse in the cemetery is no suitable analogy of the natural man. A corpse in the cemetery is incapable of performing evil! A corpse cannot 'despise and reject' Christ (*Isa.* 53:3), cannot 'resist the Holy Spirit' (*Acts* 7:51), cannot disobey the gospel (*2 Thess.* 1:8); but

[7] As A. A. Hodge writes, the attempted distinction between natural and moral ability has no warrant in Scripture, 'It is essentially ambiguous . . . misleading and confusing.' *Outlines of Theology* (reprinted Edinburgh: Banner of Truth, 1972), p. 341. Pink had picked up the theory from the writings of Jonathan Edwards or Andrew Fuller.

> the natural man can and does do these things! . . . God demands of men what they are unable to render Him. We may not understand it, but there it is . . . The gospel contains a call and command from God for all to whom it comes to obey it.[8]

In later articles on the same subject Pink confirms that his mature understanding of responsibility was *not* as in the text of the 1929 edition. In articles on 'The Doctrine of Man's Inability', published in 1940, he has no hesitation in saying that it is necessary to insist upon both the freedom of the will and free agency, and the distinction between natural and moral inability has gone.[9] He had come to recognize that man's free agency and God's control of all things are *both* biblical facts. 'These two things we must believe if the truth is not to be repudiated: that God foreordained everything that comes to pass; that He is in no way blameworthy for any man's wickedness, the criminality thereof being wholly his. The decree of God in no wise infringes upon man's moral agency, for it neither forces nor hinders man's will.' 'In all God's dealings with mankind . . . He exercises His high sovereignty but in no way destroying their moral free agency. These may present deep and insoluble mysteries to the finite mind, nevertheless they are actual facts.' 'The Fall has not resulted in the loss of man's *freedom of will*, or his power of volition as a moral faculty.'[10]

[8] *Studies*, 1927, pp. 260–1. This quotation seems to indicate that Pink did not give enough time to the revision he gave to *The Sovereignty of God* two years later.

[9] *Studies*, 1940, pp. 158–60, or *Gleanings from the Scriptures: Man's Total Depravity*, 1969, Moody Press, pp. 238–42. It has to be remembered that the phrase 'freedom of the will' has been understood in more than one sense. For a careful statement see the *Westminster Confession of Faith*, Chapter 9.

[10] *Studies*, 1951, pp. 206, 166. See also valuable remarks on pp.15–18 of the same volume.

This understanding is vital for a right understanding of the biblical teaching on conversion. In the 1929 edition of *Sovereignty*, Pink still wrote as if allowing the need for the activity of the human will in conversion would be to deny the necessity of grace, and so he spoke of God 'coercing' and 'compelling' obedience. He baulked at the idea that it lies 'within the province of man's will to accept or reject Christ' (p.169). He anticipated the objection that Joshua said to Israel, 'Choose you this day whom ye will serve,' and sought to answer it by quoting Romans 3:11, 'There is none that seeketh after God', as though the first text cannot mean what it says because 'the Word of God never contradicts itself' (p. 157).[11]

Consistent with the above, the truth that the gospel is good news to be pressed on individuals for their acceptance was absent in the 1929 edition of *Sovereignty*. Along with hyper-Calvinists, he still wanted to reject the idea that gospel invitations are an 'offer' of Christ. 'The gospel is not an 'offer' to be bandied about by evangelistic peddlers' (p. 257). Rather, he thought, it was to be presented primarily as a witness and testimony – 'no mere invitation, but a proclamation'. Gospel preaching was a statement of facts by which the elect are brought to faith while 'God suffers' it 'to fall on the ears of the non-elect'.

But even as the 1929 edition went into print, Pink's thought was developing. Perhaps such revision as he did for that edition was done the previous year. At any rate, in an article on 'Accepting Christ', published in *Studies* during 1929, he stated that there is a sense in which the call to 'accept Christ' can be justified, and that, certainly, all hearers of the gospel are to be directed to 'receive' the

[11] Yet there is inconsistency in his 1929 text for at one point he speaks of 'the liberty of man's will and the victorious efficacy of God's grace united together' (p. 164).

Saviour: 'Of our Saviour it is recorded that He wept over Jerusalem because her children would not come to Him. No heartless fatalist was He. The great apostle to the Gentiles wrote, "Knowing therefore the terror of the Lord, we persuade men" (*2 Cor.* 5:11). Do you do this, brother preacher?'[12]

By 1936 Pink speaks fully and pointedly of the error of hyper-Calvinism, and especially of its denial that 'it is the bounden duty of all who hear the gospel to savingly trust Christ'.[13] Now, instead of attempting explanations, as he had done earlier, he quotes a warning from John Newton:

> Unless we keep the plan and manner of the Scriptures constantly in view, and attend to every part of it, a design of 'consistency' may fetter our sentiments, and greatly preclude our usefulness. We may easily perplex our hearers by *nice reasonings* on the nature of human liberty, and the Divine agency on the hearts of men; but such disquisitions *are better avoided*.[14]

This is very different from his earlier confidence that the problem of human responsibility is 'capable of a simple and satisfactory conclusion'. Instead he now warned, 'If we resort to human *reasoning* it will inevitably follow that it is quite useless to exhort the unregenerate to turn unto God and come to Christ . . . the things of God cannot be encompassed by human *reason*.'[15]

[12] *Studies*, 1929, p. 144.
[13] *Studies*, 1936, p. 156. The quotation is from one of two articles defending 'Duty Faith'. [14] Ibid., pp. 93–4.
[15] Ibid., p. 253. Compare *The Sovereignty of God*, in the text of the 1929 edition, pp. 178, 198. Warnings of the above kind are constantly repeated in Pink's later writings, see, for instance, 'Reasoning Repudiated', *Studies*, 1953, pp. 92–6. Pink commented to a friend in 1944, 'The subject of Human Responsibility and Inability is a most profound and many-sided one.' *Letters to a Young Pastor*, p. 9.

By the 1930s Pink had thus come to see more clearly how hyper-Calvinism inhibited earnest gospel preaching. 'It is blankly denied that the gospel calls upon the unsaved to be reconciled to God, or that He requires anything from sinners in order to the forgiveness of their sins.'[16] Whereas true preaching must urge all hearers to respond to the gospel: 'The evangelist's message is that there is salvation in Christ for all who receive Him as He is offered in the gospel and put their trust in Him . . . God is willing to be on terms of amity with the sinner, yet He will not be so until the sinner submits to those terms.' [17] 'Life is offered in the gospel to those who believe in Christ. Under the law it was unobtainable by fallen men; in the gospel it is proffered as a free gift.'[18]

To a friend he writes: 'The gospel is as free as the air, and 1 Timothy 1:15 gives us full warrant to tell a murderer in the condemned cell that there is a Saviour for him IF he will receive Him . . . The *ground* on which any sinner is invited and commanded to believe is neither God's election, nor Christ's substitution, but his particular need of responding to the free offer of the gospel. The gospel is that Christ died for sinners as sinners (not "elect sinners") and is addressed to their responsibility.'[19]

All these, and many other quotations that could be given, show how Pink's understanding developed after 1929. After that date he plainly criticized what had been his own mistake: 'Far too many Calvinists, in their zeal to repudiate the free-willism of Arminians, have at the same time repudiated man's moral agency.'[20] He no longer saw any inconsistency in a Christian's believing in God's

[16] *Studies*, 1946, p. 20. [17] Ibid., p. 281.

[18] *Studies*, 1947, p. 203. By 'under the law' he does not mean 'under the Old Testament'.

[19] Letter to William Naismith, Nov. 16, 1949.

[20] *Studies*, 1947, p. 138.

sovereignty *and* singing

O happy day, that fixed my choice
On Thee, my Saviour and my God!

Similarly, in the correspondence with Harold J. Bradshaw, referred to earlier, Pink vigorously defends the word 'offer' over against the Gospel Standard Article that denied 'the gospel is to be offered indiscriminately to all'.[21] He wrote to Bradshaw:

> I regard Article 29 as unsatisfactory, really meaningless. The Greek word (*euaggelizo*) used for the *preaching of the gospel* signifies 'to announce glad tidings'. But what 'glad tidings' can there be in it for *sinners* unless it *presents* an all-sufficient Saviour for their *acceptance* ('worthy of all acceptation': *1 Tim.* 1:15), and what is that but an 'offer'? Again, can one *reject* unless there had been something *offered* to him? Yet Isaiah 53:3 charges the Jews with having 'rejected' Christ – see also Matthew 21:42, and John 12:48.'[22]

In the articles of 1936 on 'Duty Faith', from which we quoted above, Pink gives us some information on what had contributed to his change of understanding. As well as searching the Scriptures, he had been reading more of the Reformers and the Puritans and in doing so he reached the conclusion that, on this subject, certain

[21] See *What Gospel Standard Baptists Believe: a Commentary on the Gospel Standard Articles of Faith*, J. H. Gosden (reprinted., Chippenham: Gospel Standard Societies, 1993). 'Ministers of the present day,' it is said, are not 'to address unconverted persons, or indiscriminately all in a mixed congregation, calling upon them to savingly repent, believe, and receive Christ.'

[22] 5 September 1943.

eighteenth-century writers had departed from the teaching of 'so many eminent saints of God who preceded them'. To prove this he gives a lengthy series of quotations beginning with these words from John Calvin, 'The mercy of God is *offered equally* to those who believe and to those who believe not.'

The eighteenth-century defection, Pink believed, had begun with John Gill and others who, in turn, influenced Augustus Toplady and William Huntington. He traces to Huntington, particularly, the thinking adopted by a number of nineteenth-century Strict Baptists and Independents:

> Personally, we have often lamented the fact that Mr Gadsby, and later, Mr Philpot, followed (what we believe was) the error of Wm. Huntington, instead of adhering to that path which had been almost uniformly trodden by the Reformers and Puritans.[23]

He had himself still relied on Augustus Toplady in the 1929 text of *Sovereignty* in order to answer the appeal of the non-Calvinist based on the words, 'Why will ye die, O house of Israel?' (*Ezek.* 18:31). Anxious to avoid any impression that God sorrowed over the destiny of the lost, Toplady (following Gill) wrote on that text: 'It so happens that the "death" here alluded to is neither spiritual nor eternal death . . . the death intended by the prophet is a *political* death; a death of national prosperity, tranquillity and security.'[24] That was not Pink's later understanding.

[23] *Studies*, 1936, p. 94. Others he considered were misled in the same way were Joseph Irons and James Wells (*Studies*, 1946, p. 66). I have written further on this subject in *Spurgeon v.Hyper-Calvinism: The Battle for Gospel Preaching* (Edinburgh: Banner of Truth. 1995). Spurgeon became one of Pink's favourite authors. He wrote to a friend on 12 July 1949, 'Spurgeon is simple, but sound, wholesome and edifying.' 'Perhaps God's most valuable gift unto His people since the days of the Puritans.' (*Studies*, 1943, p.183).
[24] *Sovereignty of God* (1929 reprint), p. 125.

He specifically criticized Gill for his misinterpretation of Paul's words in 2 Corinthians 5:20, 'Now then we are ambassadors for Christ, as though God did beseech you by us: we pray you in Christ's stead, be ye reconciled to God.'[25] The statement means exactly what Paul said!

Pink's thought thus evidently matured, and it leads us to recognize a lesson: not *all* the opposition he encountered for his teaching was due to the offence of the truth. His zeal for the doctrines of grace would surely have been more effective in his early life if he had then enjoyed the more balanced understanding of later years. We have seen above how, at the age of thirty-two, he wanted to press on Herendeen the belief that the non-elect were 'necessarily created unto damnation'.[26] Herendeen was quite right to be unreceptive. Similarly Pink later had good reason to understand very differently the 'lengthy duel' he described having with Alesor Marshall, in 1921, over whether the gospel is an 'offer'.[27] At that date Pink had not learned the truth of Richard Baxter's aphorism, 'Overdoing is undoing.' He was later to be very clear in affirming that it is as the truth is presented in its biblical proportions that it is most likely to be received among believers.

[25] *Studies*, 1946, p. 23. Instead of applying the text to salvation, Gill believed that Paul was exhorting saints unto 'submission to providence and obedience to the discipline and ordinances of God'.

[26] See above p. 45. On this point also the text of the 1929 edition of *Sovereignty* is very unsatisfactory. Pink says the responsibility for damnation is man's (p. 123) but other statements are as the one quoted above, including the remark that the non-elect are 'fitted to destruction' by God, 'objectively by His eternal decrees' (p. 120). On the relevant verse in Romans 9, John Murray is surely right to say: 'The main thought is that the destruction meted out to the vessels of wrath is something for which their precedent condition suits them. There is an exact correspondence between what they were in this life and the perdition to which they are consigned.' *The Epistle to the Romans* (Grand Rapids: Eerdmans, 1965), vol. 2, p. 36.

[27] See above p. 66.

All this being so, the question arises why Pink did not revise his book on *Sovereignty* after 1929. There is probably more than one reason. First, there was no demand for the book. It was after his death that reprints multiplied. Second, Herendeen claimed the copyright, and Pink was no longer in touch with him. It was only in 1949, three years before Pink's death, that Herendeen was to reissue the 1929 edition, this time with a Foreword of his own in which there is no reference to the author. It is perhaps significant that Pink made not the slightest reference to the availability of this reprint in the pages of *Studies.*

In view of the known changes in Pink's thought, the only alternatives for the Banner of Truth Trust, which began publishing in 1957 (five years after his death), were to revise the 1929 text or to leave his *Sovereignty of God* unpublished in Britain. To reprint the edition of 1929, as we regret has continued to be done in America, would have been to misrepresent Pink's own final convictions on the issues stated above. Worse, an unrevised edition would have been calculated in places to enforce the very hyper-Calvinism which Pink came to recognize as a real danger to the biblical teaching. The revival of sovereign grace teaching for which he worked and prayed was one that would be accompanied by evangelistic passion.

To critique Pink's *Sovereignty of God* as we have done is not to question the fundamental principle of his treatment of his subject. God is sovereign, and it is to the grace that is sovereign that every believer owes his salvation. God loves the elect with a special and invincible love. To uphold that truth Pink argued in his book for the denial of any broader love in which God shows compassion to all and is not willing that any should perish. But many Calvinists, from Calvin to Spurgeon, have believed both that God is sovereign *and* that he has a love for all people.[28] Christians of Arminian persuasion believe God commands that a sincere offer of salvation be made in his name to all men, which offer may be resisted. A biblical Calvinist believes the same, only he believes more. Not all resist *because* God has chosen them to salvation, while with others he 'permits their self-destruction despite the entreaties of his benevolence'.[29]

In his 1929 text Pink had no place for this broader understanding. Dealing with the rich young ruler, concerning whom Scripture says that Christ 'loved him' (*Mark* 10:21), he there argued that it could only mean the man was 'one of God's elect', even although the last we hear of him is that he 'went away grieved: for he had great possessions'. The only support he gave for his interpretation was that the text says that the young ruler 'came' to Jesus and therefore the promise applied to him, 'him that cometh unto me I will in no wise cast out'.[30]

Thereafter we have seen Pink move a good way from handling texts in that manner. He repudiated his earlier hyper-Calvinist interpretation of such texts as Ezekiel 33:11, Matthew 23:37 and Luke 19:41. In his later thought his views of divine compassion were certainly enlarged. Thus when quoting, 'I have no pleasure in the death of the wicked,' he adds the words of Lamentations 3:33 ('For he doth not afflict willingly [from his heart] nor grieve the children of men'), and comments, 'We are told that judgment is "his strange work . . . his strange act" (*Isa*. 28:21), for it is not as agreeable to Him as His works of mercy.'[31] He had ceased to believe that Christ's

[28] For instance, see Calvin, *Sermons on Deuteronomy* (reprinted, Edinburgh: Banner of Truth, 1987), p. 167.

[29] R. C. Reed, *The Gospel as Taught by Calvin* (Grand Rapids: Baker, 1979), p. 122.

[30] *Sovereignty of God* (1929 reprint), p. 247n.

[31] *Studies*, 1951, p. 108.

compassion for the lost over whom he wept in Jerusalem was only *human* rather than divine compassion. He even went as far as saying, as we noted above, 'God is willing to be on terms of amity [friendship] with the sinner.'

Yet Pink never withdrew from his belief, stated in the 1929 text, that the only love in God is love for the elect. At this one point the Banner of Truth revisers of 1961 went beyond what Pink himself would have allowed; their revision and abridgement removed his case that the love of God is always to be understood in exclusive terms.

Arthur Pink's great concern, writing in an era when man-centred preaching was so prevailing, was to show that God is not helplessly waiting for the consent of the sinner before he can save him. He was indignant that such an impoverished view of God could ever be received. He had seen how the liberal presentation of the 'love of God' had near obliterated in the churches that 'great love' that redeems, keeps and saves to glory. For Pink sovereign grace was not an idea. It was the only explanation of all that he was, and of all that he hoped to be. The hymn he had begun to sing from his heart in 1908 he meant to sing for ever:

I stand amazed in the presence
Of Jesus the Nazarene,
And wonder how He could love me,
A sinner condemned, unclean.

How marvellous, how wonderful!
And my song shall ever be,
How marvellous, how wonderful,
Is my Saviour's love to me.

Appendix 1

Manuscript Material by A. W. Pink

The following material is in the archives of the Banner of Truth Trust, Edinburgh.

NOTEBOOKS:

1. *Small loose leaf,* with 115 pages written. Page 27 can be dated to 1913. Earlier pages precede that date and begin with sermon notes on 'Paul's Estimate of Life and Death' (*Phil.* 1:21). In addition to other sermon notes there are studies in the Gospels, furniture of the Tabernacle, unfulfilled prophecy and 'The Significance of Numerals in Scripture' (a subject he dropped in later life).

2. *Bound volume,* demy size black leather, begun at his third pastorate (1915) and perhaps not added to after he left Spartanburg (1920). There are 594 pages, a little more than 100 unused, and contents divided between 'Sermons for Saints' (pp. 11–269) and evangelistic messages (pp. 290–509).

3. *Loose leaf on unnumbered pages.* The first page, an outline sermon on Regeneration is possibly the earliest surviving from his pen and contrasts in writing and ink with what follows, 'Studies in the Gospels' (published 1921 as *Why Four Gospels?*). Other pages include various doctrinal addresses and the sermons on divine sovereignty that he gave in Spartanburg and were the substance of his book on that subject.

There are other addresses on grace, on Bible study, typology and prophecy and, in this book as in others, the emphasis that Pink gave to preaching on the resurrection of Christ is noticeable.

SEPARATE MANUSCRIPTS:
There are many loose sheets of notes and outlines, most, it would seem, from the 1920s, some on the backs of letters received. They include an extensive series of 'Lectures on Romans,' 27 pages on Acts chapters 1–10, and on parts of the book of Revelation. An absence of manuscripts for later years must be connected with the fact that Pink was then no longer preparing new material for the pulpit. All his writing was for *Studies in the Scriptures* and would not have been retained after publication.

LETTERS:
Either original or in photocopy, there are letters from Pink to those below, with the period of the extant correspondence dated. Pink kept no copies of his letters and what is listed is therefore only what has been sent to us. In all it constitutes a small part of his correspondence.

Blackburn, John C., 1929–45
Culver, John B., 1942–8.
Coleman, Mr and Mrs Horace, 1929–43
Foley, Mrs, 1939–41
Gilbey, A.V., 1951
Green, Jack, 1949–51
Green, Lowell and Evelyn, 1932–52
MacNee, John T., 1943–7
Nicholson, Wallace B., 1934

Appendix 2

'Not Ashamed of the Gospel' (Rom. 1:16)[1]

Introduction. With the one exception of the Lord Jesus the Apostle Paul was beyond doubt the greatest preacher and most successful evangelist the world has ever seen. He covered more ground, endured more hardships, displayed greater heroism and met with larger success in the salvation of souls and founding of churches than any other man.

How can we account for this? What is the explanation of these things? What was the secret of his success?

(i) In nationality he belonged to a race which was and is more hated and despised than any other.

(ii) In personality neither prepossessing or attractive. From the NT we learn he was mean and despicable – 1 Cor. 2:3; 2 Cor. 10:1, 10.

(iii) In delivery he was no orator, but probably stammered and stuttered – 2 Cor. 10:10; Acts 17:18.

The success of this man lay in his message, in the gospel he preached and his abiding confidence in its power.

In some measure at least I can make the text my own.

Truthfully I can say the text, and I will give my reasons why. I'm not ashamed of the gospel:

[1] This was the text of the first sermon Pink preached after his conversion in 1908. The following is the first of his evangelistic sermons contained in his notebook begun in 1915, when he was twenty-eight or twenty-nine. In the original the whole is contained on two pages, five and a quarter inches by eight and a quarter. In transcribing I have filled out his many abbreviations and placed what he wrote in red ink in italics.

1. BECAUSE OF THE UNIQUENESS OF THE GOSPEL

In the whole realm of literature and in all the products of man there is nothing like the gospel. It stands alone in its solitary grandeur. As there is no possible comparison between a lighted candle and the shining of mid-day sun, so the gospel surpasses in its beauty and brilliance all the creations of the human mind. Consider three elements of its uniqueness:

1. *The Gospel is Unique in its Source and Origin*

(i) This glorious gospel, this glad tidings of salvation, made known in Scripture and which God's servants proclaim is not the invention of any church, ancient or modern. It existed before the first Christian church was founded. It was the means and instrument which brought the church into existence. No! the church did not create the gospel, the gospel created the church.

(ii) This gospel [which] is now preached in every known nation on earth, and which has transformed millions of sinners into saints, was not born in the minds of apostles. The apostles were frail most sinful creatures like we are. For the most part they were unlettered and unlearned fishermen who did not conceive the gospel but received it from the lips of their Saviour and Master.

(iii) The gospel was not invented by any man or number of men, nor was it devised by the angels of heaven. It is the gospel of Christ. The Son of God is its author. So I say I am not ashamed of the gospel because of its uniqueness – Unique in its source.

2. *The Gospel is Unique in its Character*

This is best seen by contrasting it with other things. What can we compare with the gospel? Look for a moment at some of the things highly esteemed among men and then contrast the gospel!

(i) Human philosophy – which endeavours to explain the mysteries and problems of life though no two systems agree.

(ii) Poetry – paints word pictures and appeals to the imagination and emotions.

(iii) Science – utilizes God's provisions for man and harmonises the forces of nature.

(iv) Fame which enables a man to occupy a prominent position in the affairs of the world.

(v) Material wealth which secures for its possessors the things of this life.

Now contrast these different things with the gospel of Christ.

(i) The gospel explains a problem which no philosophy can solve – What must I do to be saved?

(ii) Paints a picture no poet would ever have dreamed of – gospel of Christ makes an appeal to the heart surpassing all others.

(iii) Supplies a power which no human science can provide – power of deliverance from sin.

(iv) Furnishes a place in the family of God and makes those who believe sons of the King, beside which all human fame is worthless.

(v) Secures an eternal inheritance which cannot be valued in dollars and cents.

I say then I am not ashamed of the gospel because of its uniqueness – Unique in character, solitary in grandeur and glory.

3. *The Gospel is Unique in its Simplicity and here again is different from all man made systems and schemes.*

In order to understand mathematics years of study are necessary, but the gospel is so simple the unlearned can understand it.

A child cannot fathom the mysteries of astronomy, but can believe to the saving of its soul.

An uncivilised heathen could never master the problems of metaphysics but can grasp the simple gospel of Christ.

The chief feature and beauty of the gospel is its simplicity and in this it is unique. Who ever heard of being able to secure so much on such easy terms? The simplicity of the gospel is conclusive proof of its divinity. If man had made the gospel he would have made it so difficult only few would have been able to understand it. How different the gospel as presented in the Word. 'Ho every one that thirsteth.' Matt. 11:28. Enumerate three items.

2. *BECAUSE OF THE POWER OF THE GOSPEL*

1. *Its power to overcome obstacles in the first centuries.*

Consider the difficulties faced: no means of rapid transportation, no printed Bibles, no guarantees [?] from missionary societies, no praying churches at home behind them, no previous triumphs to spur them on, but everywhere faced with relentless fanaticism and opposition.

Consider the success and victories won: in one generation the gospel carried to all parts of the known earth; the back of heathendom broken, idolatry overthrown; thousands converted; churches established everywhere.

Consider the means employed: This success not achieved by superior human evangelists[2] – preachers uncultured fishermen: not won by force of arms but by 'the sword of the Spirit'. Not by imperial edict but by gospel power.

2. *Its power to survive the assaults of its enemies and of time.*

In the early ages every possible attempt was made to exterminate the gospel but unsuccessfully. Through the 19 centuries of the Christian era the gospel has survived though most of its contemporaries long since dead. In 20th century gospel is not out of date, but new, fresh, appropriate. Why these things? How except the gospel is the **power** of God.

3. *Its power to save men from hell and transform their lives.*

'Power of God unto salvation.'

[2] Pink's abbreviation for the last three words reads 'supr. hum evis' and we are possibly misreading him.

The word 'salvation' denotes and implies a danger to be delivered from. Hear very little of it in these days: 'Flee from the wrath to come' an effete message.

Illustrations of its power to transform lives: Paul, Bunyan, Pastor Hsi.

4. *Its power to hold its converts.*

This strikingly illustrated. Early converts in Roman arena refused to apostasise. Protestant Christians in middle ages at Smithfield refused to recant.

Converted heathen today cast off by relatives and bitterly persecuted, remain true to Christ.

What is the cause of this heroism? The gospel is 'the power of God'!

3. BECAUSE OF THE BLESSINGS WHICH THE GOSPEL BESTOWS

1. Forgiveness of sins. 2. Peace of heart and conscience. 3. Eternal life. 4. Daily provision for all our need in time. 5. Ultimately being made like Christ and living with Him for ever in glory.

Application

1. *The invitation - to 'everyone that believeth'.*

Gospel is suited for all ages, nationalities, individuals, because all need a Savior.

2. *The limitation - 'to everyone that believeth.' None else benefit.*

May have been born and reared by Christian parents, taught in Sunday School, and sit under preaching of the gospel, but unless believing profits nothing – prove by analogy.

3. *Appropriation: 'Believing' means 'receiving', John 1:12.*

4. *Exhortation: Mark 8:38.*

Appendix 3
Bibliography of Major Writings[1]

After 1922 all Pink's books first appeared as articles in *Studies in the Scriptures.* From that year, the date in the left-hand column of the list below gives the period of publication in the magazine, with publication date in book form on the right. Sometimes publishers have not used the original title which Pink gave to a series; where a new title has been used we have given it in brackets. Where, to the best of our knowledge, articles had not been published in book form up to 1981, the titles have not been italicized. In some instances the articles have only been partially reprinted: we have not been able to specify every case where this has occurred. For the purpose of this bibliography Pink's *major* writings have been defined as those upon which he wrote a number of articles. Individual articles and very short series (many of which have been reprinted in booklet form at various times) are not listed, only reprints in book form.

ORIGINAL PRINTING	*MODERN REPRINTS*
1914? *The Divine Inspiration of the Bible*, Bible Truth Depot (I. C. Herendeen).	Guardian Press, 1976; also in *The Best of A. W. Pink*, Baker, 1978, 1979.
1918 *The Redeemer's Return*, Bible Truth Depot.	Klock and Klock (as the strong dispensationalism in this volume is contrary to the author's mature convictions, republication is irresponsible).

[1] Except on p. 342, this listing of editions of Pink's writings has not been updated beyond 1981. Most of Pink's writings are now available on CD-ROM as *The Arthur Pink Collection* from Ages Software, P.O. Box 216, Rio, WI 53960, USA (www.ageslibrary.com), and many are available on the World Wide Web, for example at www.pbministries.org.

1918	*The Sovereignty of God*, Bible Truth Depot	Baker; Banner of Truth (revised edition) 1961.
1919	*The Seven Sayings of the Saviour on the Cross*, Bible Truth Depot	Reiner, 15th printing, 1979; also in *The Best of A. W. Pink*, Baker, 1978, 1979.
1921	*Why Four Gospels?*	Word of Truth Publications, Canton, Georgia, 1977.
1922	*Gleanings in Genesis*, 'Our Hope', 1922	Moody Press, 17th Printing, 1979 (influenced by Pink's early dispensationalism and over-dependence on Brethren authors).
1922	STUDIES IN THE SCRIPTURES Vol.1 (published monthly and in annual volumes until December 1953).	
1922–3	*The Antichrist*	Bible Truth Depot 1923, Klock and Klock 1979 (see comment on *The Redeemer's Return*, above).
1924–9	*Gleanings in Exodus*	Moody Press, n.d. (see comment on *Genesis* above).
1922–7	*Exposition of Gospel of John*, I. C. Herendeen, first published in separate vols.; vol. 3, 1929, when a fourth concluding vol. was promised.	Zondervan, 1 vol. ed., 1968; 14th printing, 1979 (see comments on *Genesis* and *Exodus* above, but this is the best of his first three expositions).
1927–8	*Parables of Matthew 13*	Calvary Baptist Church, Covington, Kentucky (*Prophetic Parables*), n.d., c. 1978 (see comment on *The Redeemer's Return* above).

1928–38	*Exposition of Hebrews*	Baker, 3 vols, 1954, 10th edition (1 vol.), 1979.
1929	Life of Abraham	
1930–1	*The Satisfaction ('Atonement') of Christ.*	Reiner, 1969.
1930–1	*The Attributes of God*	Moody Press, 1975, 1977 (*Gleanings in the Godhead*, combined with articles on the Person of Christ) also Guardian Press, 1975, and in *The Best of A. W. Pink*, Baker, 1978–9.
1930–2	*Profiting from the Word*	Banner of Truth, 1970.
1931	*Regeneration*	Baker, 1975 (*The Doctrine of Salvation*, with articles on *Repentance* and *Coming to Christ*).
1931	*Repentance*	Baker, 1975 (as above).
1931–2	*Glories of God Our Redeemer*	Moody Press, 1975, 1977 (*Gleanings in the Godhead*, with *The Attributes of God*).
1932–9	*Life of David*	Zondervan. 1958; Reiner, 2 vols. in 1, 1977.
1932	*Saving Faith*	Reiner, n.d.
1932–3	Assurance	
1933	*Coming to Christ*	Baker, 1975 (*The Doctrine of Salvation,* see above).
1933	Heart Work	Partly printed by Guardian, 1974, 1975 (*Practical Christianity*, being a collection of various articles; same book earlier issued under the title, *Pink's Jewels*).

1933–4	Dispensationalism	
1933–7	*The Holy Spirit*	Guardian Press, 1970, 4th printing 1975.
1934	*The Doctrine of Justification*	Baker, 1974 (with *The Doctrine of Election*).
1934–8	*The Divine Covenants*	Baker, 1975.
1935–7	*The Doctrine of Sanctification*	Partly reprinted, Reiner, 1966.
1935–7	*Union and Communion*	Baker, 1971; Guardian, 1976.
1938–40	*The Doctrine of Election*	Baker, 1974 (with *The Doctrine of Justification*).
1938	*The Lord's Prayer*	Baker, 1979 (printed with *Beatitudes*).
1938–43	*The Sermon on the Mount*	1950, Bible Truth Depot; 11th printing, Baker and Evangelical Press, 1977.
1939–40	The Holy Sabbath	
1940–2	*The Life of Elijah*	Bible Truth Depot, 1956; Banner of Truth, 1963.
1940–2	*The Doctrine of Man's Impotency*	Moody Press, 1969, 5th printing, 1976 (*Gleanings from the Scriptures*, printed with *Man's Total Depravity*, see below).
1940	The Justice of God	
1941	*The Ten Commandments*	Reiner, n.d., and in *The Best of A. W. Pink*, Baker, 1978, 1979.
1942–4	*The Doctrine of the Saints' Perseverance*	Guardian and Baker, 1972, 1975, 1979 (*Eternal Security*).

1943–5	*The Life of Elisha*	Moody Press, 1972 (*Gleanings from Elisha*).
1944–9	*The Prayers of the Apostles*	Partly reprinted, Moody Press, 1967 (*Gleanings from Paul*).
1944–6	*Spiritual Growth or Christian Progress*	Baker and Evangelical Press, 1971, 1977.
1944–6	*The Doctrine of Reconciliation*	Associated Publishers, Grand Rapids, n.d.
1945–53	*The Life and Times of Joshua* (to ch. 22).	Moody Press, 1964, 13th printing, 1979 (*Gleanings in Joshua*).
1946 (& 1948)	Enjoying God's Best	Partly printed, Guardian, 1974, 1975 (*Practical Christianity*, see above).
1947–9	*The Doctrine of Revelation*	Baker, 1975, 1977.
1947	The Great Change	Partly printed by Guardian 1974, 1975 (*Practical Christianity*, see above).
1949	Glorious Sinai	
1949–50	*Divine Inspiration of the Scriptures*	Guardian Press, 1976.
1950–3	*Exposition of 1 John* (as far as ch. 3:1)	Associated Publishers, Grand Rapids, n.d.
1950–2	*The Doctrine of Human Depravity*	Moody Press, 1969, 5th printing, 1976 (*Gleanings from the Scriptures*, printed with *Doctrine of Man' Impotency*).
1950–2	*The Interpretation of the Scriptures*	Baker, 1972, 1977.

1952	*The Doctrine of Mortification*	Guardian, 1974, 1975 (*Practical Christianity*).
1953 (Dec.)	Final issue of STUDIES IN THE SCRIPTURES	

OTHER TITLES

Comfort for Christians, Reiner, 1966
(a selection of short sermons and articles)

Letters from Spartanburg,
Richbarry Press, 1993 (see pp. xi, 13)

Letters of an Itinerant Preacher, 1920–1,
Richbarry Press, 1994 (see pp. xi, 59–61)

Letters of A. W. Pink, Banner of Truth, 1978
(44 letters, chiefly from unpublished
correspondence with friends)

Letters to a Young Pastor, Grandville
Protestant Reformed Church, 1993
(see p. 27).

Index

OTHER CURRENT TITLES BY IAIN H. MURRAY FROM THE SAME PUBLISHERS

Wesley and Men Who Followed, xv + 272 pp.

'Murray's thesis is that the enormous success of the Wesleyan movements and religious movements as a whole is not about the uniquenesses, quirks, or novelties of theological insights. Instead it is based on three elements: a deep personal devotion to the Bible, an emphasis on the centrality of prayer as essential to ministerial success, and an abounding zeal in the work . . . The final chapter brings the book together with an unexpected theme. It is as remarkable and inspiring as it is unexpected.'

John D. Hannah, BIBLIOTHECA SACRA, Dallas

'As a fresh presentation of John Wesley and early Methodism this book is warmly recommended. Its further value lies in its careful contemporary application.'

Robert Oliver, EVANGELICAL TIMES

Evangelicalism Divided: A Record of Crucial Change in the Years 1950 to 2000, x + 342 pp.

'The word epiphany refers to a sudden and usually striking awareness or understanding of reality . . . Because I read so much, it is a rare event that yields a true epiphany. But this one did. As soon as I finished Murray's book, I decided to order 20 copies so I could give one to every board member of Ligonier Ministries . . . Murray's critique is as kind and gracious as it is revealing and devastating. The icons of modern evangelicalism are shown as falling into egregious strategic errors that have weakened the evangelical faith at its very core. The bridges built to reach the mainstream became a two-way street by which those who sought to influence the liberals were themselves influenced. We need to read Murray's book and read it again, because what we do today counts forever.

R. C. Sproul, TABLETALK

'This book is a page turner from first to last.'
Peter H. Breckwoldt, Church of England Newspaper

'Perceptive, highly readable, fascinating, disturbing, frustrating, but above all, extremely important; these are just some of the words to describe this latest book by Iain Murray.'
Melvin Tinker, Churchman

Pentecost Today? The Biblical Basis for Understanding Revival, 226pp.

'Some would maintain that there is no justification for a theology of revival in the Bible and see the whole revival emphasis as a distraction from the duty of seizing present opportunities. For them the subject has been worn out by its advocates and discredited by unfulfilled hopes. Yet others remain convinced that spiritual revivals are necessitated by a renewed fulfilment of 2 Chronicles 7:14 . . . *Pentecost Today?* is a different approach to such questions crucial to the present state of the churches.'
Midwest Book Review

'If you only ever read one book on revival – and all Christians should read one – read this one.'
Grace

'This is certainly a book for church leaders to read. It is written with clarity and spiritual insight, and with a sure touch theologically.'
Gordon Bridger, Evangelicals Now

'A sane, biblical, and immensely practical book on revival, and on Christian experience in general.'
Tony Gray, Themelios

For free illustrated catalogue please write to:
THE BANNER OF TRUTH TRUST
3 Murrayfield Road, Edinburgh EH12 6EL, U.K., or
P. O. Box 621, Carlisle, Pennsylvania 17013, U.S.A.

Mark 8

Not Ashamed of the Gospel. Rom 1 16

Intro n

1 With the one except n. of the Ld J. the Ap P. was bey d doubt the greatest preacher & m succ. evangt. W had ever seen. He cov d more grd, overcame greater diffs, endured more hard displayed greater heroism & met with larger succ in the savg of souls & foundg of Ch than any

2 How can we ac for this? What is the explan n of these thgs? What was the Sec. of his succ

1/ In nationality he belonged to a race wh was & is more hated & despised than any oth.

2/ In personality neither prepossessg nor attract. Fr. the N.T. we learn that in outward ap he was mean & despicable – 1 Cor 2 3, 2 Cor 10 1, 10

3/ In delivery he was no orator but prob. stamm r & stutt r – 2 Cor 10 10, Acts 17 18

The succ of this man lay in his mess, in the Gos he preached & his ab. conf. in its pow – Tx

3 In some meas. at least I can make the Tx my own.

Truthfully I can say Tx, & I'll give my reasons why. I'm not ash d of the Gos. bec:-

I Because of the Uniqueness of the Gospel.

In the whole realm of lit. & in all the product. of man there is nothg like the Gos. It stands out alone in its sol. grandeur. As there is no poss. compar n bet n a lighted cand & sking of mid-n seen, so Gos surpasses in its beauty & brill y all creat. of hum mind. Consid 3 elements of its

1 The Gospel is Unique in its Source or Origin

1/ This glor s Gos, this glad tidgs of sal n made kn in Sc & wh God's ser s proclaim is not the invent n of a anc. or mod. It existed bef the 1st Xtn Ch was founded. It was the means & instr t. wh brought Ch in exist. No! the Ch did not create the Gos, the Gos. created the Church

2/ This Gos wh is now preached to ev. kn nat n on E & wh has transformed mill s of sin s into saints was born in minds of Apos. Apos were frail mort sinful creat s like we are. For the most part were unlett d & unlearned fishermen who did not conceive the Gos. but who received it fr. lips of their Sav r & Mast

3/ The Gos was not invented by any man or numb of men nor was it devised by the angels of H. It is of Xt. The Son of God is its Author. So I say I'm not ash d of Gos bec its Uniqness – Unique in its Source

2 The Gospel is Unique in its Character

This is best seen by contrastg it with oth thgs. What can we compare with the Gos? Look for a mom t. at some of the thgs highly esteemed among men & then contrast the Gos

1/ Human Philosophy – wh endeav s to explain the mys s & prob s of life, tho no 2 sys s agree.

2/ " Poetry – " paints word pict s & appeals to the imag n. & emotions.

3/ " Science – " utilizes God's prov s for man & harnesses the forces of Nat.

4/ " Fame wh enables a man to occupy a prom t posit n in affairs of the W.

5/ Material wealth wh secures for its possessors the thgs of this life.

Now contrast these different thgs with the Gospel of Christ

1/ The Gos explains a prob wh no hum phil can solve – What must I do to be saved?

2/ " " paints a pict no poet wo d ever of dreamed of – Lf of Xt & wh makes an appeal to heart surpa

3/ " " supplies a power wh no hum Sc can provide – pow of del fr. sin

4/ " " gives place in fam of God & makes those who bel sons of King besides wh all hum fame w

5/ " " secures an eter inher wh cannot be valued in dollars & cents.